FIRST CATCH YOUR HUSBAND

Sarah Bridge is a financial journalist for the *Mail on Sunday* and has worked at the paper since 2000. She lives in London.

First Catch Your Husband

Adventures on the Dating Front Line

SARAH BRIDGE

MAINSTREAM
PUBLISHING

EDINBURGH AND LONDON

First published in Great Britain in 2012 by
MAINSTREAM PUBLISHING COMPANY
(EDINBURGH) LTD
7 Albany Street
Edinburgh EH1 3UG

ISBN 9781845967987

This book is a work of non-fiction based on the life, experiences and
recollections of the author. In some instances, names of people, places,
dates, sequences or the detail of events have been changed to protect
the privacy of others. The author has stated to the publishers that,
except in such respects, not affecting the substantial accuracy of the
work, the contents of this book are true.

A catalogue record for this book is available
from the British Library

Printed in Great Britain by
CPI Group (UK) Ltd, Croydon, CR0 4YY

1 3 5 7 9 10 8 6 4 2

For my sister Rachel, who always had faith in me

Acknowledgements

I would like to thank all the people who have helped make this book possible, including my friends and family for being so generous with their time and unfailing support. Special thanks go to Lisa Buckingham, editor of *Financial Mail on Sunday*, my agent, Robert Dudley, and my publisher, Bill Campbell of Mainstream Publishing. Thank you also to Mark Warner, Exodus Holidays and Mulbert, who kindly gave me permission to use his poem 'Body Clock'.

Contents

1

The Search Begins

As soon as I walked into the bar, I knew which one he was.

It wasn't just the fact that he was the only guy in the room sitting on his own, nor was it the quite hideous shiny green suit he was wearing, which signalled loud and clear that we were destined never to meet again.

It was the air of hopeless optimism that surrounded him, that strange combination of anticipation and resignation which is carried by all single people out on a blind date. It was the feeling that 'This could be the one; this could be the person I've been looking for, who will take me away from all this and will mean I never have to do anything as soul-destroying and torturous as this again' mixed with 'but I know it won't be and this whole evening will do nothing but put another dent in my already rather battered self-esteem'.

I'd only agreed to such an ego-crushing experience myself because the sister paper of the newspaper I worked for was running a weekly 'Blind Date' column in its magazine. The paper was finding it increasingly hard to track down volunteers prepared to go out for the evening with a complete stranger and have their picture taken, before sharing their thoughts on how it had gone with the whole of London's commuter population. Even the prospect of a free dinner and drinks wasn't enough to persuade people to apply, so the editor of the column had been reduced to sending desperate emails around the office, begging for someone – anyone! – to step forward for the good of the newspaper.

The final email had caught me at a particularly vulnerable moment. I'd not long split up with my long-term boyfriend Patrick in one of those awful 'hack into his emails and discover he's seeing other women'-type break-ups. For some reason, we were still occasionally sleeping together, partly because I still fancied him and partly because it had ended so abruptly it had thrown my whole sense of self into shock, and now I was trying to end it on a smoother gradient, in the same way that in the mornings I would often crawl back into bed for five minutes' extra sleep when I'd woken up too quickly.

Either way, I knew that in my current emotional state every decision I made was bound to be wrong. I was also aware that sleeping with my ex was not a healthy thing to be doing. A lot of my friends had been extolling the virtues of the 'rebound fling' – the brief, fun but ultimately meaningless relationship that would prove a vital distraction from my ex – and, when yet another email arrived begging for singletons willing to go out on a mystery date, I thought, 'Well, why not?'

I could think of several reasons why not as I approached his table in the bar in Old Street that had been chosen for our date, his lizardy suit being high on the list. The venue itself was nice enough, though, and I was prepared to give him the benefit of the doubt and assume that all his other suits had been swept away that very morning by a freak flash flood. Maybe he had worn it for a dare.

I was looking not too bad for a Tuesday night. I'd really made an effort and had even put on heels and some lipstick. I was bit late, though, so I arrived at his table ready to launch into a flurry of apologies.

'Hi, are you Mark?'

He nodded.

'Hi, I'm Sarah. We're supposed to be meeting tonight. I'm really, really sorry for being late. The traffic was terrible. I hope you got my message, though?'

I had sent him a text while on Shaftesbury Avenue – I'd been rather lazy and had taken a black cab across town, which as it turned out took roughly four times longer than the Tube would have done.

'No, I didn't get your message,' said Mark, but he didn't look particularly fussed about it.

'Really? But I sent it about half an hour ago. I wanted to let you know I was stuck in traffic . . .'

'I don't carry my mobile with me,' he said matter-of-factly.

'You don't carry . . .?'

'It spoils the line of my suit.'

I managed not to say, '*That* suit?', resisting the urge to point out that it was unspoilable. Nor did I mention how completely daft it was not to carry your mobile when you're meeting up with someone who might want to contact you.

'No, I left it in the car.'

'You drove here?' I said in amazement, but decided not to add: 'You drove into central London for a date where all the alcohol and food is paid for?'

'Oh, well, I'm here now!' I said as cheerfully as I could, while wishing I wasn't.

He suddenly looked a bit put out. 'Well, I'd better ask them to hold the dessert,' he said.

I laughed. I then realised that he wasn't smiling, which probably meant that he wasn't actually joking.

'I'm sorry?' I said.

'Well, when I saw you weren't here, I thought I might as well have dinner.'

I looked at my watch. It was now 7.20 p.m. Our date was to have begun at 7 p.m.

'You've already eaten?' I asked.

'Well, not dessert,' he said. 'Just the starter and the main course.'

I looked at the table. There were no obvious signs of a meal – no empty plates, no scrunched-up napkin, nothing that would have alerted me that he was over halfway through our dinner date without me. This meant that, after arriving at 7 p.m., he had managed to choose, order and eat two whole courses, which had been cleared away, and he was now waiting for dessert. If I hadn't been so astonished that he'd had most of the date on his own, I'd have been really impressed by the efficient waiters here. It usually took me 20 minutes just to get a drink! And, given that he had managed to wolf down all of his food, how long had he actually waited for me to arrive? If he was that hungry, couldn't he have ordered some olives or bread, maybe, something to tide him over until I got there? And why hadn't he carried his sodding mobile phone with him?

'Oh,' I said. There didn't seem to be much else to say.

My phone bleeped. It was a text from the magazine's photographer, who was going to take pictures of us for the article.

'On my way,' it read. 'Stuck in traffic. Be there in an hour.'

Oh, God. So now I couldn't even leave, which was what I really wanted to do. Instead, I was going to have to stay here so that the photographer, could immortalise this wonderful occasion.

After such a start, the rest of the date, like his suit, turned out to be unspoilable. I didn't mind that while I ate my three courses – well, they were paid for, after all – he ate his pudding and drank water.

I didn't mind that he turned out to be extremely interested in New Age religions and spent forever telling me about a yogic flying course that he had been on in the Nevada desert.

I didn't even mind that we had to pose for the photographer when he finally turned up, knowing that the picture of me having dinner with a guy in a shiny green suit would be viewed by a million Londoners, some of whom I might actually know. By then, I was numb to the whole experience.

Needless to say, the editor of the column, who was going to write up the 'date', thought the whole thing was utterly hilarious.

'He didn't – he didn't!' she kept gasping, as I relayed the whole sorry experience.

I tried to be diplomatic and not just have a go at the poor guy but it was hard to put a positive spin on the fact that he'd obviously viewed my arrival as fairly superfluous to the evening.

The following week, when the magazine came out, I hid every single copy that I could find in the office, which was no mean feat, considering that, as we published it, there were piles and piles of them everywhere. I scooped them up and hid them under my desk, before discreetly recycling them when everyone had gone home for the night.

I just about got away with it at work – no one seemed to notice that their copy of the *Evening Standard* had come without a magazine that week and, as journalists are not exactly a shy, retiring bunch, I would certainly have known if any of my colleagues had even had a glimpse of it.

That weekend, however, I met up with Patrick, my ex-boyfriend – arguably the cause of all of this – and a group of his mates in a pub after they'd been playing football on Tooting Common.

I bought some crisps and sat down.

'Wouldn't you rather have some olives or bread?' shouted one lad across the table.

Another guy made a pretence of trying to find his phone. 'Has anyone seen my mobile?' he asked. 'I would have taken it with me but it spoils the line of my football kit.'

The place erupted.
It was time to leave the country.

I handed in my notice at the newspaper, rented out my flat in Balham and packed up my life. It wasn't the blind date, of course, or the utter futility of still being in a relationship with my ex-boyfriend that prompted such a drastic move, but I had a growing feeling that, unless I changed my life completely, I would be in the same job, living in the same flat and going out with the same people for the rest of my life.

I loved my job, I loved my flat and I loved my friends, but it wasn't enough. I wanted excitement and adventure; I wanted to explore new places, meet new people and have new experiences, and I wasn't going to do that playing it safe in familiar old London.

So off I went. I drove to Dover and across Europe to Italy and Florence, my racing bike clinging on to the back of my tiny Fiat 500, into which I had crammed my entire life. I learned Italian, lived in gorgeous and not-so-gorgeous apartments in various flatshares across the city and worked as a freelance journalist, writing about wine-tasting in Tuscany and cycling in Siena. I got drunk with English students and dated Italian men.

After a year, I moved to Rome, staying in the beautiful cobbled district of Trastevere in a flat just round the corner from my new 'office' – a tiny café that had wi-fi and served delicious canapés each evening when they considered that it was time to start drinking. I met Hugh, an English writer, and we moved in together, living and writing in a house in the countryside outside Rome.

A year later, I had the travel bug again. Hugh and I parted amicably – I think we both knew we had become friends and nothing more – and I flew off to New York. I spent a wonderful two years there, developing a taste for dirty martinis and poker, and living in an apartment in the West Village that overlooked the Hudson River.

After five years away, I decided that it was time to come home. The recession was biting, money was tight and work was increasingly hard to find. By a stroke of good fortune, my old job at the newspaper had just become vacant and so it was back to full-time work and, this time, a shared house in Clapham.

Once again, I was single in south-west London. My memories of my blind-date horror five years earlier had just about faded. It was time to settle down and find a lovely man to fall in love with.

But two years later, nothing had happened. I went out – a lot – but with friends, not with boyfriends.

The structure of my social life had completely changed since I'd been away. No longer would I spend the weekends hanging out in one massive group of friends all day and all night, gathering people on the way in pubs and bars. Now evenings out were planned weeks, or even months, in advance and would involve dinner reservations, permission from other halves, babysitters and enquiries about the time of the last train home. A lot of my friends had got married, had babies and moved to the suburbs. It was as if there was some kind of law.

Even when I did meet a new man, it was usually only a matter of time, sometimes mere seconds, before a wife or a girlfriend or a boyfriend would enter the conversation or somehow make their presence felt, usually in the form of the dreaded 'we'.

'Where do you live?'

'*We* live in Ealing.'

Or: 'Have you been anywhere nice recently?'

'Yes, *we*'ve just come back from Australia.'

I almost wanted to look around for this invisible 'we'. It

was a roadblock in the conversation and I kept on running into them.

Being 38 and single was certainly very different from being 28 and single. The whole scenery had changed.

Now, it's not that I mind being single. I really don't. I'd much rather be on my own than with some feckless bloke with a charming smile and the morals of a bunny. But it seems that there is a whole middle ground between, on the one side, being on your own and hurtling towards 40 and, on the other, being stuck with some shag-happy Romeo. This is a place that I've yet to find.

Everyone I talk to – or who delicately approaches the subject with a 'so how's your love life then?', knowing full well that it resembles a barren desert after a particularly long drought – says in a variety of ways that they're amazed I'm in this predicament.

'I can't believe you're single!' they exclaim. 'How is that possible?' As if to other people they would easily say, 'I know exactly why you're single – it's that monobrow/extra 10 stone/man-repellent spray you use.'

Being told that you shouldn't really be single is utterly unhelpful: it's supposed to be flattering, but it's really not.

'It's a crime that no one has snapped you up' is what they think they're saying, but what they are actually saying is: 'In spite of all your great qualities, still no one on the entire planet wants to go out with you.'

And that's never a good thing to hear.

'Go on,' they persist, as if you are being deliberately annoying by not having found anyone yet, 'why are you still single?'

So I ask them, 'Well, how many single men do you actually know?'

It is at this point that they go through an entire repertoire of phrases and facial expressions starting with: 'Loads!

There's umm . . .' before tailing off into thoughtfulness. 'Well, there's . . . oh no, he's married, and, oh, he's gay and, well, there's . . . but I wouldn't recommend him . . .' Before long, they've established that they don't know anybody who is at all suitable. They then shrug and say, 'Gosh, it's difficult, isn't it?'

Is it? You don't say.

This is usually followed by a cheery: 'But don't worry, you'll meet someone!' even though they have just spent ten painful minutes helping to confirm that there is, in fact, no one out there. They inevitably conclude with: 'Well, don't think about it too much. It'll happen when you least expect it' – to which the only possible response is: '*How*, exactly?'

And then the killer: 'Well, you've just got to get out there.' I COULD NOT BE MORE OUT THERE IF MY LIFE DEPENDED ON IT.

I go out *all the time*.

My job as a financial journalist covering the leisure sector means that I am constantly meeting new people, mostly at events where copious amounts of alcohol are involved. I spend most of my time going to parties, book launches, beer-tastings, wine-tastings, trips to the races, brewery tours, awards ceremonies, PR parties, pub quizzes, distillery trips, press jaunts, poker nights, networking events, and that doesn't include all the random social drinking that goes on.

I live with three other sociable and single 30-somethings.

I have the usual number of friends, some of whom I see all the time, some of whom I see less often, but generally enough so an evening at home is a rarity.

I haven't turned down a single invitation for two years.

I am still on my own.

I am fed up with going out on my own, meeting strangers, making small talk and then going home – on my own.

It has got to the point that, if there is the slightest chance of meeting men, even if I'm exhausted and desperate to go home, curl up in front of the telly and have an early night, I don't. I make myself look as fabulous as possible (within the limits of time, finance and genetic make-up) and head on out there.

Just before I go into the event, I fight off the impulse to turn around and head off back into the night and my cosy home. Instead, I launch myself in there, chatting, laughing, listening, bonding, being fun and friendly and attentive and hoping that tonight, just maybe, I'll meet someone with whom I'll have a spark, some sort of connection. Then they say the words 'My wife . . .' or 'My girlfriend . . .' or 'My boyfriend . . .' and I'll keep on chatting and laughing, but inside I'll be raging YET AGAIN, and yet the very next night I'll do it all over again, working out what to wear, how to look, feeling glad I forced myself to go to the gym that lunchtime to counteract the effects of all these fruitless nights out. So perhaps you can understand that when someone says, 'Well, you've just got to get out there,' I just want to shout, 'Oh, FUCK OFF!'

Of course, showing rage and frustration is bad. It's not good to think about it too much, or you'll look angry and desperate. Last election night, I'd forced myself to go to a corporate bash at a casino because where there's gambling and alcohol there might also be men. I ended up sitting next to a guy who I vaguely knew through work at a poker table in Leicester Square at 2 a.m.

We were chatting away about this and that, and then, all of a sudden, he sat back in his chair, sipped his whisky and said, completely unprompted, 'You know, Sarah, you've really got to get a move on. Get out there, make things happen! You're running out of time.'

I had thought my hand of cards was bad, and now I was

being given advice that I really hadn't wanted and certainly hadn't asked for.

'But –' he leaned across to me conspiratorially '– don't look desperate. Don't look like you need it. Just be relaxed and it will happen.'

Now, I would have been quite interested to hear exactly how I could be relaxed about something that he had just declared to be a state of emergency. Was I supposed to be like an elegant swan, effortlessly and serenely gliding along the smooth waters, while frantically paddling like crazy under the surface? And how, exactly, was this miracle supposed to be achieved?

But, no, rather than backing up his helpful description of my seemingly dire predicament with some actual plan of action, my self-appointed lifestyle coach then spent the next half an hour describing how he'd met his wife while sitting on a train at Liverpool Street.

'I saw her, and I just knew,' he said, chucking gaming chips onto the green baize. 'One look at her and I just knew that I had to marry her. So I went over and said, "You must think that I'm completely insane but I've just seen you sitting there and I had to come and talk to you."' He smiled smugly. 'How could she resist?'

'Quite easily,' I thought sourly, as I folded my hand.

What did this story mean? That I shouldn't worry about finding a man because Mr Right would just come up to me one day and all my problems would be over?

Or that I should sit on trains more? Maybe he was trying to say that there was something wrong with me, because I'd sat on lots of trains and not met a potential husband on any of them.

I wondered what he would say to his wife if he hadn't met her on that train and years later she was still single and they'd met in a casino on election night.

Would it be: 'My God, you're amazing, I have to marry you and luckily for you I'm still single,' or would it more probably be: 'You've got to get a move on, you know. Get out there, make things happen! I met my wife on the train from Euston station . . .'?

There are so many more things I want to do with my life than spend all this time thinking about finding a husband. And the thing is I really enjoy my life as it is. I've got friends with lovely husbands, but also some with quite crummy ones, and I know I'd much rather have my life as it is than have to deal with a terrible relationship.

But I miss so many things about being with someone. I miss the fact that someone really wants to be with you. I miss the going to bed with someone and waking up next to them, and all the fun bits in between. I miss just spending hours doing nothing with someone because you don't mind what you do as long as you're hanging out with them. I miss going out for the evening with someone and swapping stories on the Tube home afterwards. I miss looking forward to meeting someone after a long day or a weekend away and I miss someone missing me.

It's not just about finding a man. While it would be nice to have a boyfriend, I'm also happy to wait until someone just right for me comes along.

Except, of course, my body isn't. While I'd love to have children in, say, ten years' time, I'm realistic enough to know that I've got maybe five years left, tops. For all I know, it could be five minutes left. Either way, there's no arguing that, if I want to have children, time is rapidly running out. If I want to have babies (which I do) with a partner (which I do), the fact is I'm going to be 40 next year and, as my smug and annoying casino friend said, I've got to get a move on.

I never used to have any problem finding a boyfriend.

That's not to say I was never single; I was, lots of times, but never to the point of wondering where all the men had gone. I dated at school and at university, and had three long-term relationships in my twenties and early thirties, interspersed with a healthy amount of singleness and casual flings. I lived with three guys and thought seriously about marriage with two of them, but either they broke my heart or I broke theirs. Then something happened when I reached 35: the music stopped and I was left without a partner, and not much hope of finding one. It seemed as though, practically overnight, there had been a secret cull of all the single men on the entire planet. Single men no longer walked the earth. Or, at least, not the bits where I was walking (mainly Clapham, south London – married centre of the universe).

I know that it's possible to have children without a partner. I've read enough articles and know enough people who've made that decision. I just don't want to. I want a family and I want my children to have a father. In a few years' time, I might think differently, but, if there's the slightest chance that I can have the whole package, I'm going to go for it. I know I'm not alone – there's a whole generation of Bridget Joneses out there. However, knowing that you've become a cliché doesn't make it any easier. There are poster girls for late bloomers – Mariella Frostrup, Helen Fielding, my friend Jane – so finding a guy and having a family in your late thirties and even early forties can be done. But I'm still single after two years back in London, so I'm obviously doing something wrong.

Moving to Italy – where the guys were really only interested in American college girls or Italian beauties – and then New York – where, yes, practically every man I met turned out to be gay – for five crucial years in my thirties was maybe not such a great idea husband-wise.

So I have no choice. If I want to find a man whom I can

fall in love with, plan to spend the rest of my life with and hopefully try to have children with, I've got to do everything possible to make that happen. Whether it's online dating or flirting with strangers on the bus, going on singles holidays or putting adverts in the paper, I have to do it.

I have to do everything that's worked for my friends, and everything they think might work – even things that no one thinks will work – because there is the remotest possibility that it could work for me. At the moment, it all seems completely impossible, but I don't want to be on my own in ten years' time wondering why the hell I didn't give it my best shot while I had the chance.

2

Where There's a Will

There was another reason why I might not have been looking especially hard to find a man when I moved back to London. I had found one sitting right next to me. He was called Will and he was utterly gorgeous. He was also utterly unavailable.

I had returned from my extended sabbatical in Italy and America to find everything much the same in the newsroom – same office, same colleagues wearing the same suits and telling the same anecdotes – except for Will. He was the new addition to the team, having arrived when I was away. Within a minute of meeting him, I thought he would be fun to work with; within a week, I thought he might even turn out to be a good friend; and, within the month, I realised that I had completely and utterly fallen in love with him.

We talked all day, every day. We discussed stories and leads, we talked about colleagues and rival journalists, we went to press parties together, had boozy lunches and even boozier nights. On Fridays when we worked late, we'd catch a cab afterwards and sit in his garden, drinking, smoking and putting the world to rights. Once I walked home across the common at seven in the morning when the night sky was beginning to lighten, accompanied by the chirping of the birds as they greeted another day while I was still in the previous one.

We never talked about his girlfriend. It wasn't that she was a secret, or a forbidden topic or anything like that, it was just that her name hardly ever came up in conversation. She had moved down from Manchester to live with him the week before I had come back from New York. Timing had certainly not been on my side. She sounded perfectly nice, by all accounts, of which there were few, because Will never talked about her with me; he never said anything that one half of a couple usually does, such as 'Well, I'd better go home or I'll be in trouble' or 'I'm not sure if I can come out, I'll check with the boss', or even used the dreaded pronoun 'we'.

But at weekends he would disappear into his other life and presumably that was when he became Will the boyfriend.

There was never any hint of anything more between Will and me. In spite of the hundreds of hours we spent together drinking, talking and more drinking, there was no hint of romance, no stolen kisses, no obvious flirting, no signs of regret from him that our relationship couldn't be something more, not the smallest squeak of evidence – and I looked really, really hard, believe me – that he felt anything for me in the way of love or in fact anything at all except that I was an amiable colleague. This was in spite of my yearning for him for months and months, adoring him, longing to be with him, wishing and hoping that one day he would look at me and suddenly realise that it was me who he loved. But he never did.

Every day was a fresh hell of delight and despair, a sweet torture that I dreaded but couldn't escape from. I would sit just inches away from him, practically trembling with desire, while he was all smiles, all gorgeousness, but never anything more. Every day, as I walked across the office to my seat next to him, the usual chant would go through my head.

I love him. I can't bear it. I have to leave my job. This is going to drive me crazy. But I love him. I can't bear it. I have to leave . . .

But I didn't want to leave. I really liked my job.

I had never told him how I felt and I didn't think that I ever would. It was obvious that he didn't feel even a fraction of the same way about me as I did about him, so there was no point at all in telling him and embarrassing both of us and ruining our friendship for ever.

Even the thought of telling him made my insides scrunch up in horror. A small part of me would think sometimes, 'He must like me – why else would he spend so much time with me?'

But that voice was countered by the louder, more sensible one that told me that, if he thought of me in any other way, something would have happened by now. So he obviously saw me as just a friend and colleague, and absolutely nothing more.

It was torture. Exquisite torture, but still torture. For two whole years. And it was about to get a lot worse.

I arrived in the office one day to find him already at his desk.

'Morning,' he said, not taking his eyes off his computer screen.

I peered across to see what he was looking at. It seemed to be the website of a fancy hotel somewhere in South East Asia. There were lots of pictures of boats and beaches and elephants.

'You off somewhere?'

He pushed his chair back and spun round to face me. 'Yup. Going to spend three weeks travelling round Thailand.'

'Nice.'

It was typical of Will to skip the pronouns altogether, giving no clue as to who else might be going. I could guess though.

'Know anyone out there?'

'Yes, Michelle's brother lives in Ko Samui so we're going to see him for a bit and then head off up north.'

It was one of the rare occasions that he had mentioned his girlfriend's name. I felt bold enough to get personal.

'Wow, sounds great. But, you know, taking your girlfriend on a three-week holiday to Thailand . . . you can't really do that and not propose to her at some point on the trip.'

He laughed and stood up. 'That was quick!' he said. 'It took me a little longer to come to the same conclusion.'

And with that, he headed off to make a cup of coffee. I sat there, stunned. So that was it then. He was going to propose to Michelle, she'd say yes, they'd get married and have babies and move to St Albans.

I was still totally in love with him. It was now the time not to be. This doomed, painful, fabulous, one-sided and utterly pointless relationship had to end. It was time to get out there and find someone else. Really, really quickly. But right now I had to sit there in our open-plan office and try very, very hard not to cry.

3

With a Little Help from My Friends

I have never consciously gone after men. I have fancied certain guys, of course, and flirted with them or asked them out or talked to them at parties or done whatever I could to hook up with them, but I'd never actually sought out dates.

Being British, I haven't even 'dated' as such. The accepted courtship rituals as far as they applied to me and my friends had always been to get very drunk, end up snogging or sleeping with someone, then after you'd done that a few times you were, by default, going out together.

Next, you would progress to sleeping together when you were sober, start to meet each other without your whole group of friends coming along and then you'd move in together and soon be on the slipway to marriage and babies or, in my case, discovery of infidelities or just falling out of love with each other and then back to square one.

In New York, it was done in a slightly different way. There was, of course, the 'get drunk and pull someone' option, but there was also actual dating going on, such as meeting for coffee in art galleries at ten in the morning. As an English person, I could never get my head around the concept of a date without alcohol, let alone one held in the morning. But now it was imperative that I get out there as quickly as possible and meet as many men as I could. Being in love with Will for the previous two years hadn't stopped me going out and having the occasional fling or at least being receptive to any potential advances, but it had obviously failed to work relationship-wise.

It was time to be more proactive. But where should I start?

On the way home that night, I wrote a list of everyone I knew who was in a relationship. My close friends, members of my family, work colleagues, some friends I saw very occasionally, friends I hadn't seen for years, friends of friends I'd never even met – basically everyone I had ever heard of. I then wrote down, if I knew, how they had met their partner.

There were quite a lot of names on the list, and roughly 99 per cent of them had met their other halves in one of three ways: work, friends of friends or school/university. If you hadn't lucked out through one of those routes, it seemed that your chances of success were completely limited.

This seemed very unfair. I had met boyfriends in all these ways, but none of those relationships had lasted. I'd exhausted all the school/university possibilities when I was at school and university; at work, everyone was married except the guy whom I was completely in love with and he was about to be married; and now my friends were all married and claiming not to know any single people at all. I obviously had to go down a different route.

I started canvassing my friends' opinions, subtly at first, with a 'do you know how so and so met?', but it wasn't long before it became: 'Look, I have to find a bloke. Where's the best place to look?'

It somehow seemed a bit pathetic to admit to being single and keen not to be. I don't know why, as it certainly wasn't a secret that I wasn't going out with anyone and there is nothing wrong with being single. But being unhappily single, well, that was a new feeling for me and one I was slightly embarrassed by. It seemed such an admission of failure and the solution 'Get me a man! Any man!' rather indiscriminatingly desperate. But I took the plunge. I told my friends that, yes, I wanted a boyfriend.

My closest friends were all male and we had spent all of our twenties together, getting drunk in pubs and watching one another fall in and out of relationships. Then, at some point when I wasn't looking, they had all got married. Alan now had three children and lived in Guildford, Jack had two and lived in Dorking, Clive had two and lived in Streatham, Ash had two and lived in Peckham and Max had two and lived in Twickenham.

We still hooked up for drinks, of course, but it now required a lot more planning ahead and much talk from the men about 'consulting the missus' and 'getting permission'. Having not actually been on a date themselves for years, if ever – out of the five of them, two met their wives at university and the other three met theirs through friends – they were as out of touch as I was but duly rallied round.

Thankfully, none of them said, 'There must be loads of single men out there!' because, living in married suburban bliss, none of them knew any. They had lots of suggestions though.

'Internet dating. You know, sites like *Guardian* Soulmates, Match.com. Some guy at work met someone through one of those, I think.'

'Car-maintenance classes. Although I hear that they're full of women now, trying to meet men.'

'Weddings. Loads of people meet at weddings.'

'Walking the dog. Tons of celebrities met their partners while walking their dogs.'

'Chat people up in Sainsbury's. You know, hang around the fresh fruit and veg counter and say suggestive things about your melons.'

I wasn't entirely sure whether this was helping much. There were no weddings planned for the near future, I hadn't got a dog and the thought of eyeing up strange men's cucumbers in supermarkets just made me want to run away and join a nunnery.

Internet dating – well, yes, I did think that maybe it was time to put aside all those thoughts of 'Well, it's not very romantic, is it?' and get online.

But I wanted to meet lots of men, very quickly, in the hope that at least one of them might provide a suitable distraction from my heartache over Will. I wanted a lot of single men and I wanted them now.

The guys looked at one another.

'No, I don't want to do shots down the Clapham Grand,' I said hastily. The Clapham Grand is a notorious meat market where you are pretty much guaranteed to pull but you can't be too fussy. Or over 30. The last time I went I felt at least 500 years old.

'No,' said Max. 'We have the answer. Lots of men in as short a time as possible?'

'Oh no.'

'Oh yes,' he said. 'You have to go speed-dating.'

4

So Many Men, So Little Time

I was afraid they would suggest speed-dating, but not entirely surprised. The phrase itself seems to share the same meaning as 'magic potion' to my married friends, and Max certainly wasn't the first to mention it. I'd be having a chat with someone over a drink and would mention that I'd quite like to meet a man but that I wasn't entirely sure where to start.

'You want to meet someone?' they'd say, as if this was a great revelation and they thought that you'd be perfectly happy ambling around on your own for the rest of your life. 'Well, in that case, you should definitely try speed-dating.'

They tended to announce this in much the same way that Cinderella's fairy godmother might have done, had she not gone for the whole pumpkin/coach flashiness.

'Looking for a husband, my dear? Well, in that case, you should try this magical new invention – speed-dating! Now let me just wave my magic wand . . .'

I suspected that speed-dating might not be the way to find my Prince Charming but none of my friends would hear anything against it.

The only person who seemed to think it wasn't such a great idea was one of my work colleagues who said, 'Speed-dating? That's a bit random, isn't it? I mean, it's a million-to-one shot.' He thought about it for a moment, before adding, 'Although a friend of mine got married to someone they met speed-dating.'

If that was his idea of a million-to-one shot, I would be getting him to buy my lottery tickets in future.

Of course, none of my speed-dating-recommending friends had actually been speed-dating, because they are not sad and desperate singletons, but they all seemed to have read about it in the Sunday supplements and imagined it to be a wonderful way to meet twenty dashing men and have terribly witty three-minute conversations with each of them, before choosing which one to marry.

In the real world, however, it is more like a short cut to self-loathing, depression and a massive hangover.

I had actually been speed-dating a few years earlier. It was in my brief 'hey, dating might be fun' phase (which ended abruptly with the lizardy-suit-man date). I dragged my friend Jo to a speed-dating event I had seen advertised in *Time Out* magazine. It was in a very trendy subterranean bar on the corner of Berkeley Square in central London and cost £20, not including drinks. I suspected that drinks would be an essential part of the evening.

When we arrived, there was an alarmingly large number of women queuing up to sign in and hardly any men. Where were they?

We found them by the bar, loading up on Dutch courage, all looking nervous and uncomfortable as they gulped their pints down. Some women were already chatting to some of the guys and it seemed as though we might as well forget about the dating and just get plastered at the bar, in the traditional British way.

But it was not to be. A woman blew a whistle and called us all to attention. It was all very strictly timetabled: there were twenty dates per round, and three minutes per date. The women sat at the designated tables dotted around the room, and the men moved on one table with each round. Everyone had been given a sticker with a number on it to wear and we all had a score sheet and a pen. The score sheet had a list of numbers going down the side, each number corresponding with a particular guy or girl, and after your three-minute 'date' was up, you had to tick 'yes' or 'no' next to their number, depending on whether you'd like to see them again. So make sure you make a note of the numbered sticker that your date is wearing, OK? Right, has everyone got that? Then off you go. Peeeep!

It turned out that because of the high number of people there – I couldn't believe how many people were hoping that speed-dating would be the route to romantic bliss – there was going to be not one but two rounds. Jo and I were in the second wave, so we had to sit at the bar and watch as people dated all around us.

It was fairly excruciating. It felt as if we were the B team. We hadn't even started dating and already we were feeling rejected. The tables all around us were full of couples and we were stuck at the bar like a pair of old maids. With three minutes per date, twenty seconds between dates and twenty dates in total, plus a quick break in the middle, it was going to be well over an hour before we even got round to meeting any of these men.

There was little else to do but drink and so it looked like we were going to be completely plastered when we actually did talk to any guys. Even worse, it looked as if there were only women left for the second round. So where were the rest of the men going to come from?

From the bar next door, as it turned out. Desperate for more blokes, the organisers had rushed out into the London night and lured in random males with the promise of free drinks and 20 girls to practise their chat-up lines on. There were five Italian guys in the bar next door who were scooped up in this dash for guys, so, an hour and a half later when it was our turn to join in, my first date went something like this:

'Hi, what's your name?'

'I'm Gianni. My English isn't so good ...'

'Oh! What are you doing here, Gianni?'

'Am here with friends. For a week. On holiday. I live in Rome. My English isn't so good ...'

If my heart could have sunk any further, then it would have done. This was certainly no way to find a husband. Across the room, Jo didn't seem to be faring much better. Three minutes when you didn't actually want to talk to someone at all turned out to be a really long time. Three minutes even when they seemed quite nice was also proving quite a stretch. Once you'd got through the 'what's your name, where do you live, what do you do?' type of questions and they hadn't yielded anything of interest, there was still enough time left to chat about something else, but no desire whatsoever on either part to do so.

As the dates wore on, the men became fairly indistinguishable. One guy, who was actually rather cute, slumped down in the seat opposite me.

'I'm sorry if I'm a bit tired,' he said. 'But they're asking the men who've already dated to go round again. So you are my –' he consulted his sheet '– 34th date this evening. I'm losing the ability to focus.' He smiled wearily. He was obviously completely dated out.

Across the table from us, a girl slumped forward, her head on the table. It seemed the waiting time at the bar spent drinking had finally taken its toll.

We slogged our way around the room. At the beginning, people were writing little notes on their score sheets during the changeovers, to remind themselves of whom they'd dated when it came to scoring them at the end. It was discreetly done, so as not to offend the person they'd just been talking to. Now, as the evening staggered on, people were just openly ticking 'no' in front of dates, or putting a big cross by their names. The dates got blessedly shorter – people would sit down, say hello and then say 'sorry – but no', or go off to the loo or the bar. Friends would come over mid-date to discuss the evening so far.

'Terrible, awful men,' said one to a friend. 'What a crap evening.'

Her friend's current date, who was still sitting opposite her, pretended not to have heard.

The evening, finally, thankfully, ground to a halt. Everyone was utterly plastered, because of nerves, the long wait at the bar or the early onset of drinking to forget that this evening had ever happened. I ticked a few 'yes's' for politeness' sake and got a few 'yes's' back. I didn't follow up on any of them, and neither did they.

'Never, ever again,' I said to myself.

So, of course, several years later, thanks to my friends' insistence, I found myself signing up to a speed-dating evening. Again. This time it was in Wandsworth, not far from where I lived, so at least I wouldn't be trekking across town. These things were important when you had such low expectations as I did. While booking this speed-dating evening, while persuading yet another long-suffering friend to come along and while walking down the road towards the event itself, all the time my mind was having a fairly energetic conversation with itself.

'God, I can't believe I'm doing this. Again! Remember last time? It's going to be total and utter hell.'

'Look, it might not be. You only have to meet one guy, just one, and then all this hideousness will be over and you'll never have to do anything like this again, I promise. Think of all the times that your friends have said things like: "Well, that particular evening I really didn't want to go out, I was really tired and wanted to watch telly, but my friends made me, and then I met Julie and she's now my wife . . ." Well, this could be that evening.'

'I spend my *whole life* going to things I don't want to. Just because it happened to them once, they think it's the secret to how these things work. It isn't. Smug married bastards. And if I do meet someone unexpectedly, it's certainly not going to be at a speed-dating event for thirties and forties. No one I would ever want to spend the rest of my life with would be seen dead at an event like this.'

'But *you're* going! And you're lovely, fabulous, witty, attractive. So there might be someone like you there tonight, who's been dragged along by a friend, or who's just split up with his girlfriend, or who's new in town . . .'

(In fact, imagining ways in which 'not awful' guys would have actually signed up to these things would become a full-time occupation.)

'You know that's utter bollocks. There's going to be three men there and they're all going to be crap.'

'Don't be so pessimistic. This night could be different.'

Add that constant internal monologue to the sheer effort of looking presentable and dateable for the evening – making sure that your hair, outfit, make-up, eyebrows, teeth, chin, upper lip and shoes are all in their best possible condition – and it's amazing that single women don't just turn up to these types of events and collapse on the floor, semi-comatose.

But no, we arrive and sparkle and shine and giggle and flirt, and then go home and try not to shoot ourselves.

I arrived at the bar. My equally fed-up-with-being-single friend Emma was already there buying a drink. She looked great but had *that* expression on her face. The one that said, 'I've checked out all the men here and they are all awful. Can we go home now?'

I decided to ignore it. In the spirit of openness to all sorts of different experiences, I'd decided not to instantly judge people on how awful their jumpers (*jumpers*!?) were or how bad their hair/skin/personal hygiene issues were. But the signs weren't great. Not only were the men not looking particularly fabulous on first sight, but the woman checking us off her list looked completely disorganised and admitted it was the first time she'd arranged something like this. 'Great,' I thought, 'so you thought you'd jump on the bandwagon of tragic single people and make a fast buck.' God, this dating lark was threatening to turn me even more cynical than usual, if that was possible.

The dating began, and straight away I knew that the evening was going to be a disaster. For a start, the bar was tiny, and everyone was sitting right next to one another. So you had one couple saying, 'So, what do you do?' and 'Where do you live?' at the same table as another couple saying, 'So, where do you live?' and 'What do you do?', and trying not to listen to the other person's answers, not least because they'd be dating them in three minutes' time.

Then, because, as usual, there were lots more girls than guys, for every other date the women had to sit on their own, watching people date about half a metre from them. I sat on a tiny stool at a tiny table at which two other people were asking each other things like 'So, what do you do?' while pretending that I wasn't there, listening in. It felt like a threesome that had gone terribly wrong.

Of the guys that were there, about four were genuinely single, had signed up for this online and were hoping to meet someone. The rest were – of course – friends and relatives of the organiser who had been hastily shipped in for the night from anywhere from Brighton to Bedford. Some were not even single.

I should have known. The writing was on the wall the day before when I'd checked the website to find out what time it started. 'Females tickets SOLD OUT' read a notice on the site, somewhat ungrammatically. 'Male tickets buy One get One FREE.'

The ones who were actually single and not just there as singleton ballast seemed perfectly nice but, sadly, unbelievably dull. There was an accountant who talked about how boring his job was. There was an IT guy who talked, boringly, about how interesting his job was. There was a guy who didn't have a job at all, but was on the verge of launching something so secret he couldn't even talk about it, and another guy who talked about his racing bike for three minutes solid.

After a while, all the girls and I realised that sitting on our own looking pathetic for three minutes at a time was no fun at all, so we started chatting to one another when we hadn't got dates, which actually turned out to be a lot more interesting than talking to the guys. We compared notes about the blokes present – who were generally considered to be a bit of a dead loss – and during the break we all met at the bar. Emma and I had separately come to the conclusion – by looking around and talking to the other girls about who they had already dated this evening – that there was no point whatsoever in sticking around for the second half, and so we abandoned ship to the cocktail bar across the road, where we tried not to think about how awful and pointless the evening had been.

There had to be a better way.

5

Looking for Luck

When you are single, and rather keen not to be, every little thing takes on a deeper significance than it might actually deserve.

I went to Wimbledon tennis recently on a freebie day out for journalists and joined the queue for taxis at the station to take people up to the tournament. Rather than everyone getting their own taxi, we were sharing a cab for a flat fee. Each black cab took five people, and I was on my own (of course) in between two couples, so I figured that we'd all get into a cab together.

But no.

When we got to the head of the queue, the two couples were ushered into a waiting cab, while the solitary single (me) was yanked aside and told to stand in a special line dedicated to people too pathetic to have a travelling companion. So the couples headed off up the hill, while I stood alone in the singles queue, feeling the pity of the crowd and frothing at the injustice of it all.

At these moments, the world seems against you, determined to laugh at you and make you feel small. Never mind the fact that, when returning home from the tennis that evening, I took the sad singles queue and actually queue-jumped several hundred couples to get into a cab, thus waiting for a fraction of the time, it still feels like the universe is conspiring against you to make you feel bad that you're on your own.

Even things that are supposed to help you end up making you feel even more depressed. I recently read an advice column in a newspaper that made me want to go round to the agony aunt's office and seriously ask her what planet she was living on. A woman had written in saying that she was 35 years old and had been trying internet dating for some time but hadn't met anyone suitable at all.

The advice? Try something else. So far, so good. But the 'something elses' were: join the local council! Volunteer with Help the Aged! Throw a street party and post leaflets through everyone's door with a picture of your face on it! And the pièce de résistance? 'You could always put your house on the market. A friend of mine did and she ended up marrying the person who came round to see it!'

Brilliant. A woman is seeking some sensible advice about how to meet people and she's told to look after old people (very worthy, but how really is that going to help find a boyfriend, assuming she's not into pensioners?) or to sell her house. If that advice wasn't rubbish enough, the agony aunt then embarked on a detailed description of how lucky she was to have found her gorgeous husband at a party when she was still a student, which presumably helped finish off the poor letter-writer's hopes completely.

The more I consider this whole 'dating to find a husband' quest, the more I think most, if not practically all, of it is down to sheer luck. Now I'm not saying that luck doesn't need a helping hand, of course it does. Yes, you have to get out there and meet people in the first place, and you're unlikely to meet your husband while sitting around at home (unless you are the improbably lucky friend of the agony aunt whose future husband walked in clutching a pile of sales documents). But meeting someone you can have a connection with is, I think, mainly down to luck.

I think many people who have found someone have no idea how lucky they really are. Not as in 'I'm so lucky to be living in my lovely house with my lovely husband with our lovely children'-type lucky, which most people do appreciate, but the 'I'm so lucky that my boss chose to employ us/we chose the same university/when we took up running we lived near each other so we joined the same running club' kind of luck.

And it's not just about geography but also about timing. I could have met the perfect person for me when I was 13, for example, though obviously I'd never have known it at the time, and, by the time I was thinking of settling down, 20 years and several hundred miles would have been between us.

Or I could have worked with someone wonderful but I might have been going out with someone else at the time, or he could have been with someone, or just come out of a rubbish break-up and not into dating at all, or he could have been transferred to another office or I could have left my job shortly before he joined the company or . . . In fact, there are so many reasons to miss meeting someone that I'm often amazed that people manage to get together at all.

I have a friend who met her husband in the taxi rank at Victoria station. They got chatting, ended up sharing a cab and now share three children and a house in Godalming. If they hadn't met then, would they have met another time? Unlikely, unless we're talking Hollywood romcoms here. If she had been four places behind him in the queue, would he have got married to the woman who was standing in her place next to him? Or would they both still be single, having a vague feeling that they missed out on something amazing when one of them decided to take the Tube that night, or stay in the pub for one extra drink?

Meetings like that are incredible and wonderfully romantic but really hard to replicate. At a party recently, I was told about a woman who was standing on the Tube escalator late one night and realised that she'd caught her shoe in the grating. She started getting slightly panicky – her shoe, if not her entire foot, was in danger of being mangled – and a man travelling on the up escalator saw that she was getting rather stressed. So he ran up his escalator and down hers and rescued her and the shoe before they got crunched in the mechanism.

Tearful thanks were given and phone numbers exchanged. They are now living in wedded bliss with two kids and a mortgage.

It's hard to know what to take from all this. Should I be hanging around taxi queues in the rain late at night, hoping that the be-suited executive next to me might be going to Clapham? Or maybe I should pretend to be going wherever he is? Should I check out his ring finger before getting in a cab with him? And maybe he'd quite like to get his own cab? If I get to the front of the queue and he heads off into the night on his own, should I just start again? At which point, will I get moved on for soliciting? So many questions, so many logistical imponderables . . .

Likewise with the escalator scenario. Should I just ride the escalators, risking life and limb, or at least my best pair of heels, hoping not only that a white knight will rush to my rescue but also that we'll want to get married after he yanks my foot to safety? It does seem rather a lot to ask.

But stranger things have happened. One of my acquaintances, unbelievable though it sounds, actually met her future husband when he was on his honeymoon, at the hotel bar. They are now married – he had to get divorced first, of course – have three children and live in High Wycombe.

I was certainly trying to increase my luck. I started playing social tennis at the local club where you just turned up and played with whoever happened to be there, although the first time I went it was just me and the tennis coach. I also joined a social/networking club based near me and went along to a posh drinks evening. The following weekend, we played rounders in the park. I was certainly meeting a lot of new people, but, so far, no potential partners.

Many people meet their future wives or husbands through work and that's easy to understand. You're thrown together every day, you can take your time getting to know someone and there's none of that hideous interview-style dating that goes on away from the workplace. A little light flirting over the photocopier, some banter over whose turn it is to make the coffee and you're just a Christmas-party booze-up away from picking out crockery at John Lewis for your wedding list. Of course, that also relies on your boss recruiting some suitable candidates.

I have gone out with people I've worked with before now and getting together with them was simple. But in my current job, where I've been for several years now, there have been precisely zero candidates for the role of future husband.

I mentioned this, possibly unwisely, to my boss, who entirely refuted the charge.

'What do you mean?' she said. 'I've provided lots of boys for you to get together with.'

This was news to me. Where were they hiding? 'Like who?' I asked, aware that this might be a career-limiting conversation.

'Will, Roger and Malcolm,' she said without hesitation.

'Well, thanks for that, but, erm, Will's engaged, Roger is gay and Malcolm is not only ten years younger than me but he's also completely mad.'

She sniffed contemptuously. 'Well, if you're going to be picky . . .'

My friend Amanda from school is a great example of knowing how lucky she – and of course, her husband – is. They met at the Big Chill festival, having both wandered away from their respective groups of friends, and started chatting. Eight years on, they have barely spent a night apart from each other since and have three gorgeous children.

'The thing is,' she said thoughtfully, sitting in her kitchen one afternoon while her youngest slept upstairs, 'I know that it was just luck that we met. We helped it along a bit, of course, by being there in the first place, and also by not just sticking to our group of friends. So I do feel that we helped make it happen. But the chance of him being there at exactly the same time I was there, and that we were both single, and both liked each other . . . that was complete luck. I'm totally aware of that, and that I've got lots of single friends my age, like you, who just haven't had that stroke of luck. It's really difficult out there, I do know that, and it's really hard to know what to do. How can you tell someone "be lucky"?'

I love Amanda for many reasons, but mainly because of that. There are so many people who say, 'Get out there! Go on!' (As though you are some kind of pet that needs walking.) 'Go online! Join a club! That's what you need to do!' Yet if you ask them, when they met their husbands or wives, how much 'getting out there' they actually bloody did, the answer is usually none.

'Oh, we met at work/university/school,' they'll say, sitting on their comfy sofas and simpering at each other.

Great, thanks for that.

While I had expected long-time marrieds to be smug and unhelpful, I hadn't expected the same reaction from those who had only just made it across no-man's land. One woman in my circle of friends had been single for ages and, once in her forties, was feeling utterly depressed about the fact that she would never get married and have children.

However, at a friend's house party a couple of years ago, she did actually meet a guy, started dating him, got married and has just had a baby. She is one of the success stories and gives a glimmer of hope to all my single friends. But, far from feeling lucky and happy and appreciating her good fortune, she refuses to even talk about the days when she was single and has drawn a curtain over the whole of her past life. It's as if she is so terrified of going back there that she doesn't want to 'catch' singleness from any of her still-single friends. 'She's pulled the ladder up behind her,' said a mutual friend mournfully. 'She's probably got her reasons but it doesn't help the rest of us still out here, when we listened to her tales of single life for so long.'

Maybe she's worried that, if her husband finds out how terribly single she felt before she met him, he'll wonder if she really wanted to be with him or just didn't want to be single. There is a whole relationship minefield out there, even once you have found your man.

However, after talking to Amanda, I began to think that festivals might be something worth exploring. Being way past 25 made me feel too old for Glastonbury, or Reading, or anything even slightly cool, so I decided to set my sights on something at which I wasn't going to feel too ancient and at which, hopefully, there would be some nice 30–40-something guys.

Thankfully, Alex James – Blur bassist, country gent and now cheese-maker – decided to 'invite a few people to stay in his back garden', as he put it, and hold what could possibly be the most middle-class festival ever. It even promised cooking demonstrations from Hugh Fearnley-Whittingstall, for heaven's sake. The festival's PR people had kindly given me a free ticket, so one Saturday morning I rummaged around in the cellar to find my tent and sleeping bag, borrowed a rucksack and sleeping mat from my flatmates and headed off in my Fiat to the Cotswolds.

Going to a festival on my own felt rather weird, but at such short notice – and, well, who am I kidding, a complete lack of friends who are able to go away at the drop of a hat to camp in a field for three days without organising babysitters or risking divorce lawyers – I was going to have to go it alone. However, that was nothing new.

With just a brief stop at Waitrose on the M40, where I panic-bought all manner of groceries in the way I usually feel compelled to do on entering the countryside, I arrived at the site – the one that was supposedly Alex James's back garden – by early afternoon.

It was a rather impressive back garden, I had to admit – sprawling green fields leading up to what looked like an old manor house. I tried to fight off a massive attack of lifestyle envy and parked my car among thousands of others before trudging down to the camping field.

Now, I've done a lot of camping in my life, but it soon became apparent that this was a completely different league. People had massive tents with banners and flags, furniture and kitchens, and it seemed many had basically transported their homes from the Home Counties to, well, the county next door.

I had a tiny two-man tent with not even one man to share it with.

I was untangling some guy-ropes when a couple of ten-year-old boys walked past. They were rating everyone's tents on their way to the Portaloos.

'That's good, that's not bad,' they were saying to each other authoritatively. They pointed at mine. 'That's RUBBISH,' they proclaimed decisively.

I wilted a little under their scorn.

I adopted the universal festival uniform of shorts and wellies and went off to explore. It was a beautiful sunny afternoon, the clear blue sky only occasionally punctuated by cartoon-style white fluffy clouds. I felt rather cheerful, in spite of my little tent's poor review. It was lovely to be out of London and doing something that, if it wasn't for my newfound eagerness to try something new, I wouldn't have considered doing on my own in a million years.

It was certainly one of the poshest festivals I had ever been to. Standing in the middle of the main festival field, I could count a dozen stalls selling lattes, cappuccinos, mochas and macchiatos. There would be no shortage of frothy coffees here. There was also a plethora of stalls offering such delights as goat's cheese and chorizo ciabattas, halloumi burgers, salads, curries and, of course, Alex James's own cheeses, whose tent had by far the longest queue. There was also, thankfully, a couple of beer tents that sold local ale, so I went and sampled a few of those while I debated what to do next. Being completely on your own at these types of things always puts you at a disadvantage. You might chat to people in passing, of course, to discuss food or the weather or whether that really was Alex James over there dressed in tweeds and looking like a gentleman farmer (it was), but there is a whole leap from chatting to someone in a queue to actually becoming part of their group.

You have no fixed location, as it's just you, so you wander around fairly aimlessly, chatting, drinking, eating and exploring, but there is none of the usual: 'Right, let's find a spot and set up camp here, with food and picnic rugs.' Someone heads off to get the drinks, while someone else starts handing round food, and then someone you vaguely recognise walks past and it's all 'oh, do come and join us', and before you know it you've got a whole group of people sitting around chatting and drinking and getting to know one another.

I couldn't invite anyone to join me because it was just me,

drifting around, and everyone else seemed to be so content in their own little groups that they certainly weren't going to start conversations with complete strangers, for heaven's sake. There is nothing quite so lonely as being lonely in a crowd.

So I did what I usually do in these circumstances: I turned into a journalist. Rather than breaking into the comfortable close-knit family groups queuing up for the 5 p.m. performance of *Charlie and Lola* in the Big Top, I talked to the producers and sellers of all the gorgeous cheese and meat and pâtés, made contacts and got a few stories. I was actually enjoying myself once more. It seemed that, under the guise of being a nosy reporter, I could talk to anyone and everyone, but, being just a normal person, I was, today at least, completely hopeless.

I gravitated towards one very promising-looking tent. It was selling Bloody Marys, one of my favourite drinks, but with a twist. Rather than adding vodka to a spiced tomato juice, this company made Bloody Mary-spiced vodka. All you had to do was add tomato juice, or drink it neat or with port or consommé, whatever you preferred. This was more like it.

Fortified by beer and spiced vodka, I joined the general crowd by the main stage. Darkness had fallen and the rain was starting to fall. People were clustering close together, watching the bands. Striking up a conversation was impossible as you couldn't hear or see anyone. As a way to spend a day or two with friends, I thought it was pretty good. As a way to meet new people and make new friends, well, unless you were five years old and attended the painting workshops, probably not.

After a cold and sleepless night in my little tent, which turned out to be pitched right next door to a tent full of loud, shrieking and later vomiting teenagers, I rose early, got the

Sunday papers and enjoyed one of the poshest bacon rolls I'd ever had with my morning macchiato. Then, rather than sit in a field all day on my own for the second day running, I went home.

6

The Power of Positive Thinking

There is something about being single and hoping to find someone that makes you incredibly optimistic and utterly pessimistic at exactly the same time. You have to be optimistic, or you would just go home and hide under the duvet for the rest of your life, but, deep down, you do actually secretly believe that you will meet someone special.

You know certain things to be logically true, and so you tell yourself:

'You are not that different from everyone else.'

'Other people manage to meet partners, so it'll happen for you too.'

'There is no way, out of a planet of seven billion people, that you are not going to find somebody that you want to be with and who wants to be with you.'

These are statements of fact. For everyone. Logically, statistically, rationally, subject to all the usual laws of nature and everything you know about the world, you are going to find someone some day.

Such certainty, though, lies very, very deep and can easily get hidden under the more visible layers. The layers that say: 'But you haven't found anyone yet, have you? Everyone else that you've ever known and ever met has managed to find someone and you haven't – so why should it ever happen for you? You're too old, you're too intimidating, you're too sarcastic, you're too impatient, you're too short and too ordinary-looking to ever meet anyone, unless you do some massive settling and they do too.'

However, in spite of that everyday malaise that I suspect most single people feel constantly, there is still the defiant, utterly misplaced optimism that says, 'I will not put up with this! I will go out there and seek out men. I will put myself out there and not be afraid of rejection. There is someone out there for me, it's just a case of knowing where to look and, oh, look, a speed-dating evening just down the road. Who knows, he might be there.'

Even though, all the time, you *know* he's not going to be.

No wonder single people are so exhausted all the time. Not as exhausted as new parents with jobs, childcare, night-time feeds, no sleep, relationship issues, in-laws, builders, inconsiderate bosses and pressing deadlines, and all that kind of stuff – I know that that beats anything that single people suffer in the basic exhaustion stakes. But it's the constant battling in your mind of all these different, contradictory yet simultaneously held points of view that just wears you out.

Being single wasn't something I'd particularly thought about before. During my twenties and early thirties, I wasn't actually single that often, but even when I was it wasn't anything that I dwelled on too much, or worried about, or that in any way defined me.

Now that I had decided that I really did want to meet someone and maybe, if I was lucky, spend the rest of my life with them, I was starting to think about it a whole lot more. It was hard not to really, what with every spare moment taken up with Googling new ways to meet people, before actually going off and trying them out.

However, I still really didn't want it to define me. When I was in my twenties, I'd met too many women in their thirties and forties whose very appearance screamed SINGLE as loudly as if they had been actually shouting the word through a megaphone.

They all had that air of quiet desperation, that sad, lonely look that came from living in a world where every day was bookended by waking up on their own and going home every night, still on their own.

You could tell the 'single women for whom time was running out' by the fact they overdressed for something as mundane as going to the pub for Sunday lunch, or meeting up for casual drinks after work. They would arrive looking very smart and colourful, make-up carefully applied and a silk scarf cast lightly about their shoulders in a well-thought-out 'I just threw this on' look, and they would be bright and sparkly, yet their eyes would reveal their sheer horror and shock at finding themselves in this situation. Others seemed to have totally given up and would arrive looking slightly grey and washed out, chins sprouting stray black hairs and nails and eyebrows in a state of unvarnished, unpruned neglect.

The things they would all have in common, though, were their brittle smiles, which didn't reach their eyes, and the eyes themselves, which had the sad, resigned look of the unloved strays in Battersea Dogs Home.

Now, by accepting my singleness and trying to build myself an escape ladder out of it, I was becoming one of those women. Maybe I was already; maybe I was just pretending that wasn't me yet. I began to scrutinise my face in the mirror more and more, not just for chin hairs and upper-lip forestry, but for that sad, desperate look in my eyes.

It was only a matter of time. *The Sound of Music* had been on the TV recently and for the first time of watching it I had found myself rooting for Christopher Plummer's short-lived girlfriend, the Baroness, rather than Julie Andrews. Poor woman, she didn't stand a chance, turning up smartly dressed and not knowing how to play football, while Julie was young and fresh-faced and hanging from the trees with children dressed in curtains. It would only be a matter of time before I started supporting Glenn Close in *Fatal Attraction* and that was a really alarming prospect.

I had some friends round to lunch, including my one and only single male friend Damien, who was as fed up of being single as I was (it was quite comforting to know that it wasn't just women who felt this way). We started talking about dating, as you do. One friend said she knew someone who would be perfect for Damien, and offered to set them up together.

Damien, making heavy inroads into the cheeseboard at this point, seemed fine about the idea in principle, and asked a few questions about what this woman did, where she lived, that type of thing.

Then: 'How old is she?' he asked.

'Thirty-nine.'

He winced. 'Hmmm, I don't know,' he said.

We – all the late-thirties/early-forties single women round the table – shrieked at this. 'But *you're* 39!' we chorused as one.

'I know, I know,' said Damien, taking courage from the Stilton. 'But I don't think I want to go out with someone my age. Women that age tend to be . . .'

We all waited, our hearts sinking, knowing the answer.

'You know, sad. Unhappy, desperate.'

If we hadn't been before, we certainly were after that. Even though we knew it was true, to have it said by someone so close to us, someone who knew that he was talking about our age group, and someone who knew how hard we were trying to get out of our situations, was terrible.

After people had left, I cleared up, finishing off the cheese and opening another bottle of wine.

'I don't want to be that person,' my brain was saying. 'I don't want to be sad and desperate.'

Now, even though I was actively seeking a man, I still felt rather embarrassed about actually saying that out loud. To me, it was just a short hop from admitting that I was single and not wanting to be, to becoming one of the women for whom the condition was practically terminal. But given that I was doing a lot of things I wouldn't have done in the 'real' world – and occasionally trying to rope friends into coming along with me – it seemed easiest to just come out with it. 'Hello, my name is Sarah and I'm looking for a man.'

I certainly wasn't the only one. Whenever I tentatively mentioned it, at a party, for instance, or in the pub, someone would barge into the conversation and tell me not only what else I should be doing but what they themselves were doing. People couldn't wait to reveal their single status and what they were doing about it. It was astonishing how many people – people whom I thought I knew pretty well, whom I'd chatted to and got drunk with many times over the years – were all doing this type of thing but had been doing it secretly. Now, though, the smallest mention of it was enough to set them off detailing all the ups and downs of their hunt for love.

I felt like a personal therapist, or one of those barmen in old American black and white films in whom everyone confides their troubles. The problem was that, while I was getting an awful lot of insight into other people's personal lives – and I was finding it reassuring that I wasn't the only one fed up with being single – it wasn't actually helping me find a guy of my own.

During one such conversation, someone revealed that they were so sick of being single that they'd signed up for a canoeing course.

'It worked too,' she said. 'I did actually meet someone.'

We all started wondering where our nearest canoeing centre might be, before she added, 'Unfortunately, he turned out to be a complete nutter.'

We all scrubbed 'research canoeing courses' off our mental 'to-do' lists.

'And the thing is I don't even like sodding canoeing. But you do strange things when you're desperate.'

I had to agree. I remembered when meeting new people was as easy as walking into a room or, when I was in Italy, just driving down the motorway. It became a common occurrence to be overtaken by a car driven by a good-looking bloke, who would then do a double-take when he realised that not only were you a youngish woman driving on your own, but you also appeared to be sitting on the wrong side of the car.

In fact, driving an Italian car in Italy with a right-hand drive made for a great deal of confusion. Once when I was sitting at the head of a queue of cars waiting to drive onto the ferry to Sicily, the traffic controllers seemed to be delaying boarding for some reason. Finally, they realised that I was on my own in the car. They apologised profusely. 'Sorry, signora,' they chorused. 'We were waiting for your husband.'

'You and me both,' I thought gloomily.

Sitting adjacent to other drivers on the *autostrada* meant that they could get a good look at you and would signal their approval by driving alongside you, smiling and waving. When another car wanted to pass, they would drop back and then re-emerge alongside once the way was clear, and when they saw a lay-by sign they would put their indicators on in the hope you could be enticed off the road for, well, let's politely say a picnic.

Needless to say, I was never tempted but it was typical Italy – you could never go very long without being chatted up, even while driving along the motorway at 130 kilometres an hour. Now I was back in London, if a guy even looked at me, it was some kind of minor miracle.

Actually, that's not entirely true. I was asked out just recently. I was locking my bike up outside the gym when a guy – slightly overweight, slightly hairy, but a guy nonetheless – came up to me. 'I'm sorry to ask but, well, have you got a boyfriend?'

I was slightly taken aback and gave my automatic stock response when someone whom I don't know and who doesn't look like Keanu Reeves in *Point Break* asks me out: 'Yes, I'm afraid I am seeing someone.'

He didn't look particularly bothered by this but said quite sweetly, 'Oh well, sorry to ask. I should have guessed that you were. But my sister is always saying that I should be more spontaneous and, well, I thought I'd take her advice. Sorry to bother you anyway.'

'No, not at all,' I replied, and went into the gym with my ego rather boosted by that little exchange, but just a little embarrassed when the same guy was on the bike next to mine in the spinning class.

After the class, I phoned my sister and told her what had happened. She thought for a moment and then said, 'Was he quite tall with massive eyebrows?'

'Yes, he was,' I said, surprised.

'Well, don't take this the wrong way, but he's asked me out too. I think he does it to everyone, sorry.'

Now she mentioned it, I had a feeling that he had asked me out before, about four years earlier. Still, I couldn't fault his persistence. And even if he was going round asking out every girl in south-west London, at least it had made me feel an inch more desirable, even if just for a second. It was the Italian approach all over again.

7

Fifty Ways to Find Your Lover

At home, I couldn't stop thinking about the canoeing idea. Even though it hadn't actually worked out for my friend, the concept of doing something you liked while hoping to meet someone else who liked doing it too was a pretty good one. Rather than having 'being single' as the sole common denominator, as was the case with the speed-dating events, it made sense to try the 'having things in common' approach. You know, like in *real* life, not just single life.

I wrote a list of everything I was interested in. Sport. Beer. Books. Films. Poker.

I looked at the list. I wondered, not for the first time, if I really should have been born a boy. I added some more girlish stuff to the list. Wine. Cocktails. Dancing. Acting. That seemed to be quite enough to be going on with.

More than enough, as it turned out. The good thing, I soon discovered, is that, if you are interested in wine-tasting or acting courses and live in London, there are literally hundreds of options open to you.

The bad thing is that it is easy to get totally and utterly overwhelmed by all of them.

Five minutes on the internet will throw up a whole new

world of things to 'do', a world populated by hundreds of people who want to sign up for things.

It can be utterly intimidating. From complaining of never meeting any new people, you can suddenly find yourself doing nothing but meeting new people.

The problem is not which course or event you would like to attend; it's finding which one *he* will be at. *He*, of course, is the man that I will want to spend the rest of my life with, and he with me. He is obviously no more than a concept at the moment, roughly sketched out along the lines of a 30/40-something single straight male who's looking to settle down but still wants adventure and new experiences. I think this is a pretty open category without all the usual caveats women my age are accused of making that narrow our options, such as 'must have hair' and 'must not have children'.

But even assuming this mythical man is actually into wine or poker or films, where will he actually be? Say he's into wine and actually wants to go on a wine-tasting course. A quick Google of 'wine-tasting in Clapham' yields a promising-looking venue that organises both evening events and weekend trips away to vineyards. This sounds ideal – I'm into wine, and I generally like other people who are too.

However, would the guy I'm after – and I have to keep reminding myself that it is just a concept of a guy I'm after, as it sometimes feels as though there is an actual man that I'm stalking across the internet, thinking, 'Where will I find him? What does he like?' – choose this particular place in which to learn about wine? Just this one site offers so many opportunities to meet 'him' that I'm terrified of choosing the wrong one.

With an unlimited budget and unlimited time, several repeats of my 39th year and without having to go to work every day, I could easily check out all the options offered by this one place. I could go there every Wednesday to do wine-tasting, spend every weekend on trips down to local vineyards and really thoroughly wring all the single-man-meeting potential out of it.

I could do the same for all the wine-tasting courses in Balham, then Battersea, Kensington and Wandsworth, and across the whole of London and the south-east. I could do one-off events and term-long evening classes. It wouldn't be just wine-tasting either, but wine-making too, or beer-making, food appreciation, cooking, learning a foreign language, car maintenance, dancing, public speaking, films, screenwriting or outdoor fitness classes. The list was endless, and I could spend a whole lifetime chasing my mythical guy around until I actually found him.

Of course, I haven't got an unlimited budget or unlimited time to pursue this: I have just months until I'm 40 and in that time I have to work, sleep, eat and pay rent, and what I am left with is basically several nights a week (assuming I abandon all evening work commitments and seeing my friends for the next year or two) and not very much money to track him down.

So, what's it to be? I feel overwhelmed by both choice and the hopelessness of the task. If I choose 'An Evening with New World Wines', what are the odds that he'll have booked 'An Evening with Old World Wines' instead? Or decided to go on the trip to the vineyard in Sussex, rather than Surrey? I can't afford – either in time or in money – to spend a whole day on a trip to Dorking with completely unsuitable people when my man is swigging wine in Kent, or has booked the Dorking trip for the following week when I'm in Kent. Perhaps he has decided not to do wine-tasting after all, but has plumped for brewing or a writing class, or even given up on the whole thing and either gone down the pub with his mates to watch the footie or has got a huge hangover and is spending the whole day in bed, while I've paid £100 to sit on a coach with a bunch of 60 year olds.

These are the kinds of difficulties that married people or any couple in a long-term relationship just do not understand.

'It takes a lot of effort to make a marriage successful, you know,' they'll say, annoyingly and pointlessly. 'It's not as easy as you think.'

Well, I appreciate that marriage is a lot of work and I'm sure it's really tough at times, but look – you've got something tangible to actually work with.

I, on the other hand, have just the vaguest idea of the person I'm looking for, no idea at all whether he even actually exists and barely the faintest idea of how to find him. It's like nailing fog to the wall, or throwing a dart into thin air, hoping that there is a dartboard out there for it to land on.

There are so many ways *not* to meet someone that it makes my head spin. Even assuming we both like – to continue the theme – wine-tasting, and he lives in Clapham and he's heard of this wine-tasting place and he goes to the same event that I do – there's no reason that we should meet, and chat, and bond. He could be sitting at the wrong end of the room, or at the wrong table, or at the wrong end of the coach. I could spend the entire time talking to someone who seems perfectly nice but who turns out to be mad. Or gay. Or married.

This is why I fantasise about a magical invention, a special pair of glasses that make a big brightly coloured arrow appear over someone's head showing that he has all the right sane, straight and single attributes. Think of all the time I'd no longer waste in futile conversations or attending pointless events. I could just walk into a room and there would be a flutter of glowing arrows pointing down at the people I should be talking to.

Now, of course I know that this might be the wrong approach. Just because I end up talking to someone who's the wrong age, or gay, or married, or for whatever reason not suitable, there's no reason that they might not know someone who would be perfect for me.

I know that. I realise that, if I talk to as many people as I can, some of them might turn out to be good fun to hang out with, and one day they might invite me to dinner or out for drinks and they might introduce me to someone who is exactly the kind of person that I've been looking for. But I haven't got time for that! I can't spend my time talking to people in the hope that they might introduce me to other people. I've spent the last 20 years doing that and look what's happened. Nothing. Well, not nothing, but nothing right now and that's what counts.

It's amazing how you can be single for years and yet if you end up with a bloke, it's as though the wilderness years never even happened. On the other hand, you can have had lots of perfectly respectable, long-term relationships, but because they didn't ultimately work out, you're just a sad loser who didn't end up with the prize.

Since the age of 35, my fertility – according to various terrifying newspaper articles – has been falling off a cliff. I have to find someone *right now* and there is no time for any more dead-ends or diversions.

However, even assuming I attend all the classes in the world, it's quite hard to establish over a few hours of slurping and sipping or lubing and pumping (bike-maintenance course, since you ask) whether someone is not only single, but also actively looking for someone to spend the rest of his life with. It's tricky to elicit that kind of information so soon after meeting someone without sounding desperate and sending him running for the hills.

This is, I belatedly realise, the point of internet dating. Everyone on those sites wants to meet someone. It cuts out all the unnecessary 'What brought you here?' 'Oh my wife just adores Tuscan reds' types of conversations that instantly cut short all those fantasies about marrying him that you've been indulging for the last ten minutes. But internet dating has its own horrors, just one of which is the lack of something in common. You're there to date, that's all. There is no other, diversionary activity in sight. So this means there's nothing else for it but to combine the two: interests and dating. Wine-tasting and dating. Bike maintenance and dating. Italian-language classes and dating. I think I could be on to something.

8

Anything for Love

By allowing myself to become overwhelmed by choice, I was in danger of not actually doing anything at all, which was completely daft. So I consulted my list, decided to go for the sporty option first and joined a running club. In fact, not one, but two. I joined a huge one in central London and a smaller one in Clapham. Every Wednesday night I ran around Hyde Park with hundreds of other runners and every Thursday I ran around Clapham Common with five other runners.

Both approaches had their drawbacks. The central London club was so huge it was easy to get completely lost in the crowd. It soon became obvious that the lean, keen, super-runners, who were mainly blokes, would usually go out on their own and do a quick 13-mile dash along the river and back. Those who were more on the fun-runner side of things, like me, would instead trot around Hyde Park several times. And people in this group were mainly girls. So, while I met lots of nice women on the trips round the park, chatting about this and that on our way to Kensington and back, it wasn't an ideal way to meet, or even talk to, any men.

The smaller local club was nice and friendly, and consisted of two married men and a married couple, which was not particularly promising.

I soon dropped both of those in favour of British Military Fitness, a new craze that seemed to be taking over most of London's green spaces. Every morning and evening on Clapham Common, there were groups of people in netball bibs doing shuttle runs or star jumps, much to the bemusement of passers-by. I'd recently read an article about a newly engaged couple who had met while going to a BMF session in the pouring rain one wet Wednesday night. They'd gone to the pub afterwards to dry out and, well, if someone is soaked through and covered in mud and sweat and you still fancy them, it must be love. I duly signed up.

Again, most of the fitter – in every sense – guys were in the more advanced group but, as I lined up on the common preparing for my first session, I did notice that there was quite a healthy gender mix in the blue bibs, the group for beginners and happy amateurs. We were led by a rather good-looking army type in a jacket and combat trousers, and spent an hour alternately jogging and sprinting from tree to tree, doing press-ups, squats, playing tag and generally throwing ourselves around. It was certainly a very impressive workout – one that left me feeling suitably achy the next day – but I was unsure where the opportunity was to actually talk to someone for more than a minute without one of you having to count the number of sit-ups they were doing.

After the hour, we jogged back to the car park where the BMF van was parked, handed back our netball bibs and then, well, nothing. Everyone just melted away. Undeterred, I kept on going back, running around the park in the cold, the wet and the dark, and yet the social aspect of it completely passed me by. No one seemed tempted by the pub that was so invitingly close, and, although I might have been getting fitter, I certainly wasn't meeting any men, unless you counted jogging along in a group with them while a military guy shouted, 'Ten press-ups, now!'

I continued BMF-ing but starting exploring other, less physical options. I enrolled on a rather serious wine course, which involved trekking across to the Vintners Hall every Monday evening to sit in a classroom and learn about grape varieties and the difference between viticulture and viniculture. I enjoyed the course and even got a certificate afterwards, but again the social aspect of it was non-existent. I had to practically drag some of my fellow workers along to a wine bar to celebrate after passing our exam and it was not what you would call a wild evening.

I did another wine course, in Balham this time. It was not as serious as the last one, and, in fact, drinking rather than learning was a definite priority. The course was great fun, run by an enthusiastic husband and wife team, and, after two hours of swilling and glugging in the classroom of a local school, we'd all decamp to the pub for a drunken evening followed by an even more drunken curry. This was much more sociable than the other course and it obviously worked: out of a class of fourteen, four people paired off and both couples actually ended up getting married. I didn't find a permanent drinking partner myself, it has to be said, and, after a term of turning up very hungover to work every Friday (bad news for a Sunday newspaper journalist), I decided that it would be career limiting for me to stay another term. However, it showed that there was definite husband-hunting potential out there.

Next, I moved on to acting. I quite liked the idea of doing something completely different from what I was used to, and inspired by my time in New York, where everyone was taking some sort of class or another, I signed up for six weeks of acting classes, for two hours every Tuesday. The class was taught in a disused church up the road from Clapham Junction by a very cheerful and well-spoken young man called Toby.

The first week, we played lots of word games, pretended to be animals and did activities I remembered from childhood parties such as 'concentration'. So far, so ... well, juvenile, but it was fun of sorts and probably a healthier way to decompress from a day at work than stopping off at the pub, but I was looking forward to getting down to some actual acting.

The next week, however, and the ones after that, provided more of the same. Lots of games where you had to guess what someone was miming, and lots of *Whose Line Is It Anyway?*-type activity, when you were given an object and had to pretend it was something else – a chair turned into a car, or a phone as a bomb. It all began to get a little bit tedious. I wasn't expecting to tackle *Hamlet*, but something that we could rehearse would have been nice, rather than making it all up as we went along.

Toby did get full marks for inviting us along to the pub afterwards a couple of times, and the guys on the course were nice in a dull kind of way, but at the end of the six weeks I wasn't sorry that it was over.

However, while walking home from the class each week, I had noticed a sign up across from the station. 'Ceroc every Monday,' it said. Several of my married friends had gone to ceroc classes before their weddings so they could actually perform a dance, rather than just shuffle around the floor looking awkward, begging other people to join in so they wouldn't feel so self-conscious, but that's as far as my knowledge went. But in the spirit of doing new things, I went along the following Monday, wearing some cute little pink pumps I thought I might be able to dance in and a swirly skirt.

There were far more women than men – of course – so some women had to sit out the dancing each time, but every few minutes we all moved along so it wasn't actually that bad. The dancing was fun, too, with the basic moves fairly easy to pick up thanks to our cheerful Scottish instructor who demonstrated each routine with her partner up on stage. After an hour or so of learning various different moves, we finally managed to put them all together in a proper routine and so we ended the evening on a note of achievement.

The blokes seemed to be nice, if rather serious about dancing. I was told off by one for doing something wrong and abandoned by another the moment we went to free dancing. There seemed to be little flirting and a lot of earnest learning going on, but it was pretty enjoyable nonetheless.

I went back the next week, but this time my partners were even more serious and I was nearly crippled by a rather overweight woman next to me who took off with all the poise of a baby elephant and landed full square on my poor defenceless foot. She didn't even have the grace to apologise.

All this was starting to cost me a fair bit of money, not to mention time. Running, BMF-ing, wine-tasting, acting and dancing were all fun things to do but they cut quite a swathe through my bank account, as well as taking up precious evenings, particularly the ones that required you to sign up for a whole series.

However, I was resolved to keep at it. No one was going to accuse me of not trying hard enough. I signed up to everything I could find – I even applied to go on a television dating show (although I am still waiting to hear back from them). I found a brand-new dating experience that sounded quite fun, called Come Date With Me. According to its website:

> Come Date With Me is a fun alternative to internet dating – no endless emails, no monthly fee and no first date nerves. Instead, a sumptuous meal, plentiful fine wine and the fantastic company of up to 23 other single guys and girls. What's not to love?!

What indeed? I immediately signed up for cocktail-tasting dating and a dinner party.

Alarm bells started to ring when I saw that I was the first person to sign up for either event, but maybe I was just being super-organised. Then the company sent me a confirmation email of my booking, which added: 'And please, do tell your friends about us and get them to sign up too!' This seemed a little odd. If I knew anyone I wanted to date, then surely I would be dating them already without having to sign up to this type of activity? And why would I bring along girls (competition) or boys (would take up the place of a potential husband) I knew? Alas, my concerns turned out to be justified: both events were later cancelled due to lack of interest and my money promptly returned.

Some dating companies seemed to go out of their way to make me feel bad. I would get emails saying: 'Hurry hurry hurry – sign up for this fabulous singles event! PS FEMALE PLACES ALL SOLD OUT.' Thanks for that.

It was time to try poker. Not only could you just turn up whenever you felt like it rather than having to book and pay well in advance, you might even end up winning, if not a man, then at least some money. And poker was, traditionally, a man's game. I hardly knew any women who played it. So, in theory, it was one of the few activities I could do where the men would outnumber the women.

I actually liked playing poker. I used to host a weekly game when I lived in New York. Every Wednesday, friends would turn up at my tiny apartment overlooking the Hudson River, armed with six-packs of beers and dollar bills. It was quite an expat hack pack: there were guys from *The Guardian*, *The Telegraph*, *The Independent*, *The Observer* and *The Times*, as well as the bloke from the Press Association. There was only one other woman, who freelanced for *The Financial Times*, and me, who freelanced for anyone who would have me. We would sit at my flatmate's huge round table, the size of a wagon wheel, and dole out the chips. Then we'd play for an hour or so, drinking beer and munching on corn chips and salsa, before having a break to order massive New York pizzas, which were almost as big as the table, and then play on till midnight.

Back in the UK, pub poker had been gaining in popularity and quite a few of my local pubs were now advertising poker nights. My nearest pub had a poker game there every Tuesday at 8 p.m. and I turned up at 7.50 p.m. one Tuesday to be told that it was full. It was evidently more popular than I'd thought.

The following week, I turned up at 7 p.m., paid my five pounds to get onto the table and nursed a pint for an hour. At 8 p.m. we all filed into the back room and found a seat at one of the three poker tables. There was a guy who fancied himself as a bit of a poker pro on my table and, rather to my relief, he took over the dealing rather than the duty being passed around the table, leaving me free to gamble and, of course, check out the other players.

The good news was that there were about thirty men and three women. Those were my kind of odds. The bad news was, well, they were all obviously just there to play poker. While everyone seemed quite friendly and certainly not at all hostile to a complete stranger in their midst, they were too intent on their cards and trying to win money to engage in any mid-hand banter. I didn't do too badly poker-wise, being one of the later ones to crash out of the game, but I had already crashed out in the dating stakes the moment I'd walked in the room.

I was beginning to suspect that luck was going to play a large role in my quest and, so far, it was looking as if I didn't actually have any. I read in the local paper about a new running club that had just been set up called Home Run.

The idea was aimed at busy City professionals who didn't have a great deal of spare time but still wanted to get fit. If you chose to work out by running home from work, rather than going home on the Tube and then going to the gym, you would have to run wearing a cumbersome backpack. Home Run would transport your bags home, or at least to a nearby Tube station, for you, so you could get fit while avoiding commuter hell. My forays into fitness had shown me that where there was running there were usually men, so I decided to check it out.

I logged on to the site, signed up and made my way over to the Embankment by 6 p.m. one dark Wednesday evening. The group was so small I nearly missed them. There was me, two guys and the girl from Home Run. That was it.

'Gosh, we've never been such a small group!' exclaimed the Home Run rep. 'Last night we had 25 runners!'

'Of course you did,' I thought. God, or Lady Luck, or whatever supreme being is responsible for that type of thing, obviously wanted me to remain single. It was time to get serious.

9

Kilts, Cocktails and Cardio

My flatmates Charlotte, Jeff and Alex had been watching this sudden flurry of activity with a mixture of amusement and alarm. They had often seen me come home in a mood of tortured longing, which signalled yet another lovely but utterly pointless evening in the pub with Will, and were probably quite relieved that I was starting to fill up my time with Will-free activities. They were also all in their thirties and single, but didn't seem that bothered about it. The boys especially were relaxed to the point of extreme inertia about the whole thing. They were both good-looking, fun, witty and charming guys and, when I came home from event after event where there was a chronic shortage of men, I wanted to shake them from their usual positions on the sofa and shout, 'Come on! Get out there! There are women there who need you!'

But I didn't. They were pretty happy and, let's face it, I was hardly a great example. I'd spent months quite literally running myself ragged in the search for a partner and so far it was yielding the square root of bog all results-wise.

Charlotte, on the other hand, was showing signs of thinking about jumping on board the dating bandwagon after a year of being happily single. She had taken up dancing too and stuck to it far longer than I had done and had even been asked out on a date by a guy she'd met there. She had also dipped her toe into internet dating and spent a day with one pleasant chap going round the museums in South Kensington. Now she had heard that some friends of hers were going to an evening of Scottish dancing and she decided that she should go, too, and that her friend Lisa and I should join her.

Not having been invited to many ceilidhs before, I had visions of it being held in a Scout hut off the A3 where we would be served watery beer and ham sandwiches. It turned out to be a rather more sophisticated affair at the extremely posh Hurlingham Club in Chelsea. The evening would kick off with a champagne reception, 'sumptuous' – according to the invite – three-course meal with half a bottle of wine per head, charity raffle, silent auction and live Scottish reels and DJ into the wee small hours.

I hadn't done any dancing of this nature since country dancing with Nicholas Gibson at primary school, but I was assured that the whole thing would be simple to pick up.

The event was very grand indeed. The entrance hall was packed full of posh people sporting kilts, ball dresses, wraps and a hefty amount of jewellery. Lisa, Charlotte and I, looking fairly smart ourselves after a series of increasingly panicked shopping expeditions, hung around nervously in the foyer, sipping fizz and wondering where Charlotte's friends were. Thankfully, we found them and were welcomed into the group. There was a fair amount of drinking, polite small talk and courteous flirting going on, and then we sat down to dinner, after which there was a raffle and an auction, before the dancing began.

The good thing about Scottish dancing, I soon discovered, is that you had to be partnered with a man. However, that is also the bad thing about Scottish dancing. If you knew lots of people or were in a large group of friendly men, you were likely to be fine. If you were in a group of three women who had only just met your party for the first time that night, many of whom were in couples already, then you had a problem. I was all right for the first few dances, as one of the guys I was sitting next to at dinner politely asked me to partner him. But then he went off to dance with his girlfriend, and I was left to scrabble around for a spare man. As this was what I had already been doing for some months now, I wasn't too thrilled with having to do it this evening as well. 'Bloody Scottish dancing!' I raged internally after yet another dance got under way while I was relegated to watching from the tables. Why couldn't it be like English dancing when you just all jumped around on the dance floor in one big mass to some incredibly cheesy music? Sometimes, it seemed to be deliberately annoying: some of the dances called for two women to partner one man, which meant that you lost your partner to make up a three with someone else, and then, when it reverted to a man-woman couple, you once again found yourself partnerless and banished from the dance floor. When I did manage to find myself a partner and hang on to him for more than one dance, it could be quite good fun, but I was rather relieved when the band packed up their violins and Abba came on the turntables.

The flirting was continuing intermittently, but nothing more. One guy who had shown an interest in me decided to turn his affections to Lisa instead. Charlotte was propositioned by a guy whom she had barely spoken to all night but whom she shared a cab home with. And, just a few weeks later, a guy from work whom she rather liked declared that he had completely fallen for her. Her foray into the singles world looked to be mercifully brief.

My own stay in singledom looked likely to be a rather lengthier one. And rather more alcoholic too. I discovered that the vodka bar down the road by Clapham Junction ran singles cocktail-making classes, and so dutifully headed there after work one Thursday night.

I was unfashionably prompt, and no one else had turned up yet. The event itself was to be held in a glass-fronted room just off the main bar and it was completely empty. Rather than stand there like a new scientific project – look, see the single people dating! – I lurked at the bar and drank a couple of fortifying gin and tonics. Soon, the girls had all arrived, but there were no blokes anywhere to be seen.

'Don't worry,' said the organiser cheerfully. 'They will come. Boys are always a bit last minute. It's a spur-of-the-moment thing with them.'

The women, all of whom seemed to have spent around two hours getting ready, several days on pre-date grooming and no doubt several hours at the weekend traipsing around the shops for suitable outfits, looked green with envy at the very thought of just casually turning up.

The men finally made it and they all seemed to have come on their own, whereas the girls had arrived in twos and threes for moral support. I was a good few years older than the other girls and about the same age as the guys, but in my work clothes I still felt rather old and 'mumsy'. I could tell pretty much straight away that there was next to no chance that I would end up with any of the guys who all looked, well, amiably hopeless, shuffling around in tatty jeans and trainers like perpetual students who still lived with their mothers.

However, to my surprise, the cocktail class itself was pretty good fun. Our cheerful bartender showed us various tricks, such as how to pour spirits like Tom Cruise in *Cocktail*, and the cool way to pour Red Bull (by suctioning the can onto your palm). We were let loose behind the bar to conjure up a variety of concoctions, and all got fairly plastered as we tasted our way round the optics for almost three hours. It was very enjoyable and good value for money, at least on the alcohol front. On the man front, again it seemed that I would have to go a little further afield.

And so I did – to the Isle of Wight, in fact. I had discovered that British Military Fitness, as well as doing circuit training on the common – and pretty much everywhere across the UK by now – also organised short breaks and longer holidays. This could be my chance of actually talking to some of my fellow BMF-ers rather than just counting the number of press-ups they did.

I packed a rucksack and off I went for a long weekend. I caught the ferry from Portsmouth early one morning and was met by some burly fitness instructors at Yarmouth, on the west side of the island. We all piled into a minibus and headed off to our home for the next three days, an old army barracks just by the beach. There were about 30 'civilians' in the group, mostly in their twenties or thirties and a fairly equal split between girls and guys.

It was raining hard when we arrived, so we gathered under the tarpaulin strung up over the dining area, which consisted of a long wooden table and benches. Next to the remains of the open fire were some upended logs for seats. We all bagged a bed in the dormitories and I was, in a rather teenage way, happy to see that I was sharing a room with the cutest guy there, although I did notice that another girl was rather pleased about that too. I wasn't the only one who was here hoping to meet a guy, it seemed.

We spent the weekend rambling, cycling, drinking and chatting. Everyone seemed friendly, keen and eager to chat, and it was great to get out of London and clear the cobwebs away. The cute guy was called Danny and we were getting along really well. He was interesting and intelligent and seemed to spend most of his time jetting from one ski slope to the next due to his having been paid a lot of money not to work for a year. It wasn't just that he was cute and friendly that made me really glad that I'd come on the trip – it was also the feeling that I could have stayed in London that weekend and gone out with the same people and gone to the same places, but instead I was somewhere completely new and having really interesting conversations with people I'd never met before. It felt liberating and adventurous and made me realise how easy it is to settle into a routine without even noticing it.

After doing the army's tough and extremely muddy assault course on the final morning, Danny and I stayed on to go round a second time and ended up showering in cubicles next to each other, chattering away at high volume for ages until the army boys thumped on the door, telling us to get a bloody move on as they wanted to wash. We gathered up our clothes and scampered across the field in our towels to the dormitory, but I had been rather too hasty.

Soon someone knocked on the door. 'Erm, Sarah, did you leave anything behind in the shower by any chance?'

It turned out I had, much to the army boys' delight, and my mud-soaked pants were now flying from the camp flagpole.

Everyone swapped details on the journey home, and, after arriving in Clapham Junction, Danny and I ended up spending the afternoon in the pub drinking pints and generally feeling that all was well with the world. I couldn't work out if I fancied him or not: I really liked him, that was true, but he'd just split up with his girlfriend and was obviously deeply cut up about it. It didn't seem the best time to get involved. He did invite me out to a pub quiz a few weeks later and it could have been meant as a date, but by then I had decided that it was best we were just friends. Either way, it was really nice to have made some new friends this way and BMF definitely seemed to tick a lot of boxes: interesting, intelligent, sporty people who might be in their thirties but were still up for adventure. And who didn't mind sleeping in dormitories and getting thoroughly tired and muddy.

Buoyed by the success of the Isle of Wight trip, I started thinking about going on another of the BMF trips away. The skiing holiday in particular caught my attention. Some of the guys in the Isle of Wight party had spoken very highly of last year's trip, making it sound like one non-stop party. It wasn't so much the party aspect that attracted me as the idea there would be a whole group of us hanging out in bars in the French Alps. And the skiing sounded fun too.

The slight problem was that I had never been skiing before in my life. Well, that's not entirely true. In my first year at university, a group of us went to the dry ski slope nearby. I went down a slope that was so flat it barely qualified as such, fell off my skis at the bottom, twisted my ankle and could barely walk for months.

It wasn't cheap, and what with this and all the courses and classes I was signing up for, my bank account was permanently in the red. 'However, it will all be worth it,' I told myself. 'You can start saving your money later, when you have actually found your man and you never have to go out again. Or when it finally becomes clear that there is absolutely no chance that you'll ever find a man and you retreat to your bedroom like a modern-day Miss Havisham. But until then, while there's still a chance, it's spend, spend, spend. And ignore your credit card statements.'

The ski trip turned out to be a really good week. I had expected to either like or loathe skiing, but I hadn't expected to fall completely in love with it. The beginners' instructor, Freddie, was as cute as only 21-year-old ski instructors can be, and his enthusiasm and confidence in us got us from the first day when we could barely get our skis on to going down a red run on the last day – a personal highlight. Our group of complete novices turned out to be fearless in our extreme ignorance, and were up for anything.

The days took on a very pleasant routine: we'd have breakfast and meet on the slopes for lessons from nine to eleven. Then we'd all meet up for hot chocolate in the café overlooking the nursery slopes, and plan our route towards lunch. Lunch would be on top of the world, it seemed – I had never imagined that such huge restaurants could be found so high up in the mountains, where you could sit outside and feel the sun on your face while seeing the snowy peaks rising up around you. Such views didn't come cheap, I soon discovered after paying £8 for a beer and £20 for a burger, although it was a magnificent burger. Some of us would continue skiing, while others would take the lifts back home and then we'd all meet up at various times in the pub next door for vin chaud and a game of gin rummy.

As for romance – well, apart from various crushes on the army instructors, there was surprisingly little. Debra from my skiing class fancied Gordon, a really nice guy who seemed to have no idea that he was the target of her affections. Debra tried hard all week, bless her, and they would have made a lovely couple, except for the fact, only revealed much later, that Gordon had got together with a girl the night before the trip and didn't want to either tell anyone about it to jinx it, or do something he might regret with someone else while away. It seems that it's not just my timing that's completely out of sync.

There were several other nice guys in the group who were great fun to be around but who showed absolutely no sign of being interested in girls, or guys for that matter. They only had eyes for snowboarding. So for me, still no man. So far, the BMF score ran rather like this: cute guys met – quite a few; cute guys 'more than met' – absolutely none. I was having a great time, that was true, but, when it came to sealing the deal, my dating was very much like my skiing – completely amateur.

10

Love's Labours Lost

I watched my ex-boyfriend, Patrick, from the pub window as he walked alongside the canal, talking intently on his mobile. I gathered the drinks and went outside to a table in the sunny beer garden and read a discarded newspaper while he finished his call.

He joined me a few minutes later, smiling sheepishly and helping himself to his drink.

'How is she?' I asked.

I hadn't been told who it was on the phone but I could guess.

He shrugged. 'She's OK,' he said, downing a third of his pint. 'She's a bit annoyed, though. She bashed her phone the other day and now it's playing up.'

'How did she bash it?'

He looked even more sheepish. 'She threw it at me.' He finished his pint. 'Would you like another?'

I had barely sipped mine. 'No, I'm fine, thanks.'

As he went inside, I had a bit of a think. I could make a fairly accurate guess at why Patrick's girlfriend had thrown a phone at him. While it had been years since our relationship – and the post-break-up stuff – had ended, we, against all the odds, had become good friends. When Patrick asked if I'd like to cycle along the Thames to Oxford during one hot summer weekend, I thought it was a lovely idea. Now, I suspected that Patrick's girlfriend had thought it was less lovely and I couldn't really blame her. Still, that was his business, not mine.

Cycling for hours and miles along the canal turned out to be great thinking time. This was the kind of thing Patrick and I did a lot when we were going out together. We had met on a corporate freebie during Wimbledon fortnight and, after a day spent drinking Pimm's, we ended up kissing during a game of pool in a pub in Wimbledon Village. The next day, he came round to my flat to compare hangovers and it went from there. He was everything I found attractive in a man – he was fit, sporty, loud, friendly, cheerful and would talk to anyone, anywhere. He radiated fun and energy. We spent our weekends cycling off to cosy countryside pubs, or watching the rugby in our local pubs, or I'd watch him play football on the common, before ending up in the pub. It was fairly pub orientated but pubs meant loud, cheerful conversations, or hectic debates over the Sunday newspapers, or an attempt to win money from the quiz machines, and then a lazy cycle home along the river.

Within a week, I felt so comfortable with him, it was as though I'd known him for years; within a month, we'd met each other's friends and family, and within the year, we'd moved in together and I knew – just *knew* – that this relationship was going somewhere. We talked about where we would get married and what our children would be called, and we made plans for our future together.

Within two years, of course, he was showing an alarming attachment to his phone, would disappear off for the evening and be caught out in an obvious lie about where he had been, had gone off sex, would hide away in the spare room and basically behaved so badly that, when I finally hacked into his email account and discovered that he had a very loose attitude to fidelity, it was only really a shock that I was actually still shocked about it.

Now, years down the line, we were on friendly terms again – great mate, useless boyfriend was my general view – and having what to outsiders would seem a very romantic weekend in the country. We stayed in a lovely country pub, had a very nice meal with lots of wine and kept chastely to our own sides of the bed. Lying next to him while he watched *Match of the Day* on Saturday evening was like going back in time.

The next day, we were poring over the Sunday papers at breakfast when I said, 'Did Jennifer throw her phone at you because she was annoyed that we were going away this weekend?'

Patrick looked up from the sports section. 'Er, well, yes. She was a bit put out.'

'I can imagine. I'm just impressed you told her, to be honest. You would have spun me a line about going on a footie weekend with the boys.'

Patrick assumed his sheepish look again. Sometimes it could be endearing, sometimes it could be really annoying. I wasn't quite sure which it was this time.

'Is everything going all right, apart from the phone throwing?'

'Yes, it's fine, it's just . . .'

'Just what?'

'Well, it's just that sometimes I need my own space and yet that seems to make her really possessive and clingy and that makes me need my own space even more.'

This sounded very familiar. Patrick seemed to be one of those boys who were super-keen and eager and all bouncy like Tigger when they were trying to woo you, but the moment you succumbed or they became sure about your affections they would start craving 'space'. And, if your boyfriend goes from being super-keen to distant and aloof, it's really hard to be relaxed about that. Instead, you're likely to wonder what you did wrong, or panic about whether he's cooling on the whole relationship, and get even more attached and need to see him all the time.

'The thing about you, Patrick,' I said, feeling that he probably didn't want to know but I was going to tell him anyway, 'is that you always give the air of being just about to float away. And, if you're in love with someone like that, it's completely terrifying. You think all the time that that's the last time you're ever going to see them. So, it makes you go completely bonkers and paranoid and you do pretty much everything you can to get completely involved in their life and that's even more likely to make them sprint in totally the opposite direction.'

Gosh, it was all coming back now – the feeling of dread when he went off, the joy when he returned, the feeling of happy privilege he was spending time with me. The times when I got fed up and ended it, only for him to suddenly become ultra-keen and lovely again.

'Why didn't you end our relationship?' I said. I knew this was a rather heavy conversation for breakfast-time in a little country pub but I couldn't help it. It was also probably the best time to have it, years after the event, once most of the emotion had gone, and with no alcohol involved. We were hardly likely to start shouting at or sleeping with each other this early in the morning, no matter how emotional the conversation got. 'You obviously didn't want to be with me, so why didn't you end it? Instead, you behaved so badly that I had to do it.'

'Cowardice, I suppose,' he said. 'I hate ending relationships.'

'Well, so do I,' I said angrily. 'And it seems rather unfair for me first to have to find out that you've been shagging all over town and then to have to bloody end the relationship as well.'

'I was hardly shagging all over town,' said Patrick, and then held up a hand to defend himself as he caught the look in my eye and realised there was sharp cutlery to hand. 'I know I was completely in the wrong. But that's what I do. I let things deteriorate so badly but try to ignore it until there's just no way back. But I should have acted much sooner.'

I felt exhausted just remembering all the emotional turmoil. What a waste. What was it all for?

'You know, I really thought that we were going to get married,' I said. I became aware that the rest of the breakfast room was completely silent apart from the sounds of the other guests pouring cereal and buttering toast, no doubt wondering if they were part of some new hidden-camera soap opera.

He nodded. 'I know, I'm sorry. But you know that I'm really not the marrying kind. I don't think I'm ever going to get married.'

'I know that *now*!' I practically shouted. 'After me and the girlfriend before me and the girl after me and the girl after that, I do know that you're not the marrying kind. But I didn't know that then! I really thought we had a future. And now it turns out that we didn't, but I went out with you at a really crucial time in my life, from when I was 29 to 33 and then all the aftermath . . . those were really crucial husband-hunting years, you know. All wasted.'

He nodded again. 'I know. I'm really, really sorry.'

I poured some more coffee. There really didn't seem anything else I could do.

11

Desperately Seeking Soulmates

I don't think that it was the bottle of champagne and heart-shaped chocolates left lying around the kitchen just before Valentine's Day that set me off, although I'm prepared to accept that they probably didn't help. I was glad Charlotte and Matthew, the guy from her office, had hooked up, and obviously when you're in a new relationship you do all that kind of stuff, from the overtly cheesy Valentine's Day stuff (done in a coolly ironic way, of course) to having really huge breakfasts at the weekends, with the very best food and orange juice money can buy.

When you're single, or have been going out with someone for a while, cheap unbranded bacon and eggs from the garage or corner shop will do fine. But, when you've just started going out together, you have to get the poshest stoneground loaf of bread, the smoked-over-hickory-chips bacon, which costs five times as much, the organic, corn-fed eggs and as for juice – well, our fridge was groaning with cartons of freshly squeezed orange juice, with juicy bits, without juicy bits, with mango, with pineapple and some gloopy mango and coconut concoction for when even posh orange juice just wouldn't do. Now that Charlotte and Matthew were dating, our fridge door, burdened by all this extra weight, would swing all the way round and smash into the cupboard, threatening to bring the entire fridge crashing down with it.

Again, I couldn't blame them. When Patrick and I lived together, we would sometimes spend entire Saturdays making breakfast. We'd wake up slowly, have a snuggle, maybe some sex, then he would amble off to the kitchen and come back to bed with a pot of tea. We'd finally get up and plan to pop to the shops for some breakfast, but the quick trip out would turn into a two-person, hour-long trip to Waitrose, where we'd load up with eggs, bacon, sausages, posh bread, tomatoes, hash-browns and, if we were feeling particularly flash, smoked salmon and bagels, and maybe even a bottle of champagne, so we could make buck's fizz with our posh carton of orange juice.

By the time we'd staggered back to the flat with all this, then cooked it, while drinking posh coffee and reading the papers, it would be about 3 p.m. The table would be groaning with food, with newspapers everywhere, and it would be just perfect, apart from that nagging feeling that most of the day had passed us by. We'd feel so full and lardy and lethargic that there was nothing else to do but watch whatever sport was on the telly, or head out to the pub to meet up with friends. Then, of course, the whole thing would be repeated on Sunday.

Whole weekends would be spent just making breakfast, or that other great couples meal, a Sunday roast. I look back on that time and marvel about how much time we spent on these rituals. So, as I say, I can hardly blame Charlotte and Matthew for doing this too, or for doing the cheesy Valentine's thing.

However, this year, seeing the champagne and chocolates standing so proudly on the middle of the kitchen table for a week before Valentine's Day (I kept on hiding them in Charlotte's cupboard, feeling rather annoyed that she was creating an unnecessarily long build-up to the whole hideous business of the actual day by flaunting her new girlfriend status) sent me further down a single-feeling spiral till I just wanted to lie on the kitchen floor and howl, 'I want a boyfriend too!' every time Matthew walked through the door.

But I had my pride.

For about two days.

On the third day, I carried my laptop downstairs. It was time to enter the world of online dating.

It had the feeling of a particularly difficult homework assignment that I'd finally faced up to. It had been hanging over me like a cloud for ages and now I was finally going to do it. It surprised me that I'd put it off for so long. It was the first thing that anyone ever said to me when I mentioned I might be looking for a bloke, and yet something had always made me resistant to the idea. I don't know what it is really – it's not the idea that it's somehow embarrassing or tragic to go online looking for love, as, well, to be honest, I'd been doing a lot more tragic and embarrassing things recently.

I know that online dating is becoming a totally socially acceptable thing to do, that there isn't the stigma about it that there used to be, that . . . Oh, who am I kidding? I think it's tacky. I think it's unromantic to go shopping for your boyfriend in the same way that you'd buy books or toilet roll. I hate the idea of people scrolling dismissively past my profile, of taking roughly a tenth of a second to think 'Nope' and move on. It is so completely at odds with what being a human being is all about – and, more importantly, I think it only really works for good-looking people and I'm just not good-looking enough.

Still, even I have to admit that it works for some people. Not just any people in that vague 'some guy I once heard about' kind of way. A friend of my sister's met his wife through *Guardian* Soulmates after a dedicated trawl through practically every profile on the site, while an old university friend of mine recently revealed that she'd met her husband – with whom she has just had a gorgeous baby girl – through Mysinglefriend.com.

'He was completely out of my age range,' she said happily, 'but thankfully that didn't put him off getting in touch with me. It was my first date and his second and that was it.'

So I did know that it could work. I also knew that my friend Damien had been working really hard at online dating and so far nothing had worked out for him. And my friend Sue had spent, on and off, the best part of ten years on various dating websites and was financially and emotionally exhausted.

For me, the thought of it was just so clinical, completely the opposite of how I'd imagined meeting someone. It was like being picked out from a police line-up or an Argos catalogue. And it wasn't just that, it was the fact that he, by definition, would be a complete stranger, who didn't know you and wouldn't know any of your friends or family either.

I suppose, now that I was thinking seriously about it, that I had always imagined I would end up with someone with whom I had friends in common. Lots of my own friends had done that: they'd met as part of our larger social group and gradually become their own little group, but were both still part of our crowd so that nobody could really remember whose friends they were originally. Weddings were great because everyone you knew would be there. Online dating would mean that just wasn't going to happen.

I was being an idiot, of course. Unless I started looking at Damien – my only single male friend left from those days when we all shared friends – in an entirely different light, and he did the same with me, then the days when I was going to marry an old friend had long gone.

What finally clinched it for me was finding the profile of an instructor at British Military Fitness on one of the sites. He was utterly gorgeous, and looked like he would be fighting off hundreds of girls any time he walked into a bar. If he was on it, then the whole world could be.

So the internet it was.

I sat down on the sofa – Jeff was watching telly – with my laptop and a large glass of wine.

I started off with *Guardian* Soulmates, the most recommended in a very unscientific survey of my friends. Everyone seemed to know someone who was on it or who had met someone on it. I browsed for a bit. There must have been hundreds of guys from south London alone on the site. From thinking that this idea would be a dead loss, I was now overwhelmed with choice.

Some of them sounded quite mad, to be honest: 'I have matured like a ripe cheese,' claimed one. 'Sheep like me,' claimed another.

It was obviously going to be hard to separate the potentials from the unlikelys from the absolutely no-ways. It looked like it could be a full-time job to manage just one site.

As for creating my own profile, the site didn't like any of the pictures that I had of myself – it strongly took against hats, or sunglasses, which ruled out any pictures taken when I was actually looking smart and dressy – so I moved on to the words, which turned out to be even worse.

'For God's sake, what are you doing?' Jeff exclaimed, as my sighing threatened to drown out the latest episode of *House*.

'I'm trying to do my flipping bloody crapping profile, like you told me to do,' I said, blaming him for everything because he was the only other person nearby.

He instantly paused the telly. 'Oh, goody! What have you written so far?'

He lay back on the sofa with his eyes shut to listen, like a psychiatrist in reverse.

> I love meeting new people, exploring new places . . . ['Sounds a bit sexual,' said Jeff. I ignored him] and finding new fun things to do ['too many news'] especially discovering cosy traditional pubs ['wow, that's adventurous'] and trying their guest ales ['you sound like an old man'].
>
> I like spending the weekends reading the papers and meeting up with friends ['who doesn't?'] and during the week tend to be busy attending work functions ['workaholic'] or meeting up for wine and cocktails with friends ['alcoholic'].
>
> Otherwise I run marathons ['freaky sports nut'] or do triathlons ['even freakier sports nut'], go cycling ['that's a lot of sport'] or watch rugby in the pub with my friends ['you seem to be a bloke'].

I looked up. Jeff's one-man Greek chorus was starting to get on my nerves. It was really hard to write this kind of stuff without sounding like a show-off or a complete moron and it was also rather personal. It was my life I was trying to describe, after all.

'Thanks, Jeff, you've been a lot of help,' I said bitterly.

He looked up. 'Have I?' He caught sight of my face. 'Oh. Obviously not.'

He came over and gave me a big hug. 'Sorry, I'm being a prick. Read some more stuff out, it was great.'

'It obviously wasn't!' I said, feeling like the whole internet thing was a really bad idea. 'You objected to practically every word!'

I slammed my laptop shut, and the noise brought Charlotte in from the kitchen. 'What's going on?'

Jeff held his hands up. 'I'm sorry. I'm being nasty to Sarah. I wasn't taking this whole dating thing seriously enough.'

'What dating thing?' said Charlotte. 'Ooh, are you finally doing online dating! Hurray! What have you written then?'

She prised open my laptop.

'Why hurray?' Jeff and I asked simultaneously.

'Well, you know, it's a great way to meet men!' she said cheerfully.

'How would you know?' said Jeff, having spotted the flaw in her argument. 'You met your man while walking across the office to the photocopier.'

'Good point,' I thought, but didn't say so.

Charlotte ignored him. 'It *is* a good way to meet people,' she said. 'Loads of people do it. And, for the record, I did go on one date with a guy I met online that was very nice.'

There was an expectant pause.

'Yes, all right, the following week I met Matthew at work,' she said hastily. 'But this is about Sarah now . . .'

She read my profile.

'It's not bad,' she said finally. I shot Jeff a triumphant look. 'But you do sound a bit too sporty,' she added. 'And a bit of an old man who likes ale and pubs.' Jeff shot me a similar look in return.

'But I do like ale and pubs,' I said. 'And I'm not that sporty. It just sounds that way.'

'Well, we can work on that,' she said briskly.

'I'm not working on anything,' I said miserably. 'It's just too awful. I don't want to do it any more.'

There was a general uproar, Jeff's apologies mingling with Charlotte's headmistressy 'Oh, come on now'.

'Look, I didn't want to do any of this in the first place,' I pointed out tearfully. 'The whole idea of being single is rubbish and the whole idea of looking on the internet for a boyfriend is rubbish. Added to that, my entire personality and all the things I like doing appear to be rubbish. So none of this is actually making me feel very good at all.'

Charlotte started clicking away on the computer. 'Look, it is difficult but it'll be completely worth it,' she said. 'Come on, let's do your profile questions.'

She rattled through the categories. 'Right, you have a degree, yes? And you work in . . . media. Standard 40-hour week – ish. How would you like to spend your retirement?'

'I'm sorry?'

'Presumably not doing this,' Jeff remarked, back in his prone position on the sofa.

'Backpacking around the globe, doing voluntary work, enjoying the comforts of home, finally writing that novel, living in the country, sailing the seven seas, seeing the world in style, sipping margaritas on a beach, travelling cross country in a mobile home,' she rattled off.

'Blimey, what a list!' I said, slightly overwhelmed. 'I think I'd like to do them all. Apart from the mobile home one. Can you choose more than one?'

Charlotte consulted the website. 'Nope, just one.'

'Well, that's a bit daft then,' I said. 'What happens if I'd like to sail the seven seas in style, stopping off to drink margaritas on the beaches that we pass?'

'I'm not sure you . . .'

'And what if you put "finally writing that novel"?' I continued, warming to my theme. 'Is that supposed to be good, because you're arty and creative, or bad, because you should have already written it by then?'

'Well, I . . .'

'And what about if you've already sailed the world and backpacked and written the novel and done all that? You might say mobile home because you've done the rest, but the people reading your profile won't know that, they'll just think you're sad.'

'JUST PICK ONE,' Charlotte said through gritted teeth.

'Seeing the world in style,' I said grumpily.

'Good,' she said, in a certain kind of voice. 'We'll move on.'

There was a small part of me that quite liked the fact that, even though she had a very nice boyfriend who was giving her all sorts of Valentine's loveliness, she still wasn't escaping at least some of the torture of online dating.

'Do you have a special diet?'

'No.'

'Right – would rather not say,' she said, clicking on the box.

'Hang on, I just said that I haven't got a special diet.'

'Well, there's no answer saying that,' she said. 'It's either halal, kosher, vegetarian, vegan or would rather not say.'

'But rather not say sounds really suspect,' I said. 'As though I'm only going to reveal that I eat fried locusts after the third date.'

Charlotte started, understandably, to get a little ratty. 'Well, I'm not responsible for the flipping options, am I?'

'No, no, fair enough. All right, put "I'm keeping it top secret until we're married".'

She ignored me. 'Do you smoke?'

'No. Not really. Only when I'm completely plastered.'

'Is that three answers?' Jeff asked unhelpfully.

'Shall I put trying to quit then, or occasionally?'

'Put occasionally. No, put no. No one wants to go out with a smoker. Sorry, Jeff.'

'What are your spiritual beliefs?'

'Gosh, I don't know. What should I put?'

'Well, what are you?'

'Well, I'm nothing really. I mean, I'm Church of England, or at least my family are, so Protestant, I suppose. What are the options?'

'Well, you've got all the major religions, plus agnostic, atheist, other, spiritual but not religious, and rather not say.'

'Which one should I put?'

'Well, which one do you want to put?'

'I want to put whichever will make me the most attractive to men.'

'It's not a question of being the most attractive option to men, you have to be true to yourself,' Charlotte said.

'That's not true!' I said. 'It's *all* about being attractive to men, otherwise you guys would let me put lots of stuff about beer and pubs in my profile blurb.'

There was a pause. It seemed that we had reached some kind of impasse.

I took the computer back. 'Maybe I'll do this tomorrow,' I said.

I finally got a not too awful profile together and added a not entirely horrific picture to go with it. We were good to go.

Now there was a whole new hurdle.

There were a lot of men out there, it was true. However, they just didn't seem to want to go out with me.

I sifted through hundreds of profiles and clicked 'Add to your favourites' dozens of times. No one wrote to me. I sent people cheerful smiles and winks, and, when that didn't work, I emailed people cheerful messages. Still nothing.

'Are you doing it right?' said Damien, my online-dating expert. 'You've got to know how the system works. You go higher up people's searches the more recently you've edited your profile, so you have got to tweak something, even if it's just a word, every day. If you don't go online for a while, that will show too. Then you've got to keep track of who you've emailed, who you've looked at, who's looked at you. Then there are all the new people coming onto the site too – you've got to get in quick for those people. Then there are your photos . . .'

I felt exhausted just listening to him. And that was just my *Guardian* Soulmates account. In a fit of 'if you can't beat them, join them', I had also signed up to Match.com, LoveandFriends.com and Mysinglefriend.com. Then friends started recommending other sites to me, which I felt obliged to join too, so I had also registered with SpeedDater.com, Love@Lycos, Cupid.com and Quiverz.

As well as juggling all those sites, I was also on Ivory Towers – intelligent dating for UK graduates – and Movie Lover Dating – not to be confused with Movie Lovers Dating, FilmLoverDating, Movie Lover Dating UK and Date Movie Lovers – which, in theory, linked up people according to their film preferences. Having got used to receiving no emails at all, I was now getting hundreds of them from Movie Lover Dating, which was very exciting, until I realised you could send one email to hundreds of people in a mass round-robin email. I felt decidedly less special then. The company behind Movie Lover Dating was also responsible for Pet Lover Dating, Fitness Lover Dating and a whole range of other sites including gay dating, Christian dating, military dating, black dating and BBW dating, whatever that was.

I had already signed up to Fitness Singles, the dating website for sporty types, as well as PerfectMatch, and even, rather improbably due to being egged on by friends one drunken evening, SugarDaddy-Dating.com. To be fair, the guys on the site all seemed to be gorgeous but, according to one friend, who claimed some kind of inside knowledge, 'Everyone on there is married and looking for affairs.'

I was certainly learning a lot. But it was practically taking over my life. All these profiles had to be written, maintained and updated, as well as questions answered and photos uploaded. Then there were all the men to sort through, prod, poke, smile or wink at, depending on what the site told you to do. On the sites that recommended men to you, I was receiving dozens of emails a week, which meant more profiles to check, and, if they sounded nice, email conversations to strike up. I was losing track of what I'd said to whom and what stages we were at. One guy 'dumped' me before we'd even met up because I'd forgotten the password to the site he was on and by the time I'd managed to log back in he'd lost patience and abandoned me.

I wasn't the only one on multiple sites: I started recognising profiles from other sites, so people from Match.com would pop up on *Guardian* Soulmates or Mysinglefriend.com. It seemed as though we were all on one big, rather sad merry-go-round.

The pressure really ratcheted up when I joined eHarmony, which was fast becoming the giant of the internet-dating world. Not only were there seemingly hundreds of questions, which took the best part of a week to answer, before you could sign up to the site, but they also matched you up with men whose profiles you had to check out every day. If you didn't keep on top of the workload, it really piled up. It wasn't long before I had 400 men sitting in my inbox waiting to be dealt with. If you liked the look of a particular guy, you were supposed to send them five multiple-choice questions, such as:

If I took you to a party where you knew no one, what would you do:

a) stay close to my date, letting her introduce me,

b) find a spot at the bar and relax alone, letting her work the room,

c) strike out on my own, introducing myself and making friends,

d) ask my partner if I could skip this particular event,

or

e) something completely different?

So I would send questions over to people and they would

send theirs back for me. We'd then move on to a list of likes and dislikes – 'I can't stand someone who is not clean' was one of the possible statements – and then on to three longer, more detailed questions, such as: 'Of what in your life are you most proud?'

The time and effort spent doing all this was immense and exhausting and not particularly productive. I once spent hours ploughing through all these stages with one guy who seemed really nice, but by the time we'd made it to the open communication stage, where we could actually email each other, we were both so exhausted by the whole process that we never even got round to meeting up.

I was actually going on some dates, albeit with varying degrees of success. I met up with one guy in Kensington who turned out to be very short and very Spanish and who barely spoke English. He was perfectly sweet, and to be fair he had put his short Spanishness on his profile, which I hadn't read properly, so it was completely my fault that he wasn't quite what I was looking for.

I went out with a teacher in Borough market, but, within three seconds, I knew it just wasn't going to work. It was the sad eyes again. It was the depressed air of resignation that people get when they spend too much time going on online dates and getting rejected. On paper, well, email, he was lovely – a witty, interesting guy who obviously cared a lot about the children he taught. In a Southwark pub, he just seemed battered down by life.

I got along really well with a guy I met in a pub in Balham. We chatted, laughed, drank beer and played pool. We moved on to another pub and did the same, but table football this time. He seemed a really nice, lively bloke with a lot going for him.

I waited, in vain, for another email from him.

Finally, I emailed him. 'I think I already know the answer,'

I wrote, 'but in case you were waiting for me to email or weren't sure what I thought, I just wanted to say I had a lovely night and would love to meet up again some time.'

When a reply finally arrived, he confirmed I was right, but not harshly. He'd had a great evening too but just wasn't getting that spark. Ah, that elusive spark.

Undaunted, I met up with another guy, this time in Clapham. We went for a drink, and then a curry, followed by some more drinks. We seemed to have a really good night but I got the feeling he was more keen on me than I was on him. However, a week went by and no email. I was starting to get rather annoyed with how acceptable it seemed to be to spend an entire evening with someone, sharing anecdotes and life stories, and then never get in touch with them again.

It seemed just basic courtesy to say thank you for a lovely time or acknowledge what a good evening it had been, if nothing else. Or was I being too middle class?

I finally emailed him to say what a nice evening it had been and maybe we should keep in touch. He emailed back saying that he'd assumed that, as I hadn't been in touch, I wasn't interested. Well, that swung it. I wasn't now.

All this dating was, quite frankly, a real palaver, from arranging a time, a day and a place to meet in, to working out what to wear, not to mention making sure every visible part of me was groomed to, well, if not perfection then as good as it could be, which meant spending a small fortune on haircuts, hair colours, manicures, eyebrow plucking, eyelash dyeing and make-up. I felt as if I had to be permanently prepared for a job interview.

As I was losing hope, *Guardian* Soulmates finally turned up trumps. A guy called Phil got in touch. He seemed perfect in every way. He was Irish, lived in Clapham and was a freelance journalist who supplemented his income in a variety of wacky and interesting ways, including being a tour guide for rich Russians around the English 'season', including Royal Ascot. His emails were witty, interesting and perfectly punctuated. Having exchanged fun, lively emails for a while, we planned to meet up.

And then he vanished. Not in a 'he just didn't reply to my emails again' way, but his entire profile disappeared off the site. He'd mentioned there had been some technical problems with the site's redesign, but they'd been fixed and he'd been given another month free to make up for it. But now, just as I was writing to him to say yes to his suggestion that we meet, he'd completely disappeared.

'Look forward to hearing from you' had been his last words to me. Now I couldn't even write back. 'Profile unavailable' was all that was left of him.

'That's a bid odd,' Damien said, when I phoned him in a panic. 'Even if someone doesn't pay their subscription, you should still be able to see their profile.'

I contacted *The Guardian*. 'It should be a temporary thing,' they said breezily. 'Give it a week and see if he comes back.'

I gave it a week and he hadn't come back. So I emailed them again, pointing out that he'd disappeared mid-chat.

'It appears that this Soulmate is no longer on the service, or changed their Soulmates username. I'm not able to provide any further details, I'm afraid.'

And that was that. I only knew his first name, and how many Irish guys called Phil live in London? He did his freelancing under a different name, so I had completely lost him.

That was it. I totally lost faith in internet dating. I shouldn't have to work so hard for heartbreak.

12

Sex and the City

I was at my mother's house for the weekend. She lives in a small village on the south coast and I often popped down there for the weekend, bringing my bike on the train so I could cycle once I was free of London.

I enjoyed spending time down there – on Sundays, we'd head off to a country pub and pore over the Sunday papers, while enjoying a massive roast lunch, before returning home to play Scrabble in the back garden and drink gin and tonics. It was all very nice and comfortable, and I would head back to London on the train feeling very relaxed and content and ready for the working week ahead.

Enjoyable though it was, hanging out drinking in my mum's garden wasn't exactly the perfect way to meet a husband. Even I, in my most optimistic 'Look, this week we might actually win the lottery' moments, had to admit that a suitable candidate was unlikely to suddenly spring over the garden fence. I went away to my mum's on the weekends that there was nothing planned in London, no parties, no barbecues, no Sunday brunches or lunches, but, even so, I started to feel as though I was missing out, that I should be spending every second of my free time getting out there and meeting men.

But what was I supposed to do? Head off to hit the pubs and bars of Clapham on my own, before ending up in the Clapham Grand, hoping for that 2 a.m. snog when everyone suddenly starts panicking that they haven't pulled yet and makes a beeline for the most drunk person there?

Well, yes, that was probably exactly what I was supposed to do. But without the group of friends that I'd had in my twenties and early thirties, the kind that just assumes you are going out on a Saturday night and the only question is where next – or, more usually, since you'd been in the pub since lunchtime, the only questions were whose round was it and who had already passed out in the toilets – it seemed that I just hadn't got anyone to do that kind of stuff with any more.

My married friends were exhausted from having babies and moving to the Home Counties. If they socialised at all, they went to dinner parties in the suburbs that ended at 10 p.m. and to which only other couples were invited. They had become completely incapable of doing anything spontaneous and would feel utterly traumatised by the idea of going out on Saturday night without at least three months' notice and multiple entries in various electronic diaries, and would invariably cancel at the last minute anyway. I understood that their lives had changed and I was happy for them, but it left me unable to rustle up large groups of friends at a moment's notice, which used to be the simplest thing to do.

The only set of friends I did have who went out till 4 a.m. on the spur of the moment were my gay friends and 18 months of living in New York and going out to gay clubs every week – Ass Wednesday on 1st Avenue was a particular high point in the social calendar – had taught me that there was really no point in my being there. My friend Adrian had once persuaded me that gay clubs were full of straight men who'd been dragged there by their gay friends and who'd be overjoyed to meet a straight, single girl in Paradise or Club X or wherever we'd ended up that night. It took a lot of clubbing and fruitless talking to beautiful men before I realised that his theory was total bollocks. I don't think I've ever met a straight guy in a gay club, or, at least, one who wasn't already part of our group and who'd been dragged along because 'gay clubs are full of single women who've been dragged there by their gay friends'. So, while Adrian was chatting up men, I would hang around feeling utterly invisible and fail to get served at the bar.

There was only one place in New York where I felt even more invisible. Cubby Hole was a fairly cool but supposedly approachable lesbian bar just round the corner from me in the West Village in New York. It was packed every time I went there, hundreds of girls crammed into a tiny room with a bar running along one side and all sorts of clutter and trinkets hanging off the ceiling.

The first time I went was with my friend Fiona. She's tall and dark and striking, and so she often gets a certain amount of attention. At Cubby Hole, though, she was – well, I'm not sure what the appropriate metaphor in this context is – but it was as though the Queen of all Lesbians had turned up and everyone in the bar had to pay homage to her. She was mobbed the entire time we were in there. People approached her at the bar, while we were sitting down having drinks, while she was outside watching me have a cigarette, even while she was queuing for the loo.

I, meanwhile, have never been so utterly invisible in my entire life. It was as though I wasn't even in the room. Had I ever considered becoming a lesbian, my time at Cubby Hole would have convinced me that it would be a completely wasted effort.

Anyway, it had begun to occur to me that if I wanted to meet someone – and I did – West Sussex wasn't the place to do it. And it seemed my mum had been thinking the same thing.

We were in my mum's garden one weekend, setting up the Scrabble and fixing some more gin and tonics, when she said, 'Oh, I cut something out from *The Telegraph* for you. I'll just go and find it.'

She beetled off and I sat there wondering what it could be. She is always cutting things out of newspapers when she comes across something she thinks someone would be interested in and it can be quite handy, if fairly random – a book or restaurant review, for example, or some shopping vouchers.

After much rummaging around, she came back and handed me a scrap of newspaper. While she set up the Scrabble board, I read the cutting:

'CitySocialising. A fun, relaxing way to meet people.'

After I'd lost at Scrabble, I went online to check it out further.

> Meet people, make friends, share interests & socialise in London. We're the UK's leading network, now in 50 cities, dedicated to connecting laid-back, outgoing people with new friends to socialise with in their city.

As if to back up the point, there were umpteen pictures of happy, beautiful people laughing and hanging out in bars.

At moments like this, my mind splits into two completely opposing views.

Half of me is thinking: 'This is utterly tragic. I've lived in London practically all my life. I don't need or want to join a group like this that's going to be full of Antipodeans and Europeans coming to London for the first time. Moreover, what kind of person would ever go along to these events? It's like book clubs or knitting circles, full of sad, lonely types who have no friends and will have that sad, desperate look in their eyes. I've got friends. I'm not lonely. I can go out every night if I want to and frankly most of my life is spent trying to avoid going out and getting blasted all the time. The man of my dreams – or, indeed, any guy with more than half an ounce of self-respect – is not going to be seen dead at something like this and it'll just make me want to shoot myself even more than I already do.'

The other half usually argues a more reasoned approach: 'OK, so you have friends and you're not lonely. But all your friends have disappeared to the suburbs and are a dead loss when it comes to going out on a Saturday night. Yes, you spend a lot of time in bars and pubs anyway but that's during the week when you're with friends from work and you're not meeting any new people that way. This is exactly the kind of thing you did in Italy and New York to meet people so there's no shame in it, it's actually quite a sensible thing to do.

'And –' this is the mantra to which I always return, always keep telling myself, always willing myself to believe it '– *you just have to meet one bloke*. Just one. It doesn't matter if all the rest of them are utter losers – if there is just one nice guy there that you connect with, who is maybe looking at the same newspaper cutting and thinking, "Well, it sounds terrible, but I may as well give it a try, just once," and if he's there, and you meet, and you bond about how awful it is, and then you ditch the others and go off to a bar on your own, and start talking, and . . .'

That's the dream, the – I try to convince myself – *possible* dream and, if I'm not there in the bar when he's there, well, there's just no chance of our meeting. It is this dream that keeps me going throughout all this hideousness, that there is someone out there, someone for me, and I just have to keep plugging away until I find him.

Obviously, I try not to think of the possibility that he doesn't exist and it'll never happen.

Later that evening, as I signed up to the site, I realised that I had reached the point where there was very little I would not do to try to find this elusive guy.

No matter how tragic the proposition, no matter how unlikely it might seem, if there is the slightest chance that I will meet someone, then I will be there. I have to silence all the negative voices in my head that say, 'He doesn't exist, you will never find someone for you,' because the odds are that someone, somewhere, might be the right one for me. I'm not talking soulmates, I'm just talking someone that I have a spark or a connection with. Let's say out of 10 million people in London half are men, a tenth of those the right age and a tenth of those are single, that's still – oh, God, financial journalists are notoriously crap at arithmetic – 50,000 single men within 20 miles of me. So not bad at all, says the optimist inside me. Practically a dead cert. Which is probably why I never win at the races.

The pessimist/realist in me says that there is no way in hell that a guy I'd want to meet will go to these events. That's a harder voice to silence, because that's much more believable. If *I* don't want to go to them, what makes my ideal man likely to be there? The only answer is, well, if I'm doing it, then he might be too. But is that true? If I knew where the single men in their thirties and forties were, I'd be there, not handing over my credit card details to a company that will enable me to go to pubs I already go to, but this time with people I don't know and whom I probably won't ever want to see again.

I was clearly thinking too much. I should just flipping do it.

So, the next Saturday night, when the rest of the country was watching England play the USA in the World Cup, I walked down the road to the All Bar One on Northcote Road in Clapham. I passed about five pubs bursting at the seams with exactly the kind of guys I'd like to meet – sporty, sociable, good-looking, fun to be with – and wondered whether I wouldn't be better off ditching the losers (I had an open mind, as you can tell) and going on a one-person pub crawl instead.

I abandoned the idea as soon as I poked my nose around the door of one pub. The men had eyes for nothing but the football and, even if they did, this wasn't one of those films where you started chatting to a guy at the bar and he came and found you afterwards to ask for your phone number and buy you a drink. No one I've ever met in my entire life has gone to a pub on their own and ended up with a guy. With friends, of course, lots of times. There's a group of you, a group of them, and someone starts chatting and then you're all hanging out together and things happen . . . that's not what I'm talking about. I'm talking about a single girl going into a bar, obviously on her own, and someone making the effort to talk to her. It just doesn't happen.

People drink in packs, they hang out in packs and they hunt in packs too. Guys don't go into pubs on their own; they barely go into coffee shops on their own and, if they do, they're plugged into all manner of gadgets such as laptops and iPods to prevent themselves from feeling alone, and women are equally likely to ignore the outside world in favour of a book or chatting away on a phone. In films, of course, it is completely impossible for a woman to walk into a bar alone and not get chatted up by the good-looking guy who is also there on his own, but this wasn't Hollywood. This was Battersea Rise.

I resignedly carried on to All Bar One. It was the only pub on the whole street not showing the football. This meant that it was fairly quiet, which was good, and full of women, which wasn't so good. There were two fairly large groups of people there, both of which looked as if they could be the CitySocialising lot, and I thought it was pretty poor that the member who'd organised the night out hadn't at least put a sign on the table, or had someone looking out for people wandering in on their own and looking a bit lost. The odds of my crashing into completely the wrong party were pretty high. Fighting the very strong impulse to just turn round and flee home, I walked up to one of the groups. 'Excuse me,' I said, 'are you guys from CitySocialising?'

Thankfully, they were, and no one said, 'CityWhat?' or 'Do we look like we are total and utter losers?' In fact, this bunch seemed very friendly and shuffled up the benches to make room for me. Around ten people had arrived so far, with a mix of ages and accents from Scottish to Australian and back via Surrey, but most of them seemed to be in their twenties or early thirties, which was younger than I'd expected. Everyone introduced themselves and we sat rather earnestly facing one another across the long table, making polite small talk, mainly along the lines of 'Well, it's a good job they are not showing the football in here'.

So far, not bad. It was all quite stilted but presumably the evening might get better once we'd all had a drink or two. Or, at least, *my* evening would improve considerably. It suddenly became top priority to get a drink. Unsure of the etiquette in buying large rounds for complete strangers, I offered a drink to my nearest neighbours – both of whom politely declined – and I popped off to the bar where I was told Cath, the girl who'd set the evening up, would be.

I found her chatting to a bloke.

'Hi,' I said cheerfully. 'I'm Sarah, one of the people who signed up for tonight. Are you Cath?'

Cath looked at me with a complete lack of interest. 'Er, yeah,' she said.

I hovered, anticipating some hostess-like small talk – 'So glad you could make it!' or 'Did you find us OK?' – but it soon became obvious that there would be none. She had turned back to the guy she had been talking to, without introducing us, and I was dismissed.

I got my drink and sloped rather pathetically back to the group. At least people here were friendly.

The evening passed pleasantly enough, but I was certainly not convinced that this was the brave new world of dating that I'd been looking for. There was a lot of small talk, nervous laughter and quickly rushing to fill in any silences in the conversation that made it feel like after-work drinks organised by the boss at which no one can actually relax.

A new guy arrived in the bar, looking around in that lost and apprehensive way that signalled a new CitySocialiser. Like a velociraptor stalking her prey, Cath was onto him in a flash.

My neighbour clocked my glance. 'She does that,' he said. 'That's her style. She organises loads of these things and yet she only talks to the guys she fancies.'

'That explains her lack of hostess skills,' I thought. I remembered seeing her profile on the CitySocialising site – she had posted a pretty striking picture of herself in a red dress and lipstick, and was 41, or so she said. I had to admire her single-minded focus. If she wanted to meet a man, then certainly one way to go about it was to commandeer the entire CitySocialising network as your personal dating agency.

The evening began to improve. The drinks were going down well, everyone was starting to relax and there was something quite nice about being able to talk to anyone at the table without getting the 'Who on earth are you and why are you talking to me?' look. There was a nice Australian guy to flirt with, a couple of women to talk to about men and a guy called Sanjay who was up for partying all night, so it did seem as if there were worse ways to spend the evening.

At around 10 p.m. Cath and her man – who was never allowed to talk to any of us – announced they were leaving to go drinking in the pub across the road and that we were welcome to follow them. None of us felt like taking them up on the offer and by now we had all bonded as one little team against the world.

When All Bar One closed at 11 p.m. it felt like the night was still young. Cath and her man had disappeared, but when Sanjay cried, 'More drinking!' off we went, down Northcote Road with the rest of the Saturday-night crowds who were hopping from bar to bar, following the alcohol and staying one step ahead of closing time.

We ended up heading down an unlikely alley to a bar that seemed to have no closing time at all, and which served a variety of haphazardly made cocktails by some enthusiastic staff. We sat up on the ramshackle balcony, which looked as though it had been put up by the staff in their lunch break, and drank martinis and talked nonsense. We soon discovered that there was an entire dance floor downstairs and so we did silly dancing in between tequila shots.

I stopped flirting with the charming Australian guy, suspecting him to be a bit of a playboy, so he promptly turned his attention to a sweet young thing who had barely uttered a word all evening but who was instantly smitten. Within minutes, they were kissing vigorously on the dance floor.

He joined me at the bar in between snogs.

'Please don't take advantage of her tonight,' I said, suddenly feeling like a Victorian governess. 'She's very nice and I'm sure she'd be lovely to see another time when we're all less drunk, but, if you go home with her tonight, you'll sleep with her, never see her again and make her feel rubbish.'

The cute Australian agreed. 'I know,' he said. 'But it seems silly to pass up such an opportunity . . .'

He leaned over, very close to me. He was pretty sexy but knew it too.

'I would much rather go home with you,' he said softly. 'But I knew you'd say no.'

There was a pause. We looked at each other.

'Yes, well, you'd have been right,' I said loftily, and almost believed it too.

It was 2.30 a.m. and time for me to leave. I declined Sanjay's invite to continue dancing at Infernos in Clapham – he sent me an email the next day saying they danced until 4 a.m. – and walked home, feeling toxic from alcohol and cigarettes but also that the whole evening had gone rather well. I wasn't convinced it was the best way to find a husband, but, as a way to go out, get trashed and meet some fun people for the evening, it was pretty successful.

13

A Question of Dating

If I ever have the time and inclination to set up a dating company, I have two perfect – well, I think so anyway – ideas.

The first one addresses the fundamental problem with dating websites and agencies and singles events, and anything even vaguely associated with such ventures: men do not want to be associated with them in any way.

Women don't either, to be fair, but they tend to be much more proactive about just getting out there regardless.

Men haven't got the ticking clock that drives many women of a certain age to do desperate things, such as Brazilian waxes or rock-climbing lessons or signing up to dinner dates with complete strangers when they'd much rather be drinking wine with their friends or curled up with a box set of *Mad Men*.

Not only do men not have the panicked 'oh my God, I've got a week to find a man or I will die alone' mentality, but they also seem to be a lot better at dealing with single life even if they would rather not be.

They either go down to the nearest tacky nightclub with their mates and pull, or they stay at home drinking beer, eating takeaway pizza and playing Grand Theft Auto: This

Time It's Personal (I may have made that one up). And they are probably very happy doing so.

Oddly enough, this doesn't seem to apply to men who have been married and are now single. Studies have shown that divorced men are completely hopeless at adjusting back to the bachelor life, possibly because they handed over all responsibility for children, housekeeping, holidays and their social diaries to their wives, and they can't remember how their lives work any more.

Single guys are a completely different story and not one that helps equal out the gender balance when it comes to the dating scene. Which is why every organised singles/dating event I have ever been to has been desperately short on men.

There is also the problem – to paraphrase Groucho Marx – that I wouldn't particularly want to date the kind of guy who would actually be happy to join dating sites or go to singles events. If *I* don't want to be there, why should I admire or fancy someone who voluntarily turns up to these things? I know it may be illogical but it's true. So, even if I joined every single dating agency in the country, went out with every single guy on *Guardian* Soulmates or Match.com or SadSingleLosersOnTheVergeofShootingThemselves.com, I'm still not sure I would find someone for me. My ideal guy would run a mile from these places, or more likely wouldn't even have them on his radar. He'd be too busy running his own business, writing his best-selling novels, editing a newspaper, putting out fires, healing small children, looking after cute furry animals or training for triathlons and . . . well, you get the (wholly unrealistic) idea.

So my dating agency would employ 100 good-looking, intelligent women who would go into every bar, pub, sports club and gym across the country and stand on the sidelines of every football, rugby and cricket match and make sure that they persuaded every single guy they met to answer a few questions about who they were and what they were looking for, and then I'd sign them up to my agency.

Because that is how to get the guys – not by waiting for them to come to you.

I would then match each of them up with a suitable girl and put them in touch with each other. They'd go out for a quick drink, all very casual, and see if they got along.

As a premium service, you could hire two women to hang out in bars with you, to act as wingmen. They'd spy a likely target, move in on his friends and, bingo, you've got your introduction. Get his number, move on, and within a week you would have more nice, eligible guys than you would in an entire year of trawling the singles scene.

(If anyone wants to take this idea and run with it, please be my guest. Just do it in south-west London first, please?)

There are dating agencies – of which more later – who say they advertise in the classifieds and you can search the online sites but, again, you're fishing in a very small self-selecting pool. No, outreach to the local pubs and football fields! That's the way forward.

My second idea is also, in my view, quite brilliant – and one that I actually did for a while. Quiz-dating. Now, veterans of the singles scene might point out that there are some companies who offer quiz-dating for singles, the idea being that it's more relaxed and fun than just speed-dating.

Having been speed-dating, I can say without fear of contradiction that root canal surgery is more relaxing and fun than speed-dating by a factor of about a million. But, again, as with any dating concept, it all depends on the quality of people you meet there. You can have all the speed-dating, quiz-dating, wine-tasting, lock and key, cowboys and Indians, Samson and Delilah parties in the world, but, if everyone there is an utter disaster, it's not going to be much cop.

When I started organising quiz nights for singles, there wasn't such a thing as quiz-dating. (Again, if anyone wants to take my idea and make it even more brilliant, be my guest. My reward will be being known as the Cilla Black of pub quizzes.)

One wintry Sunday afternoon, I'd just come back from a long lunch with friends and didn't feel like going back to my flat just yet. So I took the Sunday papers off to the pub down the road and sat there with a drink.

The pub had these long, farmhouse-kitchen-style tables and, while I was happily absorbed in the magazines, a couple of guys sat at the end of the table. It turned out that they were there for the pub quiz that was just about to start and, although I wasn't going to do the quiz on my own, I kept half an ear out for the questions.

The guys were completely stumped by one of the questions and one of them looked up hopefully at me, presumably on the lookout for anyone who might know the answer. I did actually know this one – it was something like 'What is the only X-rated film to have won the Best Picture Oscar?' and as I'd just watched *Midnight Cowboy* it wasn't that difficult.

After that, they asked me whenever they didn't know the answer and so I ended up joining their team. They were nice blokes and quite chatty and in the half-time interval they included me in the round and it was assumed I would stick around for the second half. We actually ended up coming second, which they told me was a record for them. We celebrated with more beers and several games of table football, and it was pretty late when I reeled off into the night.

This seemed a perfect way to meet people, but I wasn't going to sit around a pub all Sunday on the off-chance that someone might again invite me to join their team, so I decided to put an advert on the classified-ads website

Gumtree. It basically said: 'Looking for single people for a pub quiz' and detailed how I was going to try to get a team together to do the quiz the following week.

The response was amazing – about 20 people replied within 24 hours, saying things like 'This is the business' and 'I've been waiting for ages for someone to come up with an idea like this.'

They were mostly men, too, which was a first. There were some, of course, who didn't seem to be quite what I was looking for: 'Horny 1800' replied to the ad with: 'Hello I'm gigolo who want sex with me waiting I live in Turkey but mine very big', while another guy wrote to me with the name 'NaughtyButtNice'. I declined the Turkish gigolo's kind offer, but replied back to NaughtyButtNice – who seemed by his email, if not his online name, to be a fairly normal bloke – and several others, all of whom seemed nice, normal and up for something new.

We all arranged to meet up for the next quiz, and on the night there was a large group of us, sixteen people in all, so we had to split into two teams. This worked even better, as we could all chat in our smaller groups and then come together at the end for some more drinks and to compare our answers.

The pub-quiz format was ideal for a dating event, as it turned out. Unlike on a blind date or speed-dating, you instantly had something to discuss, whether it was what was the capital of New Zealand or who directed *North by Northwest*. Not only was there a ready-made topic of conversation, but it also led easily on to more personal disclosures, such as your recent trip to Australia or what films you liked watching.

Everyone seemed to be getting along really well and one of our teams even won, which was a bonus. We all felt very proud of ourselves, both for winning and for actually daring to come along, and thus a whole new way to spend Tuesday nights had begun.

Every week there would be a different group of people, some old, some new. I invited my single friends along and so did the regulars like Andy (formerly known as NaughtyButtNice). My sister even started going out with Pete, a guy she'd met on one of our quiz nights. So it worked, which was good, but not for me, which was not.

We had a fond farewell before I left to go and live in Italy but, without me there to organise it, I think the whole thing just ran out of steam.

Now I was back in the country, I decided that I would give quiz-dating another go. Since I'd been away, a dating company had started running quiz nights of its own, so I signed up. The event was held in a subterranean bar just south of Oxford Street, and was gloomy to the point of rendering everyone but your nearest neighbours completely invisible, which rather defeated the purpose of the evening. We were allocated teams and sat around rather nervously waiting for it to begin, while the organisers battled with the sound system.

It soon became obvious that this evening wasn't going to work as well as my quiz evenings had. For a start, the room was so dark and cramped that you felt like some kind of pariah, being shunted to a secret den away from the sight of normal, sociable people. Being part of an existing pub quiz meant that you actually felt part of the real world, rather than some tragic singles colony off to one side of it, and you were there because you liked pub quizzes, not just to meet someone. Here, the whole reason we were there was to find a mate and so the quiz seemed completely irrelevant.

The quiz itself was a bit of a let-down too. The questions veered dramatically between the completely easy: 'What is the capital of Great Britain?' and the near-impossible: 'What is the circumference of the moon to the nearest hundred miles?' so we were either bored or flummoxed. They also moved everyone around between rounds, which, while good for the meeting-people aspect, made it impossible to build a team, so when the winning team was announced it was very much 'Well, who are they?'

And I didn't even fancy anyone.

Undeterred, I signed up for a CitySocialising pub quiz, this time in Putney. I was having a lovely post-work drink with my colleagues, which was turning into a rather pleasant evening, and was very reluctant to leave them and trek off across town to do a pub quiz with a bunch of random people. But, with the old 'this could be the night and you'll never know if you don't go' mantra of desperate singles everywhere ringing in my ears, I headed off to Putney.

The moment I got there, I just knew it was a bad idea. The pub was old and depressing, with an air of faded grandeur, signalling that its best days were very much behind it. Sadly, the people on my team weren't much better. I know it sounds harsh and incredibly impolite, but it felt like an OAP night out. Everyone had an air of fussiness and bossy fidgetiness that comes with being very set in your ways, and, although I joined in, I just thought, 'I don't belong here. Please don't let me belong here.'

There was only one other team in the pub doing the quiz and it took hours. The whole night was torture.

During the quiz, Patrick had texted that he fancied a drink and I texted back to meet me in the pub. He turned up just as we finished, took one look at how I had chosen to spend my evening and his face was a picture. He bought me a drink and led me outside. 'Who on earth were those people?' he said. 'And what were you doing with them?'

I leaned against the railings and looked out onto the river. I remember that we'd once stood at this very same spot,

Patrick and I, when we had been going out together. We had spent the whole night and morning in bed, and then we'd cycled over here for a drink and to meet up with some friends. The sun was shining and it had been a glorious day. We felt young, energetic, full of life and love, and radiated contentment from every pore. Now I felt old, sad, lonely and single, and was reduced to spending my evenings with people with whom I had nothing in common. I was pathetically relieved that Patrick had come and rescued me. What on earth had happened?

Despite the disastrous evening, I decided to give quiz-dating one more try, but I organised my own in a pub on Lavender Hill, and put the event up on the CitySocialising website. That way, I figured, I could be in control over who was there.

The event was oversubscribed, with sixteen people – the maximum number – signing up, fortunately leaving no room for one guy who had wanted to come but rather doubted he could find the pub on his own.

'Why don't you come and meet me at the Tube and we could go there together?' he suggested.

If you are 41 years old and still can't read a map or walk into a pub on your own, you are certainly not worth a place on my pub quiz, I decided. So it was a no for him.

Everyone who did make it was very nice, cheerful and keen to get along with everyone else, but there was not a potential boyfriend among them.

This was clearly getting me nowhere. Going to single-specific events was too depressing, while general socialising was just too hit and miss. I needed another strategy.

14

Painting the Town Red

My mother – again, trying desperately to come up with something, *anything*, that could get me off the single stage for good – had recently read an article about parties where everyone sips their drinks through red straws to show that they're single and therefore are eligible to be approached at random to be chatted up. This sounded like a good idea – the equivalent of my own glowing arrows to highlight all the single people – and she ferreted out the article for me.

The red-straw events were organised by a company called Lovestruck. As well as being a standard online dating site, with various hopeful people's pictures plastered all over the screen, Lovestruck also organised what it called 'Laissez-faire parties':

> Every so often, we 'ghost-host' drinks nights. This means that we won't make a big thing about being there. Or a small thing. We'll just . . . be. (It's terribly Zen.) So, as we won't be rolling up, there's no entry fee, no RSVP, no nametags, no games and no rules. Just the knowledge that a higher-than-average number of single people will be there on that particular night.

I quite liked the sound of going to an event in a 'normal' bar where other 'normal' people might be as well as the tragic singleton crowd. Having gone to so many of these single-specific events, I'd started to feel completely disconnected from the real world, not helped by the fact that many of them were held in a specially cornered-off area of a bar, as if we were carrying some dreadful 'singles' disease that might suddenly contaminate the happy, coupled-up folk and cause them to be suddenly single too.

The more I was out, hanging in the right kind of bar, the more chance I had of bumping into a guy I liked. And, if all the singles themselves were utterly horrendous, I could always pretend that I was a regular person just popping into the bar for a few on my way home.

So this sounded like one of the least appalling options on the dating circuit. There was only a slight clanging of alarm bells when I read the instructions, as it were, behind the whole red-straw thing on the website:

> Simply ask for a red straw or write an 'L' on the back of your drinking hand (entirely optional), drink and enjoy the higher-than-average chance of some gorgeous Lovestrucker spotting your straw or 'L' and chatting you up. (Or chatting up someone with a straw or 'L', if you're feeling proactive.)

Now red straws were OK, but writing an L on the back of your hand? No, no and no once more. There was hardly any difference between writing an L for Lovestruck on the back of your hand and writing an L for loser on your forehead, particularly as this whole process was making me feel enough of a loser already.

However, nothing ventured, and it would at least stop my mum from going on about it all the time.

Having been to so many of these events on my own, I knew that this one definitely required a wingman. You needed someone to have a few drinks with first, someone to debrief with after and someone to act as a mothership to which you could return after your brief forays into the intergalactic dating minefield and replenish your confidence, before striking off once again towards a designated target. And they had to be single. I wasn't going to put myself through all this once again only to have my sole support standing there and obviously thinking, 'Thank God I'm not out there, having to do this.'

A woman would be good too, so we could work as a team. The more I thought like this, the more I realised that this is what other people did all the time, but I'd never approached dating quite so deliberately before. I'd never gone out 'on the pull'; I'd never – except maybe a few times at university – got dressed up specially to go out on a Saturday night. I've probably gone out drinking more than the average person but I suppose it wasn't the 'right' kind of drinking: it wasn't 'pulling' drinking, it was 'chatting to your mates' drinking.

While all my friends had managed to hook up with someone in the course of the 'mates drinking' years, I somehow never did. Well, I did, but not long-lasting, not permanently, so it feels like it doesn't count. In fact, it feels as if your past counts for nothing if you are single in the present. Not only does being single in my late thirties make me feel as if I have been single for ever, but I'm often surprised to remember that I have actually been in relationships: I have gone out with people, lived with them, gone on holiday with them and made plans for the future, but because I feel so single now it's as if they never happened.

I have been in lovely relationships with fabulous people in which we did amazingly wonderful and romantic things, but, because that's all in the past and I'm single now, it just doesn't seem to matter. It feels as if people who have been single for ages but have now finally found 'the one', got married to them or moved in with them are the successful ones who can 'do' relationships, whereas I'm just the sad single one who's an utter flipping failure at everything.

Or maybe that's just how I feel in this particular decade.

Anyway, back to my quest. It was time to find my wingman and, thankfully, I knew the ideal person for the job. I'd met Alison just a few weeks earlier. She was a long-lost school friend of Jo who had been tracked down at a recent school reunion; she was living in London and keen to hook up with old friends again. She was also utterly fed up with being single and we had bonded over our 'we are going to be single for ever and what are we going to do about it?' panic. She possessed other admirable wingman qualities too, being tall, pretty, blonde and outgoing. Ideal, in fact.

She turned out to be even more perfect, as she not only replied instantly to my email with enthusiasm, but also turned up outside the venue the very next day at 6 p.m. sharp. This was so far removed from the rest of my friends who couldn't even consider meeting up unless it had been in their BlackBerrys for at least a month, and who would then reschedule anyway, that the evening already seemed like a minor miracle.

We walked into the bar feeling rather self-conscious, even though absolutely no one looked at us when we arrived. It was one of those trendy City places with a 17-page list of cocktails, which no one will ever buy, and ultra-modern chairs, which are impossible to sit on. It was fairly small and empty; there were only a few people there and no one was drinking out of red straws. This wasn't looking good.

Alison volunteered to get the drinks and I nipped to the loo. I found the toilets downstairs, as well as a whole other bar in which a crowd of people were sipping their drinks through little red straws. The whole evening was suddenly looking a lot more positive. There was even a big 'Lovestruck' banner. Jackpot.

We relocated downstairs and sipped our G&Ts to fortify ourselves. I even went to fetch a couple of red straws from the bar to show willing. There were a few people queuing for their half-price happy-hour cocktails, while the rest of the daters were sitting around the edge of the room in ones and twos, looking as if they were waiting to conduct a series of interviews. It would be a brave person to plonk themselves down in front of a group of strangers, however many red straws they were festooned with, and just start rabbiting away.

There was also, I now saw, a fundamental flaw in the whole 'red straw' idea. It was OK for girls drinking cocktails, because a straw was a standard part of the package, but, for the blokes, a red straw in a pint or a bottle of beer just looked, well, silly. Possibly even a bit camp. Which presumably wasn't the look they were going for. So quite a few had already abandoned the straw idea altogether, although a few others were being rather more creative with it, displaying it in their top pockets or even behind their ears like Brazilian hula girls.

'We should really start talking to some of these guys,' I said rather unenthusiastically, nursing my G&T.

Alison leaped to her feet. 'You're right. Let's do it!'

I was rather impressed. Most of my friends would have said, 'Oh yeah, sure, maybe in a bit,' and then sat there like lemons. But here we were, prowling around the room like women on a mission. Our red straws weren't exactly proving to be man-magnets but they did at least instil a certain sense of confidence.

'This is a red-straw event and here is my straw,' it declared. 'We are meant to be here.'

We chose two guys who looked friendly and unthreateningly normal. They turned out to be first-timers too and had taken the 'sit there and do nothing' approach to this event. Men! What's wrong with them? Do they never approach anyone? Anyway, they were very nice and, after it became clear that none of us fancied one another, we formed a great little mutual support group.

Thrown out of our corner by people who claimed to have reserved a table and who had no time for lovelorn Lovestruckers, we occupied the centre of the room, which was perfect, as we could survey both the bar and the doorway.

'So who do you like then?' we'd say to one another and, having spotted a suitable target, would shove one another out of our group safety net to go and chat. Even at a singles event, it seemed surprisingly difficult to approach people. I was the first to venture out, having caught sight of a tall, good-looking bloke in skinny trousers and a blazer who looked like an early Beatle, Paul probably. I bowled up to him and we started chatting about the event, as you do, the problem of the red straws and how scary it is to approach someone. The strange thing was we just couldn't get off the subject.

'It's just so terrifying talking to people,' he bleated, looking around him rather pathetically. 'I didn't really want to come, but I came anyway, and I'm really not sure if I want to be here. I don't feel I can just go up to someone.'

This was all rather disappointing. There is nothing that makes your already low expectations plummet more than a man who moans about how awful the event is, *the event that he's just met you at*.

'And you don't have to worry about approaching people, you dingbat,' I wanted to shout at him after several more minutes of his whining. 'I approached you, didn't I?'

Some more torturous chat later, I bade him farewell and good luck. Cute but utterly wet.

After a few more circuits of the room and various desultory conversations with other people, we met again. He seemed a bit more cheerful to see me this time and we even had a vaguely decent conversation about what he did and about something other than the event itself.

It turned out he worked quite near me. 'We should have a coffee some time then,' I said, suspecting that he might be better away from the trauma of the red-straw evening. I got out my phone. 'What's your number?'

He readily gave it to me, but made no effort to get mine. Shortly afterwards, he got rather flappy again. 'Oh, God,' he said. 'I don't think I can take this place any longer. I've just got to get out of here. I need to go to the loo. I've got an early start tomorrow.' Then he practically ran out of the door.

I texted him anyway later on, more out of politeness than anything else, but he never replied.

Alison had found a nice group of men to talk to. All tall, good-looking, confident and friendly, they stood out from the rest of the pack like gleaming specimens of man. This was more like it: some normal people! But no. They turned out to be the founders of Lovestruck, here to show clients how popular their events were. They were all very nice and chatty . . . and they were all very married. It felt wrong for them to be standing in the middle of the bar, masquerading as real, dateable people.

By now, I was ready to call it a night, but, as I was waiting for Alison to finish her conversation, I propped myself up against the bar and thought about ordering another drink. A guy stood next to me, seemingly alone, and with a bottle of red wine in front of him. Two people, standing alone, at a bar, at an event for singles . . . I waited for him to say something. *Anything*. But nothing. It seemed that men across the whole of London were incapable of starting a conversation with a woman. So I started talking. I said something about the red straws in a suitably witty way. He responded with alacrity and we were off, chatting and bantering and swapping information as if we were born to be in a romcom.

Even now I am still baffled as to why, if he was so ready to chat and talk and flirt, he did not even attempt to start the conversation.

Still, it was going swimmingly now, and he completely redeemed himself by saying it would be great to see me again; he asked for my phone number and said he'd call me.

Alison came over at that moment, perfect timing, and I floated off up the stairs for a debrief over Japanese noodles, feeling that the evening hadn't been an entire waste of time after all.

He never called.

I wasn't ready to give up yet, though, and decided to give it another try. Alison wasn't able to make the next event so I roped Damien in instead. He had been rather put out that I'd gone to the first event without him and was sold on what a success it had been – well, it was one of the few events I'd come out of not wanting to shoot myself, which shows how low the bar is in singledom – so he was quite up for this one.

However, it turned out that a West End bar on a Thursday night at 8 p.m. is a very different proposition from a City bar at 6 p.m. on a Tuesday.

For a start, it was already completely packed. Heaving, in fact. And dark, *very* dark. Singles and civilians mingled together in the gloom without any indication which was which. People were chatting, that was obvious, but to whom? To friends? Work colleagues? Singles? The red-straw theme had been almost entirely abandoned and it was completely impossible to tell whose conversation you could just barge in on and whose you couldn't. You could argue that that is the very point, but in the real world, when I'm out with friends or work colleagues, no one would be particularly happy if a lone singleton suddenly appeared and started asking where we all came from and how we got here. At the same time, I defy anyone, particularly an ego-crushed single, to be able to crash in on a conversation without the slightest of hints that such an interruption would be welcomed.

Damien and I stood outside and chatted to each other. That in itself was bad and I realised the wisdom of same-sex wingmen. A couple of guys might conceivably approach me and Alison, but me and a guy? It looked like we were already chatting each other up. And, as all the other pairs of friends seemed to be two girls or two guys, if Damien and I had gone on the hunt ourselves, it would have left the other one standing around like a spare part.

When it was Damien's turn to get the drinks, I loitered by the bar in a very obvious 'I'm on my own, please talk to me' kind of way. I looked smiley, friendly and approachable, and I twirled red straws like a drum majorette with no muscle tone. Still nothing.

I started talking to a couple of guys who were also loitering by the door. They seemed perfectly nice, and we talked about Lovestruck, how we'd got here and where they lived and so on. Then one of them said that he wanted a cigarette and they went outside. Not invited to join them, I stayed put.

I started talking to another guy, on his own this time. After ten seconds, I realised he was unbelievably dull. When Damien came back with the drinks, he said hello to the guy and started chatting, but quickly I said that we were very sorry but we had to get back to our friends outside. Fortunately, Damien – rather than saying, 'What friends, you utter fantasist?' – took the hint and we trooped outside.

It was obvious that this evening was a washout. I was tired and not in the mood. It was half nine by now, and I wanted to go home, eat some food and go to bed. I hated the dark and crowded bar, and the fact you didn't know who was here to date or not, but most of all I hated the flipping pain and effort, the torture and the sheer hard work I was constantly putting myself through, and for what? To make small talk with boring, hopeless people in horrible bars.

I left Damien to it and went home.

A glutton for punishment, I decided to try it for a third and final time. No one could accuse me of not putting the effort in, at least. This time, the event was in super-trendy Hoxton and I arrived bang on time, dressed to kill, or, at least, maim, in heels, LBD, eyebrows tamed, lippy on and generally looking as smart as I have ever done.

The bar was closed.

There appeared to be people working inside, but they certainly hadn't got round to doing anything quite so mundane as actually opening the doors and letting people in.

I wasn't going to stand around outside looking like the world's most desperate single, so wandered off to rather half-heartedly check out the local shops.

After half an hour of window-shopping, I forced myself to return to the fray. The bar was actually open now and there seemed to be people drinking inside. I steeled myself to go in. But where was my wingman?

He was held up at work, it turned out, once I'd checked my phone. Damien wasn't going to be here for at least another hour. I couldn't keep on traipsing backwards and forwards from posh bar to the shops until he showed up, but I *really* didn't want to go inside.

I phoned Damien and started wailing rather pathetically down the phone. 'I don't want to go in there!' I whined, sounding like a two year old not keen on Santa's Grotto. 'Don't make me go! I don't want to go to yet another event where I walk in on my own and don't know anyone and I have to go up to people I'll never see again and make pointless small talk and where there'll be a million women and no men, and even if there is one and we start talking and we get on and swap phone numbers he'll never ever bloody call so what on earth is the point?'

Damien kindly let me witter on and then pointed out that there might just be one person here who ...

'That's all I ever hear! This is the night that I'm going to meet the one! But it never is, it never happens and it never will. God, I hate all this.'

'Look, do whatever you want,' said Damien hurriedly, anticipating a shift in gear from how I hate singles events to how I hated being single, which was a whole separate and well-worn rant and could have gone on for hours. 'Just text me what you decide.'

I clomped miserably around the block several times. I think I'd reached one of those moments where I was so bloody fed up with the whole thing that I just wanted to go home and jump under the duvet. The duvet that, it seemed, I was destined to sleep under alone.

That one thought propelled me straight through the doors and up to the bar before I could wallow any further. 'Just one nice guy,' my brain was feverishly chanting, 'just one nice guy, please let there be just one nice guy.'

I looked around. There were women everywhere. Women in pairs and threes, chatting away nervously to one another and subtly looking around the room every now and then. The only men in the place were the ones working behind the bar and two old men sitting in the corner who had clearly walked in by mistake but had bought a drink anyway.

I had a choice. No, in fact, I had several. I could stand on my own at the bar like a lemon, waiting for the blokes to turn up. I could get a drink and start talking to some of the other desperate women to hear them moan about how hard it was to meet men. Or I could give up completely and go home.

I chose a fourth option. I went to the pub. I may have looked slightly overdressed for the Dog and Duck but I was really in need of a drink. The first one went down so well that I ordered another one to keep it company. It was then I actually looked around me. *Men!* Straight men! Loads of them! All rather good-looking, all just finished work for the day, all chatting away animatedly in little groups, and all looking exactly like the kind of men I was after.

I sat there, quite obviously on my own at the bar, for three whole drinks. Not one guy started chatting to me, or asked for my phone number, as would have happened within two seconds to Carrie or Miranda. I might as well have been invisible. Well, I was.

Within ten minutes of my arriving, the Arsenal–Manchester United game had kicked off. The guys had no eyes for anyone but Rooney. I was left to my G&T and packet of crisps, and the thought: 'Who on earth schedules a dating evening when the football is on?'

It was clear that pubs were where men were, not dating evenings or singles events. But it seemed actually getting to talk to any of them was an entirely different matter.

15

Don't Come Dine with Me

Sometimes, I was beginning to discover, your low expectations are just not low enough. Just Dine and Date was one of those evenings.

It had been recommended to me by a girl I'd met at a party, who had gone there with her sister some years ago.

'We had such a great time,' she gushed cheerfully, as we queued up for barbecued sausages. 'I think the men weren't up to much, but all the girls got together and got completely wrecked. It was hilarious!'

As a way of finding a husband, it wasn't exactly a glowing recommendation and the sight that greeted me on arrival at the Italian restaurant just off Oxford Street wasn't of people having a hilarious evening. It was full of people who seemed determined to convince themselves, despite evidence to the contrary, that they were having a nice time, as if acknowledging the reality of what they were doing and why they were there would have been too much to bear and they'd have all been impelled as one to rush out in the street to throw themselves under the wheels of the nearest bus.

The premise of Just Dine and Date was, as stated on its website: 'Dinner dating at the heart of London – a unique dinner dating concept.' You signed up to one of several dinner dates that were tailored to various groups, such as 'Thoroughly Thirties' or 'Fabulous Forties', or dinners for travel or film buffs, and then you turned up to meet a tableful of like-minded singles.

The idea wasn't an entirely bad one: rather than the pressure cooker of a one-to-one date or the mindless blur of speed-dating, there would be three men and three women. You would all sit together around a table and take it in turns to sparkle over the wine and pasta.

'Just Dine and Date offers a guaranteed fun and memorable experience,' enthused the site.

I signed up for dinner in the 'Thoroughly Thirties' group, lured by the website's promise:

> If you're single and in your thirties, this dinner is for you! No more scary one-on-one blind dates, or time-consuming profile browsing. Take a break from the bar scene. We have a great new dinner date concept that works and is great fun.

This was illustrated with a group of beautiful 30-somethings resembling the cast of *Friends*.

It cost £14 for one dinner date and on the evening the bill would be split between the diners equally. Having submitted my credit card details to the website, I received a confirmation of my payment and awaited an email saying exactly where my 'date' would be held. It all felt extremely impersonal, as if I had just bought an easyJet flight or a book. There was no attempt to find out anything about me at all – likes, dislikes, background and so on – so it looked like I'd just be lumped together with any other 30-somethings who happened to book for the same night. Or so I thought.

Five past eight on a Thursday evening in June and the table was already full. I squeezed myself on the end. We were seated at a long rectangular table, rather than a round one, which was less than ideal as you could only talk to the people immediately next to you. I was sitting next to a woman who looked at least ten years older than me, and opposite what turned out to be her best friend of a similar age. Next to her was a guy who, well, made my heart sink to look at him is the kindest way to describe him. He had thick, bottle-end glasses and a wispy beard, and he was wearing a bright-pink polo-neck jumper. Next to him was a smart-looking lady with long brown hair, and opposite her was a very glamorous-looking blonde City type, the only woman who looked anything like my age. At the far end of the table, and therefore impossible to talk to, was a depressed-looking guy with sad eyes and droopy mouth. None of the guys had hair.

So, to sum up, there were five women and two men. It was indeed a good job that my expectations were practically at zero before I'd even walked in. Even so, they quickly plummeted.

The Just Dine and Date website had pictured a dinner table at which beautiful people engaged in sophisticated flirting and witty banter. However, in reality, it was obvious that everyone had mentally written off the men the moment they arrived and could see no point in engaging in flirting or banter. Instead, we all talked about dating in a rather gloomy and serious way.

All the women started chatting among themselves about what other dating sites they'd been on: singles holidays, singles social events. This seemed to be a strange new world when it was perfectly acceptable to talk about your endless quest for a man in front of the bloke you were theoretically on a date with.

The older-looking women sitting near me were best friends Anne and Sandra, who turned out to be old hands at this.

'The singles balls organised by Solo are great,' said Anne, in a 'mustn't grumble' kind of way. 'You meet some really nice people there, don't you? And because you're all in the same hotel, you don't have to worry about how you're going to get home afterwards.'

'Yes, we didn't get on the last one because they had too many women and not enough men,' said Sandra, sighing. 'It's always the way, isn't it?'

Everyone nodded forlornly, as I resisted the urge to rush outside and howl.

'What am I doing here?' I thought, not for the first time. 'I don't belong here, with all these people, do I? Do I?'

I had the awful feeling that, as I was here, I probably did.

The small talk continued painfully. The table thought I was 'very brave' to cycle in London. We discussed *EastEnders* and *Homes under the Hammer*. The corporate-looking woman talked at great length about how crucial she was to her company and how she shouldn't really be here because she had a major project to hand in tomorrow that she hadn't started yet. She then ordered some more wine. We swapped typical London stories, such as 'the time my train got stuck in a tunnel on the Underground' and 'the time my car got towed'. Then the food arrived and so we could talk about that.

Halfway through the meal, the guy sitting at the end of the table whom I hadn't even spoken to had a whispered discussion with the waiter over his share of the bill, and then simply walked out.

We looked up from our plates in astonishment.

'Has he gone home?' one woman asked. It turned out he had.

'He said he was bored and then he just got up and left,' said the woman sitting nearest to him. 'What a cheek! And, if anything, *he* was the boring one.'

'It seems slightly strange to leave halfway through the evening if you haven't even spoken to everyone,' I volunteered, thinking it fairly rude that he had not even waited until we had finished eating. 'Bit of a waste of money, surely?'

'Oh, it doesn't cost anything,' said the guy in the pink polo-neck. 'They are so short of men that we get to come along for free. Well, we have to pay for our food, of course.' He snorted with laughter and forked up another mouthful of pasta.

I couldn't believe it. That was hardly fair. I looked around the table to see all the other women nodding. Clearly, this was a widely known fact.

'There is always a shortage of men, not just these people but all these types of dating companies,' said Sandra. 'Men just don't tend to sign up to these things.'

Well, if they tended not to sign up to this type of thing, what was I doing here?

'So we've all paid £14 for a night with other 30-somethings apart from the blokes?' I said, thinking I might as well get down to the nitty gritty.

'Thirty-somethings?' chorused the other women. 'We're all in the forties group.'

Anne patted me on the arm. 'Poor you,' she said sympathetically, 'stuck here with us oldies.'

'No, not at all,' I protested, hopefully convincingly. Inside I was fuming. I'd forked out for a ticket and trekked all the way across town to have dinner with two blokes – sorry, one bloke – and a bunch of women in their forties. This was giving a new, deeper resonance to the word pointless.

There was a flurry of activity. A guy with a massive paunch, a gold medallion round his neck and more wrinkles than Methuselah had arrived. 'Sorry I'm late, darlings,' he said, beaming. 'Is there room for a little one?'

Astonishingly, all the ladies perked up no end at the sight

of the late arrival, who at least seemed to be up for a laugh about it all. They all clicked straight back into flirt mode and started showing lots of teeth and flicking their hair about.

I stayed as little time as was politely possible and then left, pleading an early start in the morning. I was really hacked off. It was bad enough having to take part in the hideous concept of singles evenings in the first place without feeling ripped off as well as being bored and depressed beyond belief at the same time. People desperate enough to go to this kind of evening were obviously vulnerable and easy pickings for all sorts of bad deals.

I cycled home furiously. I was pissed off at having to endure such an evening but there was also a deeper, darker feeling. I didn't want to be one of those women who had an encyclopaedic knowledge about singles events and which ones were 'good' or not. I didn't want to be one of those women who accepted with stoical resignation that there were always going to be more women than men and that the ones that did turn up – for free – weren't going to be any good. I just didn't want to be here, at all.

I fired off a complaint to Just Dine and Date. To their credit, they apologised straight away, refunded my money and said that one guy had dropped out at the last minute while another woman must have turned up without booking, hence the imbalance in numbers. Either way, it was a rubbish evening. I wanted to give up on the whole idea. But I had to keep on going. So I ran away to an island instead.

16

Nothing Ventured

My friends had been generally supportive of my attempts to find this elusive man with whom I would hopefully spend the rest of my life. But when I told them that I was going to battle with rhododendron bushes on an island in the middle of the Bristol Channel, then even they started to question my motives. And my sanity.

'You're doing what?'

'Why?'

'Is it for an article?'

'You are actually using up a week of holiday to do this?'

It was time to explain that I wanted to meet new people. And possibly someone in particular. I wasn't going to do that hanging around gay clubs or working with the same people I'd worked with for the last ten years. And I certainly wasn't going to do that just sitting around moping about Will.

The reason behind the Lundy Island trip was that I'd had a lot of fun when, at the age of 15, I'd joined the Venture Scouts. So much fun, in fact, that I look back on my teenage years as being, well, just perfect. They weren't, of course; there were parents and exams and youthful angst to cope with, but those were also my Venture Scout years, and if I think about them too much I get all knotted up inside with the kind of nostalgic longing that comes from remembering wonderful times that are lost for ever.

The Wednesday nights in the Scout hut were great fun – me and next-door-neighbour-but-two Sarah, whose two older brothers were in the Scouts too, would walk up the road to the Scout meeting and then spend the next few hours building stuff, making fires, pitching tents, planning expeditions and generally hanging out with boys and having a really good laugh. I still have the friends I made there now, and the benefit of having a group of such close friends, mainly boys, when I went to an all-girls' school, was just great.

The trips away were the best. The whole pack would head off to the Lake District or Snowdonia or North Devon and spend two glorious weeks camping in the open air, a particular highlight of which would be the hiking trips. We would split into groups of four and plan a route, buy our food, pack our rucksacks and head off with our tents and camping stoves and disappear into the mountains for days. They were wonderful times. Maybe it was time to get back in touch with what I used to love doing.

I fished around on the internet and discovered that the National Trust runs volunteer weeks in various parts of the UK, ranging from sweeping up historic buildings to dry-stone walling in the Lake District. One stood out for me – a week on the Isle of Lundy in the Bristol Channel. It didn't cost that much – just £179 for a week, all in – and I liked the sound of Lundy. I knew virtually nothing about it, but a friend of mine had been for a 40th birthday party – where they'd spent the day 'dead letter boxing', whatever that was – and they said it was a lovely place.

The Lundy trip was a way of going back to doing all the things I loved – such as hiking, climbing, generally being out in the fresh open countryside and getting thoroughly dirty and exhausted before heading to the pub at the end of a long day – while hopefully meeting someone who enjoyed doing those types of things too. Once again, I had the feeling that I was just looking for someone who was going to be doing the exact same thing as me for the exact same reasons, and there were times when I thought this was entirely likely, and other times when I thought there's no way anyone would be doing that. But how do you find someone who you have something in common with without at least trying it out yourself?

That was in my more optimistic moments. The rest of the time, I just remembered the guys – still my best friends – who were in the Venture Scouts with me. All now married, all with multiple children. They certainly weren't trying to find their life partners by heading off for a week's scrabbling around in the dirt with a bunch of strangers.

Still, nothing ventured . . . I booked the trip and some time off work, then caught the helicopter over to the island. I was joining the group a few days late as I couldn't take that much time off work, but I'd still be there for the main bulk of the week, and there was always a chance they'd be so bored with one another that they'd be delighted to see me. Of course, they could have all partnered up by the time I got there, but that was a risk I'd have to take. There was also a third alternative: that people on the trip were genuinely just interested in spending a week clearing rhododendron bushes and digging ditches. But I had become so blinkered by this dating quest that it didn't actually occur to me.

The helicopter flight to the island was fabulous fun – it felt like the opening credits of *The Apprentice*. The ground shot away from beneath us and then we were scurrying along, high above the sea. Twenty minutes later, we were on Lundy.

As I chatted to other visitors to Lundy, I started to have a clearer idea about the island. I had thought that Lundy was a smaller version of the Isle of Wight in the sense of being a place where people live and work and lead regular lives, but Lundy is actually more of a holiday island, where visitors are checked in when they arrive, and the only people working are the ones who are there to serve the guests, from the bar staff in the island's only pub to the staff of the island's only shop. There are people around maintaining the land, of course, but the whole impression I got was like a short-stay version of *The Prisoner* – a slightly unreal environment where everyone arrives one day and leaves exactly a week later.

I checked into the island's reception, which was next to the pub, and found that our accommodation, a large hut, was precisely 15 steps from the pub's front door. The shop was halfway between the two, and it seemed as if the whole of island life was right there, in a space no bigger than two tennis courts. Fighting off a feeling of impending claustrophobia, I set off to find the others.

As I strolled off through the fields, the trapped feeling left me and, when the footpath twisted round to run along the coast, about 20 metres up from the sea, it began to feel as if I were on some Mediterranean island. The scenery was absolutely incredible. The sea sparkled under the deep-blue cloudless sky, and I felt a million miles from London and work. As if to emphasise the point, a bunch of deer suddenly appeared just above me and sprang along cheerfully as if choreographed by the Lundy tourist board for the occasion.

I found the group on the coast path. Two men in their late thirties were sweating away just by the path, cutting branches and stacking them in a neat pile. These, I was to learn, were the dreaded rhodi bushes, which were an unstoppable force taking over the island.

I called out a hello and was duly greeted and introduced. The pair at the top were Jez, with a cheerful, smiling face, and Colin, the group leader. Jez was chatty, and he was pleased as punch to discover that I was a former Venture Scout. He'd also been a Venture Scout and he instantly regaled me with the trips he'd been on, the adventures they'd had and the 'just crazy' people he'd met. Colin joined in, and they were soon both starting anecdotes that the other would finish.

It was pleasant enough background music to listen to, and I enjoyed the novel sensation of working the muscles in my arms without being attached to a machine at the gym.

At half four, Colin decided to call it a day. The team downed tools and started emerging out of the bushes from far down the steep slope. We seemed a mixed group – some couples, most single travellers – with quite an age range. I seemed to be one of the youngest – there was one guy, Charlie from Canterbury, who I think was 29 – but the rest were either my age or older. We all said hello and then headed back to our hut.

It was, quite literally, just a hut. There was a massive open space that started off with a kitchen, then turned into a large dining-room area with two long tables, and then ended up with a sitting room with a fireplace and various comfy chairs placed around. It reminded me more than ever of Scouts – there were various socks and wet jackets drying all over the place, a mountain of walking boots by the front door and industrial-sized pans in the kitchen to make gallons of porridge in the morning.

The men's room was a separate room off the main living space, whereas the women's sleeping area was on the mezzanine floor above the kitchen, which didn't make for a great deal of privacy, but it seemed comfortable enough.

Colin and Jez had organised a rota and menu plan for the week and mealtimes were organised with military precision, down to who was laying the table and who was washing up afterwards, although it was all done with a fairly relaxed air.

However, when you put a load of British strangers together in this kind of environment, you do get an endless amount of chatter. Incessant, pointless chatter.

'Oo, I could do with a cup of tea. I might put the kettle on.'

'Oh, are you putting the kettle on? That's a good idea. I could do with a cuppa.'

'A cup of tea! What a great idea. Whose idea was that?'

'JUST MAKE THE TEA!' I managed, by some heroic effort of self-control, not to say.

'I thought I might check out the pub,' I said instead.

This provoked a whole new round of chatter.

'Oh, she's been here for five minutes and she's off down the pub!'

'Well, she is from London, you know, that's the kind of thing they do in London . . .'

Finally, I managed to get a small party to come to the pub and, thankfully, they seemed quite normal. Charlie, the youngest of us, was enthusiastic and cheerful in a bouncy, puppy-dog way and seemed fun and friendly. Rosie was fortyish and quite beautiful, with short dark hair, cheeks flushed in the wind and a bright, wide smile. And, most encouragingly, Jill and John, a couple who lived in Devon, had actually met on a National Trust volunteering week. 'So it can be done!' I thought triumphantly. I didn't see it happening for me on this trip, but it was nice to know I was on the right lines at least.

The week developed a natural rhythm. Everyone would get up insanely early, chatter loudly about tea for a while and have breakfast, and then we'd all head out at nine. We dug ditches for cables, we cleared scrub and we shifted rocks; in fact, we did anything that needed doing around the island. Working outdoors was great – some days were sunny and we'd sit at the top of the lighthouse having our lunch and admiring the view, and on days that were cold and wet we'd eat huddled together against a dry-stone wall, sheltered from the wind.

When we had a free day, we hiked to the other side of the mountain and watched seals playing in the waves and deer cantering over the hills. It felt great to be outside, sweeping all the London cobwebs away. There is a special feeling you only get when you have been doing hard physical labour in the teeth of a gale all day and then you come back into the warmth, prise your boots off and sit by the fire, clothes gently steaming.

After dinner, we'd either read or play card games in the hut, or venture the ten yards to the pub, where we'd play drinking games or just, well, drink. Charlie and I developed a passion for Yahtzee and would play that for hours. Then it would be back to the hut and bed, with the earplugs in to try to combat the deafening snoring that shook the women's room each night.

I began to suspect that Charlie might be rather keen on me. I thought he was lovely too, but way too young and bouncy for me. Everywhere I went he seemed to be there too: 'What shall we do now? Shall we play Yahtzee? Shall we go for a walk? Shall we, shall we, shall we?'

I was starting to feeling slightly stalked. It was a small island and there was nowhere really to go. If you walked beyond our cluster of buildings, you were walking into the wild remoteness of the rest of the island. Every time I went somewhere, to the pub, or even the loo, Charlie would either turn up and say, 'What are you up to?' or greet me afterwards with 'Where have you been?'

While I enjoyed his company, it was all getting a bit too much. So I was quite relieved when the final day dawned.

We, along with the entire island, had to pack our bags and meet in the pub to wait for the helicopter. At 10 a.m. we'd cleaned, swept and mopped the hut and were playing cards in the pub. Two hours later, we were still playing cards and getting rather bored and impatient. Four hours later, we were told that the helicopter was fogbound and we couldn't get off the island that day. Everyone got their bags and trooped back to the hut.

'What shall we do now?' said Charlie, bobbing up beside me as usual.

We went for a walk in the rain.

That evening was a real anti-climax. We'd had the final big night the night before, we'd all said our piece about what a great week it had been and we'd eaten all the food, drunk all the wine and cleared the whole place up. Now we were back, stuck in our hut, and not even sure we would be able to make it off the island the next day.

Sunday dawned and we did the whole thing all over again. We had breakfast, cleaned up, swept, mopped, packed our bags and then sat in the pub, waiting for the news. After another four-hour wait, it came: no flights today either.

I was starting to go slightly mad. Not only was my precious holiday ebbing away but also the prospect of another day stuck indoors playing Yahtzee before waking up to the tea-making chorus the next day was doing my head in.

I had a chat with Rosie and found that she was also keen to get home.

'By the way,' she said, 'Charlie's looking for you. In fact, he's *always* looking for you. Every time I see him he's looking for you.'

I sighed. 'This island is much too small for the both of us.'

'No chance then?'

I shook my head. 'Nope. He's lovely but way too intense for me.'

It seemed very annoying that I was in a potentially very romantic situation but without the right man to share it with. Stuck on a fogbound island for days – what could be better? There was nothing else to do but talk, and walk, and drink and hang out . . . if my feelings towards Charlie had been different, it would have been perfect.

But they weren't, and I was about to go completely out of my mind.

We walked back into the pub and, like a vision in yellow waterproofs, there they were.

Rosie grabbed my arm. 'Sailors!' she breathed.

I looked. There were three of them, clad head to toe in sou'westers and scoffing down egg and chips like their lives depended on it.

'Let's hitch a lift!' said Rosie. 'You up for it?'

Anything to get off the island. 'Yes, of course,' I said. My sailing experience was next to nil – no, I think it *was* nil – but I was fairly sure I could sit on a boat without falling off.

We approached them cautiously, as if not to scare them off.

'Are you sailors?' Rosie asked rather unnecessarily.

The guys laughed and nodded. 'In a manner of speaking, I suppose we are,' said one.

I couldn't help but notice that they were all remarkably cute.

It turned out that they were all doctors from Cardiff, who had sailed to Lundy overnight. They were now heading back to the English mainland for dinner, and then would head back across the Bristol Channel to land in the early hours of the following morning. It sounded completely barmy to me but, well, each to their own. The main thing was that they were perfectly happy to take two random females with them to North Devon.

We rushed outside to retrieve our bags from the general luggage pile and to tell the others that there would be two fewer for dinner that evening. Colin was most unsure about the plan, most unsure indeed; he pursed his lips and shook his head, looking most disapproving. Charlie, poor thing, looked absolutely gutted. But we promised to keep in touch and he very sweetly lent me his hat. I hugged him goodbye and promised to keep in touch. It's all about timing, luck and timing . . .

Charlie came down to wave us off and to watch us make the perilous leap from the jetty onto the sailing boat. Rosie was quite a keen sailor and immediately made herself useful by doing things with ropes. I had already warned them I barely knew the front of a boat from the back and so sat where I was told and tried not to get in the way.

Sailing, as far as I could work out, seemed to consist of a massive initial flurry, when things would be furled and unfurled and other things tied and untied, followed by a period of about three hours when absolutely nothing happened at all and then, at the other end, there would be a massive flurry of activity again. It seemed a pleasant enough way to spend an afternoon but I couldn't see myself making this a regular habit. However, the feeling of relief when we were on the boat and we could see Lundy getting further and further away was amazing. We'd escaped!

Once all the sailing necessaries had been done, one guy disappeared downstairs for a sleep. There was nothing else to do but chat. The cute doctors turned out to be married, of course, but were currently all agog about a friend of theirs who was supposed to have come on this trip but whose wife had just discovered that he was having an affair. They were torn between disapproval of their friend's behaviour and concern for his wellbeing, and thought it rather fortuitous that they had picked up two women to canvass their opinions.

There was something about being on a yacht in the middle of the sea with no land in sight with complete strangers to make all sorts of conversation seem possible. We talked about infidelity and whether or not it should break up a marriage. I told them about my rather disastrous love life, which provoked gratifying gasps of astonishment among the captive audience. Rosie talked about the various temptations that she and her husband had faced throughout their marriage, and their decision not to have children.

We talked about Charlie ('He was really sweet on you') and how I really wanted to meet someone. I thought of how lovely these guys were and how annoying and typical it was that they were already married. It seemed that I was being thrown into some incredibly romantic situations – I could imagine my mum's delight: 'You met a Welsh doctor! On a boat!' – but without the romantic ending.

We arrived at the beautiful village of Clovelly, which looked from afar as if it were plunging down the steep cliffs and into the sea, and headed to the pub after the palaver of parking, or whatever it is you do with the boat. It was then I got the point of sailing – walking into a warm, bustling pub where everyone wants to know where you've come from or to tell you about their day's sailing, and after the fresh air and the exercise, the pint and the roaring fire warm you right down to your toes.

We said a heartfelt thank you to the Welsh doctors for rescuing us, and we got a lift back to where our cars were parked. It was a long drive ahead.

17

Supermarket Sweep

The world seemed to have tilted slightly, now that I'd decided to go all out on this dating quest. I couldn't walk down the street without checking out all the suitable-looking blokes. It was the same on the train, in the supermarket or in the pub. (Is this what blokes feel like all the time? It's amazing they actually get anything done.)

I kept on thinking: 'Should I be chatting to him? Or him? Or what about him?' Simply doing my shopping in Sainsbury's rather than finding my husband there seemed like a wasted opportunity. A voice in my head would say, 'Quick! Hurry up! Time is fleeting! The clock is ticking!' as if I'm in some terrible game show where I have to find three men before getting to the checkout.

My flatmates had gone on a shopping trip for food one Saturday and practically threw themselves at me when I came through the door.

'You've got to go to the supermarket!' they chorused as one.

I was confused. 'Why, what have you forgotten?' I asked.

They shared exasperated looks.

'Nothing,' said Alex, 'but the supermarket is full of men! Shopping! Loads of them – it's a perfect place to meet. We saw two guys shopping together who would have been perfect for you.'

This didn't sound particularly helpful to me, and an element of doubt must have shown on my face.

'They weren't *together*,' clarified Charlotte. 'Well, they were together, but not *together*, if you see what I mean.'

'You want me to go and chat up gay men in Tesco?' I asked.

'Not gay men!' said Alex, buzzing with enthusiasm. 'You know, you just go up to likely-looking guys and say, well, you say . . .'

'Yes?' I asked.

He faltered. 'Well, you know, ask them where the echinacea is, or something.'

This sounded even less likely.

'Well, I'm sure you'll be able to think of something better,' said Charlotte briskly, without giving much idea what that might actually be. 'But there's loads of them out there.'

It all sounded rather like a step back to the start of my quest when my non-dating, happily married friends had suggested I hover around the fruit and veg section, asking guys if my melons were ripe enough. It may have worked in *Animal House* but I couldn't see it actually working in real life. Yet my usually rational flatmates thought this completely – in my opinion – loopy idea was the way forward. They weren't prepared to try it out for themselves, naturally, but were more than happy for me to go and make a fool of myself.

Pondering all this, I went off a few days later to my local Sainsbury's to do some actual shopping, and found myself – as I always seemed to be doing nowadays – checking out the single guys. It was 3 p.m. on a Monday, so probably not the greatest selection to be fair, but there was a surprising number of single guys in there and not all wearing builders' overalls.

But how would you actually go ahead and approach

someone without looking like an utter weirdo? I thought I wouldn't really mind the rejection of someone being brusque or just walking away, but I didn't think I could handle the pity. The 'I know you've just asked me where the tomatoes are, but we both know that you're just really hanging around supermarkets trying to chat people up, and that's really quite sad' look. Especially if they were cute.

However, I did dimly recall seeing a programme on TV in which people were sent off around supermarkets to try to chat people up and, while most of them found it excruciating to begin with, with a bit of help and encouragement from the show's presenters, they were actually quite successful. Maybe there was something in this after all. If only I knew what to say.

The ringing of my phone broke into my thoughts. It was my sister.

'Where are you?'

'I'm in the supermarket, thinking about picking up single guys,' I hissed into my phone. A woman walking past gave me an odd look.

'Which supermarket?'

'Eh? The Sainsbury's on the corner . . .'

There was a shriek from the other end of the phone. 'Don't go to Sainsbury's! You've got to go to Waitrose. There'll be much nicer men in there.'

'But that's miles away! And it's all a bit stressful in Waitrose – it gets really busy there . . . Anyway that's not the point. What on earth do I say?'

'Just ask them to get things down from high shelves. But don't pick up any weirdos who are going to follow you home.'

It seemed unlikely that people would start to stalk me merely because I'd asked them to pass me down a jar of olives. And, looking around, it didn't seem like the right store for that either. The shelves were all annoyingly low, so not to be able to get something down for myself would have positioned me firmly in the pygmy category. I decided to put it off for another day. Or when I was very, very drunk.

This latest episode had, yet again, made me consider the power of fate and luck in all this – what if the guy I'm destined to be with is in Waitrose, while I'm in Sainsbury's? Or on the same train but a different carriage? Or getting a coffee on the platform or decided to cycle to work today but will be on this train tomorrow? While the world seemed to have opened up to include all these possible ways to meet men, there seemed to be even more ways to miss meeting Mr Right than to find him.

A friend of mine met his wife to be in a pub in Clapham. Does he ever wonder what would have happened if they hadn't met? Does she thank her lucky stars that she was there that night, with friends, the same night that he was there, that night, with friends? The friends met and then so did they . . . With my luck, I would have been there, but five hours too early, having a drink after work, absorbed in my newspaper or the quiz machine, without any friends to act as wingmen and conversation starters.

Maybe it doesn't matter. Perhaps they would have met someone else and been just as happy. I don't believe, or at least I don't think I do, that there is just one person for you or that some people find their soulmates, while others just make do or find no one. But maybe the type of person who is attractive to someone in a rainy taxi queue or a crowded bar is someone who will never be short of dates. Maybe I'm just not that kind of person, the kind who stands out. To try to improve that, I actually started carrying a make-up bag with me – unheard of for most of my adult life – and even spent time putting the stuff on my face, with varying degrees of success. When it worked I actually looked more sophisticated, more glamorous, and I'd think, 'Why haven't I been doing this for years? Why deliberately avoid something that does actually make you more attractive, you fool?' And then I'd catch sight of myself half an hour later with mascara smeared across my forehead or eye shadow on my nose, and I'd remember exactly why.

I'd feel ridiculously smart and overdressed, wearing lipstick to work ('What is the point? I know these people') but I thought that maybe this was a good habit to get into, that the more I practised wearing make-up the better I would get. I suppose that there's no harm in looking as good as I can, as often as I can. You never know, someone could spot me buying my lunch in Pret, for example, and be so bowled away by my carefully applied foundation and Rimmel eyeliner that he'd stop dithering over sandwiches and wraps and come and talk to me instead. Some chance.

My friend Kathryn, whom I'd met at one of these dating events and who had become a very useful person to discuss all these things with, not only looked extremely well groomed whatever she was doing, but had also taken my whole 'what happens if you meet somewhere when you're out and about?' to the next stage.

'You will never meet people when you're at home,' she explained over drinks one evening. 'So I've started deliberately being out as much as possible, even for small things. So, instead of making myself a coffee in the morning at home, I'll go out and have one in my local café, for example, or in the Starbucks near work. And then if I'm on my way home and would normally have a glass of wine when I get in, I actually stop off in the nice pub at the end of my road and have a drink there. I just think it's really important to get over the embarrassment about doing all these things on your own, and it's much more likely I'll start chatting to people when I'm in the pub or café rather than when I'm at home alone and there's no chance of meeting anyone.'

I thought that all made rather good sense. And it was a nice balance too to the 'big-ticket' items such as ski holidays and mountain treks. Just little tweaks to one's life and then, who knows?

Far from being terminally single, Kathryn had actually been with someone for ten years. 'We were one of the first in our group to get married and everyone thought we were the perfect couple,' she said. 'But within a year of us getting married he ran off with someone else. So you think that, once you're married, that's the solution to everything, that you've got it sorted now. Well, you haven't. I'm back out here again and, at this age, it's so much more difficult.'

Some people I've spoken to have found love, or lust, in some rather unlikely places. One girl I know was dumped so abruptly by her boyfriend that she hadn't wanted to even go near another bloke for years and years. Then, just recently, she travelled up north for a friend's birthday party and was having a drink in the hotel bar before going round to her friend's house. She started chatting to a guy and swapped phone numbers. When the party turned out to be utterly tedious, she texted him to ask if he was still around for a drink. He certainly was and, three days' happy bonking later, she trooped back to London, shag-happy and glowing, and attracting men all over the place because of her newfound confidence. Her gorgeous stranger, improbably enough, turned out to have been a gravedigger from Newport Pagnell. Who knows when you'll meet the person who switches your life around?

Another friend met her boyfriend in equally unlikely circumstances, on Twitter. Now I know very little about Twitter but I was under the impression that it was an online thing, not a 'real world' thing. How wrong could I be?

'We met at a Tweet-up!' said Francesca, who laughed at my baffled look.

'A what?' I asked, feeling hopelessly out of date.

It turned out that Francesca is building a career as a comedian and had started putting some of her jokes on her Twitter feed. As people re-tweeted her jokes, her followers grew, and started corresponding with her and so she thought it would be a good idea to meet up with them for drinks one night.

'Real drinks?' I asked, suspecting she might be talking about some kind of virtual pub session done by webcams.

Francesca nodded vigorously. 'Yes, real drinks in a real pub! We all met up, and one of the guys was very cute and we started talking and . . .'

A year later, they are still going out together. Not only that but a producer also came along that night and Francesca is now getting regular radio and television credits for her writing. Quite a productive evening, really.

I sat there and marvelled at the world and how many ways there were to meet people.

There were, of course, more old-fashioned ways. One unexpected ice-breaker, I discovered, is to wear a very fancy hat to your local pub. I didn't do this deliberately, of course, but I'd been to Royal Ascot that day and there is a very strict dress code. 'Ladies will wear a hat or a substantial fascinator' declared the ticket. I experimented with wearing some substantial fascinators in John Lewis – once I'd worked out what they actually were – and decided that most of them made it look as if some small birds had built their nest in the side of my head. A hat it was then.

After a day's racing and drinking and Royal-spotting, I met a friend for a drink in a pub in Clapham Junction. Needless to say, in my heels, posh frock and massive pink hat, I looked rather overdressed for a pint in the local boozer on a Monday evening. But it was amazing how much attention I got. Men smiled at me, struck up conversations with me at the bar, offered to carry my drinks, spontaneously barged into our conversation to comment on my appearance or – for those who worked out why I was dressed to the nines – ask if I'd actually backed any winners that day. It was quite astonishing. I made a mental note for next year that, even if I hadn't been to the races, I should just dress up and go down the pub anyway.

But would I be able to do that, knowing that it was such an obvious ploy to meet men? I feel perfectly comfortable looking out of place if there's a reason for it, but it would seem rather sad to actively dress up and pretend you're something you're not. Or maybe that's the whole point.

Of course, there is a far simpler way to get talking to complete strangers in the pub without having to dress as if you're an extra from *Downton Abbey*, which is why I'm seriously considering taking up smoking again.

Now that smoking has been banned from pretty much everywhere, it has become a brilliant way to meet people.

I was given a pack of ten Silk Cut on my sixteenth birthday, along with a pack of condoms, in one of those rites of passage gifts, although I didn't get round to using either for a year or two. Smoking in the sixth form was the thing that the cool kids did, and meant you got to hang around and chat to boys, and, by the time I went to university, smoking was such a sociable thing to do I'm astonished that students who didn't smoke actually had any friends at all.

There was the chatty 'have you got a light?' opening gambit, the sharing of cigarettes, the move into roll-ups and the whole ritual that went into that, and of course the progression on to smoking hash with its whole new set of rituals and paraphernalia.

Throughout my year travelling round Australia, smoking

was the social equivalent of making a cup of tea – you'd arrive at the backpackers hostel, dump your rucksack on your bed and then head outside for a puff and a chat with the other cool guys. At parties back home, there were several occasions when I ended up going out with someone simply because we'd started chatting over a smoke.

In my memory, it's always standing outside places, although I'm sure that can't be correct, unless I'm only remembering the times when we couldn't smoke inside because it was someone's parents' house, but there was something about smoking that meant you could just start a conversation with anyone just because you were both standing outside a building and it would always be perfectly acceptable.

When I moved to Italy, the smoking ban was just coming into force, a few years before Britain went the same way. It was widely predicted that there would be, if not full-scale rioting, at least very widespread disobedience of the smoking ban, as Italians loved smoking and they were not particularly keen on obeying rules. However, it turned out to be a resounding success and, from my first-floor room just off Santa Croce in Florence, it wasn't hard to see why. My window looked out onto two bars, a restaurant and a nightclub, and the pavements were packed every night.

Driving Italians out onto the streets to smoke meant that they could indulge their dearest passions, showing off and flirting, even more than usual. The bars liked it because a crush outside made it look incredibly popular, even if, once you'd fought your way through the crowds to the inside, there was just one lonely bartender forlornly polishing glasses, and the Florentine men preened and puffed and trotted out their patter as if they were born to it, which they probably were.

When I moved to New York a year later, I discovered a

different benefit to smoking. New York bars as a rule tend to be tiny, dark and crowded one-room venues, particularly in West Village where I lived, and so, once you were in, you were huddled up with the friends you arrived with and you'd shout into one another's ears all night for conversation. It was lively but could be quite oppressive and occasionally I'd miss the comparatively vast spaces of the British pub.

But add smoking into the mix and, suddenly, the problem is solved. You wouldn't stand outside a bar just to get some air – you'd look like a bit of an oddball – but go out for a cigarette and suddenly there would be a whole new set of people to talk to, other people who have also briefly stepped away from their friends and are free to talk about everything and anything. You bond in those five minutes and, when you re-enter the crush, you briefly meet their friends before rejoining yours. Then you meet a whole new bunch of people with the next cigarette. Before you know it, you've made friends with practically everyone in the bar while you were outside it, and all your non-smoking friends are bored with talking to the same people all evening and are thinking of calling it a night.

Of course, with chatting, there comes flirting, and, with flirting, there's romance. You don't have to have watched Bette Davis and Paul Henreid flirting over cigarettes in *Now, Voyager* to know that 'smirting' (smoking and flirting) may be a new word but it's certainly not a new concept.

And, if the person you fancy smokes, well, you'd be mad not to spark up. Saying to the object of your desires, 'Let's go and stand somewhere else for a while for no particular reason so we can talk to each other about nothing in particular' won't get you very far, but say, 'Fancy a smoke?' and they're exclusively yours for the next five minutes.

I, along with the rest of the British public since the dawn of time, have always viewed approaching a random stranger in a bar as something akin to flying – i.e. impossible and risky – but with a cigarette in your hand anything is possible. So it gives you cancer, bad breath, yellow teeth and a hacking cough, not to mention being insanely expensive nowadays. Yes, but to the unhappily single, it might just be the way forward.

I might do it. Take it up again. Just for a year.

18

Losing the Plot

The good thing about meeting lots of new people at all these dating events is that, well, you're meeting lots of new people. The bad thing is that you can actually start to lose your marbles.

The other day, I received a cheerful text that said: 'Hello, just got back from work! How are you doing?'

I didn't recognise the number, or more accurately my phone didn't, so I left it. I assumed that the sender had either got the wrong number or would send another text later complaining that I was ignoring them. I saved the details under 'Mystery number' and forgot all about it.

A few days later, on a Sunday morning, my phone rang. It was 'Mystery number'. I started to get slightly alarmed. Who was it? It could be a close friend who had changed their number without telling me, or equally it could be some annoying PR guy who was about to ruin my Sunday by taking issue with one of my stories. Or it could be a rival reporter about to do the same. I decided to let it go to voicemail.

'Aren't you going to answer that?' asked Alex, who was making coffee, while watching me watching my phone ring.

'No, I'm trying to see who it is,' I replied, not explaining things very well.

'Eh?'

'I don't know who it is, so I'm hoping they will leave a message,' I explained. The phone stopped ringing. We both watched intently.

Charlotte came into the kitchen. 'What on earth are you doing?' she asked.

Alex held up a hand. 'Hang on,' he said.

The phone bleeped. A voicemail message. Alex and I gave a sigh of relief.

'He left a message, perfect,' I said, snatching it up to play it back.

Charlotte was still mystified.

'Sarah has a mystery caller,' explained Alex.

I put the phone on speaker and put it on the kitchen table.

'Hi Sarah!' came a man's cheerful voice. 'It's John, I've just woken up, I'm a bit hungover – busy night last night – and well, I was wondering if you were still up for that lunch we talked about? I could jump on the Tube to central London, could be there in an hour or so. Anyway, let me know what you think, would be nice to see you, speak to you soon.'

The message ended.

Alex and Charlotte looked at me. 'Well?'

I was completely baffled. I still had no idea who it was. But he obviously knew me. 'I haven't a clue who it is!' I said, feeling a bit stupid. 'I don't think I know anyone called John, do I?'

'It must be someone you know,' said Charlotte. 'He knows your name and everything.'

Alex, livened up by his coffee, started to investigate. 'Do you have your name on your voicemail message?' he asked. 'That could have told him.'

'Well, yes, I think I do,' I said, wondering if I actually did. 'But presumably he knew it already. I mean, it's not as if you want to go out for lunch with, I don't know, a Kate or something and then the voicemail says, "Hi, this is Sarah,"

162

and you suddenly decide to have lunch with someone called Sarah instead.'

'Well, it must be someone you know then,' he concluded. 'Have you talked about having lunch today with anyone recently?'

'Er, I don't think so,' I said, feeling more and more uncertain. 'I mean, not consciously, but it's the type of thing I might have said.'

'And what Johns have you met recently?' Charlotte asked, making some toast and getting involved in the investigation. 'What about any of the guys from the dating things you've been on, you know, the speed-dating, the singles nights . . .'

'. . . the pub quiz, the drinks thing, the poker thing,' added Alex.

I couldn't work out if my life sounded quite exciting or utterly pathetic when listed like this. I suspected the latter.

'What about your online guys?' Charlotte asked.

'Oh yes, what about the guy with the hair? Or the one with the dog? Or the sad-eyed guy. The first one. Or the running guy?'

God, they all sounded utterly awful. This conversation was making me rather depressed. On the other hand, this guy John actually sounded quite nice on the phone.

I called my sister. 'Look, do I know anyone called John? Some guy has left me a message and I don't know who it's from.'

'Could it be the running guy?' she said. 'Or the guy with the hair? Or the one with sad eyes? The first one?'

Clearly, she was going to be no help. And I made a note to myself to keep the details of my internet dates to myself in future.

'You've got to go for lunch with him!' said Charlotte, suddenly enthusiastic about the whole idea. 'It'll be fun!'

'How will it be fun? I'll walk in and see him and still not have the faintest idea who he is, or, worse, I'll walk in and think, "Oh my God, that's the pillock I stupidly gave my number to the other day and never want to see again."'

'Well, in that case, you quickly remember something else you have to do, or suddenly become violently ill, you know, that type of thing.'

'Yes, well, that does sound like a rather fabulous way to spend a Sunday ...'

I was still trying to think of any Johns I had met recently. Or ever. There was one guy I'd met recently who had given me his card and who I thought was called John, but he was about 70 and unlikely to be crawling out of bed at midday with a hangover.

I had an idea. 'I know. One of us calls him and says it's a wrong number or something, and then the other one of us phones him at the same time. It'll go straight to voicemail and his message will hopefully say something helpful like "Hi, this is John Interestingname" and then we can Google him and hopefully it'll all come zooming back to me.'

The others looked at me as if I were mad.

'No, come on, it's a great idea!' I said, rushing off to get the home landline. 'I saw it in one of the *Bourne* films.'

'Count me out,' said Alex, hastily finishing his coffee before scooting out of the kitchen.

'What! Coward. Right, Charlotte, you ring from this phone and then I'll ring from my phone, or, better still, your phone ...'

'But it might not go straight to voicemail,' Charlotte pointed out. 'Mine always shows up as call waiting.'

'Oh bollocks.'

That put paid to that idea.

So I decided to send a nice, neutral text. 'Hi. I'm sorry but my phone has lost all my numbers so I'm asking everyone who's sent me a text to say who they are – technology, eh?'

The phone bleeped. 'Lol Hello its me John!'

He dropped a few notches in my esteem with the 'lol' and the missing punctuation but I still didn't know who my potential lunch date was.

'John who?' I texted back.

'John you are having lunch with at 2!'

I was getting nowhere, so I phoned him and got his voicemail.

I left him a message. 'Hi John, it's me, Sarah, do give me a call back.'

I sat on the stairs, still completely at a loss. The fact that I couldn't instantly say 'this must be a wrong number' meant that I was totally losing track of my life. A mysterious guy called John thinks we're having lunch, so I assume that we are, and I've just failed to put it in my diary. I tried to work out how many men I'd met during my deliberate man-hunting months. It must be several hundred. And not one of them the one for me. Clearly, I was either very choosy or looking in completely the wrong places.

My phone bleeped again. 'Ooops . . . I'm texting the wrong Sarah – how silly!'

So there it was. Mystery solved.

I reported back to the flatmates. 'So he was the nutcase, not me,' I concluded.

I felt relieved but also slightly bereft. It would have been nice to have a cute-sounding guy phone me and ask me out for lunch.

I said as much to Charlotte, who looked at me thoughtfully. 'You know,' she said, echoing my thoughts, 'if this was a movie, you guys would hook up anyway and it would be terribly romantic.'

I texted John back: 'No problem – I started wondering if I did have a lunch today and had completely forgotten about it!'

'Lol!' came the answer. 'Sorry I feel like such a muppet!'

'Not at all!' I texted, more in hope than expectation. 'You sounded v nice on the phone – was tempted to meet up anyway!'

Now, if that didn't inspire him to Hollywood-type behaviour, nothing would.

My phone bleeped. 'Lol,' it said.

And that was it. So much for Hollywood endings.

However, it did bring home to me how much I was hoping for a miracle. A tiny hint of hope and I was in there straight away, picturing happy endings and tales told at our wedding of what an amazing stroke of luck it was that we had ended up together.

19

The Ones That Got Away

It seemed as if I was spending large portions of my life walking home from Clapham Common station after a late Tube home from whatever traumatic dating evening I'd just been on. I took to calling my mum, who is a night owl, to decompress from the evening and try to talk myself out of my impending depression about the whole thing. It was during one of these talks that I had bemoaned the fact that all the decent men seem to have happily hooked up with their childhood sweethearts at least a decade ago.

There was a contemplative silence at the end of the phone. Then: 'So, which was the one that got away?'

'I'm sorry?'

'You know, the one you regret splitting up with. The one you wish you were married to now.'

It was a good question. I hadn't really thought about it in those terms before. In recent months, I had been thinking, 'Why hasn't this happened to me yet?' but I certainly hadn't been completing the sentence with '...because I should have got married to Nicholas Gibson who I kissed at the school fair when I was eight'.

I went home and lay in bed, thinking about it.

There was Nicholas Gibson, of course, but I didn't think

our brief experiment with this kissing lark really formed the basis of a long-lasting relationship.

There was also Jonny, who played the viola in the local youth orchestra. I used to look longingly over the music stands at the back of his head, which was all I could see of him, stuck as I was several rows behind him with the other clarinets. He was the epitome of cool. He had long, sleek runner's legs, big brown eyes and a long curly ponytail that was the most amazing thing I'd ever seen. All of my classmates fancied him but, astonishingly, it was me he chose. We would walk for hours and hours around the local streets in the evenings, debating politics and philosophy, and kissing as if it was our own private invention. Then he went away to university and disappeared out of my life for ever. I recently heard that he was doing something very cool and outdoorsy, managing Snowdonia or something, and had an improbable number of children. Maybe he could have been the one.

Then there was Scott.

Scott was my first. You know, in that way. We met at school in the sixth form and spent two deliciously chaste years flirting and chatting and longing and talking before finally getting together on the very last day of school before going to universities hundreds of miles away. Great timing.

Scott was the last of four brothers to go to our school and was practically school establishment. He played rugby and cricket, was a keen runner and managed to do all this while maintaining an impressive drinking and smoking habit. He had a big smile and a big laugh and nothing could faze him. His father was a lawyer, his brothers were all training to be lawyers and he was going to be a lawyer – it was all mapped out and he couldn't be happier with this.

We got together while camping with school friends in Cornwall, just after our A-levels. The others went for hikes along the coast, explored the local pubs and spent the week sunbathing and getting stoned. Scott and I spent the entire week bathed in the orange glow of our tent – kissing, sleeping, talking. We emerged only for meals and at the end of the week were as white and pasty as if it were the depths of winter, while the rest of the group were sporting impressive tans. We couldn't believe we had finally made it, had finally got to a point when we were both free, both here, both in love with each other and finally able to talk about all those times over the past two years where we'd nearly, but not quite, got together.

But we still hadn't had sex. We returned to school and the Leavers' Ball. It was wonderful knowing that Scott was mine now, not just for the night but for ever and he looked gorgeous in his dinner jacket. As it was the last night of school, there was a general feeling that going to sleep – at least, on your own – would be a terrible waste.

I waited for Scott in the garage of the other girls' boarding house, which had been turned into a lounge area for the ball. It smelled of coffee and extinguished candles and the floor was strewn with cushions and collapsed tinsel. I heard Scott before I saw him, clicking his way down the lane towards me in the moonlight in his smart shoes, still wearing his suit but with his black bow tie undone. It was the most incredibly sexy thing I had ever seen.

We arranged the cushions on the floor of the garage – which was huge, more like an old stable block – in a makeshift bed. Our teeth were chattering with both nerves and the cold.

It was wonderfully romantic.

We had a wonderful summer of commuting between each other's houses – me in London, he in Brighton – and in the autumn I went off to Sheffield University to study English, while he went to Bristol to study law. The only way he could call me was via a pay phone in the laundry block, about ten minutes from my room. It would ring and ring for ages until someone took pity and answered it, and they would then have to trek back to the flats to see if I was in. It was the same for him – one phone, a hundred students, all of whom were usually studying or drinking. So we wrote to each other – lengthy, usually drunken outpourings of the minutiae of student life and how much we missed each other. I still have a whole bundle of them, written in Scott's large sprawl, about three words to a line and five lines to a page. When it got too much, one of us would just jump on a coach and head up or down the M1. We loved turning up unannounced and surprising each other, and we'd then spend days in bed, or drinking in the student bar before heading back to bed. We never did anything 'normal', such as going shopping, or meeting up at the end of the day to swap the day's news – it was weeks of absence, followed by days of being there 24/7. Finally, we'd leave the room and go off to the coach station for painful farewells – often we'd get halfway there and then say 'just one more day . . .' and turn back.

Towards the end of the second year, our goodbyes became less painful, our meetings less exciting, and when he said that he'd kissed someone else I knew that it was the beginning of the end. I think I was sad, but not surprised. He was such a lovely bloke, the perfect first proper boyfriend, and, had I been in a relationship like that in my early thirties, I would have worked harder at it and fought harder to keep it. But we were young. The world was ahead of us. There would be other relationships like this one. Or so I had thought.

Then, there was Daniel.

I can still clearly remember the day we broke up. We had been living together for a year and going out for a year before that. He was handsome, sporty and sexy, and we were practically inseparable. But he was having a kind of – I don't know – mid-life crisis or general boredom with his job, and had decided to take off for a week to Gran Canaria to 'think about things, you know, chill out, relax, recharge the batteries'. I couldn't take the time off work so he was going on his own.

At the same time, my flatmate Carly was moving out and going to live with a friend in west London nearer to where she worked. When I got up to make breakfast, I noticed her room was empty, so she must have left really early. I decided to give her a call to wish her good luck.

'Oh, cheers, mate,' she said.

'So when's the house-warming?'

'Not for a while at least,' she said. 'I'm off on holiday for a few weeks first.'

'Oh, are you going somewhere nice?'

'I'm going to the Canary Isles,' she trilled.

I paused. There was something tugging at my brain. Something I didn't want to think about. I just felt the need to get off the phone.

'Oh. Bye then,' I said, and hung up.

Something was really wrong. I couldn't quite put my finger on it but something was not right. Was the Canary Isles the same thing as Gran Canaria? Or was one part of the other? Why was I even thinking that? Was I being really suspicious? Was I being really blind? Where the fuck was the Canary Isles? Why would she tell me where she was going if she was going with my boyfriend? Why wouldn't she?

My other flatmate Jean came down the stairs. 'Are you all right? What's wrong?'

I stood there feeling really weird but couldn't say anything. I couldn't quite pin down the reason for the niggling, worrying feeling that was prickling all over me and I was not sure I wanted to.

'What is it?'

'Nothing. I don't know.'

Deep shaky breath.

'I know this sounds weird, and I know it's just me being paranoid . . .'

'You're not being paranoid.'

'No, I'm being paranoid . . .'

'You're not, you're not.'

Even then I didn't get it. I knew that nothing was really wrong, that I was getting wound up about nothing, and I was starting to become slightly annoyed that Jean wasn't listening to me.

Then I started listening to her. 'What do you mean?'

'You're not being paranoid. Daniel and Carly . . .'

At those words, my whole stomach plunged and tilted as if I'd been pushed off a cliff, a huge lurch as I tipped over the edge and everything slowed down to cope with this new sensation that my stomach was simultaneously plummeting hundreds of feet while also blocking up my throat.

'. . . have been seeing each other for a month now . . .'

A huge crashing wave of shock hit me right in the face, taking my breath away with the coldness of it.

'. . . but it won't last. It won't last.'

What won't last? There's something to last?

And all of a sudden it hit me that *they* were the couple now; they were already being spoken of as an item and I never knew. It had been going on for a month and I never knew. He'd been seeing her for a month and it was solid and real enough to be called a 'thing' . . .

That's all I had time for before I could feel my face crumpling and distorting, and I was howling and sobbing in great gasping chokes and there wasn't enough room in me to contain all the tears. All I could say was: 'Oh my God, oh my God,' and I felt like I was going to throw up.

I couldn't even sit down because this whoosh of adrenalin was zooming through me so I was pacing and choking and gasping and no doubt looking like a complete sight. Jean was sitting down, looking very calm and matter of fact, as if every week two of her flatmates fuck off to the Canary Isles with each other, leaving the other one behind falling apart right in front of her like some weird Hollywood melodrama. Her calmness just made my reaction seem so over the top in comparison, and that was the only rational thought that I could manage before the whole thing hit me once more. The Daniel and Carly mantra started up in my head over and over and I was lurching and choking again.

After a while, I didn't even want to think about anything any more and just wished I could stop feeling sick. I was feeling so sick that I thought it was going to last for ever. I'd already grasped that this particular happening was an *event* and, once you're the other side of the event, everything changes and you can never go back to the time before. I felt I'd crossed some huge boundary that I never wanted to cross and the loss I felt sent me gasping and howling once more while Jean looked placidly on.

That was the first moment. All other moments after that were just versions of that first gut-wrenching, sickening, horrible moment.

In a rough order: I called work and told them that I wouldn't be able to come in today. I tried to sound calm and collected, but I hadn't considered how difficult it was to talk when it felt like someone was pulling out your throat through the top of your head.

'Good God, what's happened to you? Are you all right? My God, what's the matter?' my worried editor asked.

I phoned my friend Alan and honked and wrenched down the phone at him. Immediately, he said he'd come round, which impressed on me how bad I must have sounded, as it was 10 a.m. on a weekday and he's a pretty important accountant. He later admitted he hadn't been able to understand a word I'd said and had to be filled in by Jean on his way up the stairs.

I phoned Carly. I don't know why. I think I was rather peeved that I'd been so polite to her on the phone. The small details seemed easier to deal with for a start. I wanted to do the phone call again and this time shout at her when she mentioned the Canary fucking Isles. She didn't answer.

I phoned Daniel. He didn't answer.

I phoned Tony, his former flatmate and the only friend of his that I'd met. I managed to speak slightly more coherently at this point.

'Tony. It's Sarah. I just want to know . . .' Big breath, how can I say this, how can I say this out loud? 'How long have Daniel and Carly been going on for?'

'Oh. Well, hmmm –' clearing of throat, sounding abashed '– I don't really know, um, you know . . .'

'It's at least a month, isn't it?'

'Look, possibly, um, I don't know . . .'

I wondered why I'd phoned him. I think I just needed some other confirmation that everything really was as screwed up as I thought it was. I also wanted him to say, 'What? Don't be ridiculous? Daniel? Never!' and I'd know that I was getting completely worked up over nothing.

'Look, I can understand why you're upset . . .'

'You can understand why I'm upset?' I bleated, and then stopped. I had a feeling I should be saying, 'Upset? You call this upset? I'll show you upset!' like in some '70s television sitcom but the sheer stupidity of his comment had thrown me. *Upset* didn't seem to bear any resemblance to what I was feeling.

'I just want to talk to him.'

'You want to talk?'

Of course I wanted to talk to him. He seemed to be the only person who actually knew what was going on. He knew all sides of the story. I thought I knew the whole story too but now it seems I only knew half of it. And that was probably the wrong half, the untrue half, the lying half. And we had told each other everything. We'd been proud of our honest, open relationship. We always talked, him more than me. He'd told me everything about himself, right from the beginning. I felt miffed that he hadn't told me he was going out with Carly. He had a secret from me? How . . . impolite.

Alan arrived, and I could hear him and Jean discussing me in hushed tones reserved for children or psychos.

I went downstairs.

'You all right?' asked Alan. He looked ridiculously out of place in our scuzzy living room, with its overflowing ashtrays, empty beer cans and soggy kebab wrappers. In between Jean, placidly curled up on the sofa in her new role as Earth Mother, and me, a baggy, blotchy, recently single, crumbling, wheezing sack of tears, Alan loomed tall and lanky in a crisp blue chalk-stripe suit, with a black briefcase in one hand and a long black rolled-up umbrella in the other. I half-expected to see a bowler hat.

He gave me an awkward hug, encumbered by his work trappings. 'I think we should go and get some food,' he said. Alan always turns to pie and squashy cheese in times of crisis.

Jean started thinking. Aloud, unfortunately. 'The thing is,' she said, 'it's not just that you've been lied to for the past month, but what makes it much worse is that you've really been lied to for the whole time you've been going out with him.'

We looked at her dumbly. She appeared to have turned into my mother, who could always be relied on to make you feel better with choice phrases such as: 'Do you feel that everything's all your fault?' and 'Do you wish you'd done everything differently?' (When I did finally tell my mum, she consoled me with: 'Gosh, it's going to take you years to get over this one.')

Jean plunged on. 'They must have been having sex together all the time. I mean, when you think about the number of times they were both out at the same time, they must have been secretly meeting up and going back to Tony's house to shag constantly. Isn't that awful?'

We left her and went to get some food.

It took me a long time to get over Daniel, the feelings of rage and pain and betrayal. And then I met Patrick, the man I thought I was going to marry until I posed online as a health-club receptionist and he asked me out on a date, in spite of the fact that we were living together at the time.

Is it any wonder that I'm where I am?

20

Heading into the Clouds

Charlotte's boyfriend Matthew was in a very strange mood one Sunday morning. We'd had a house party the previous night – I had tried to turn it into a 'bring along a single friend' party, an idea that failed dismally because none of my flatmates seemed to know any single people at all – and so it had been a rather late night.

Not as late as the parties of our twenties, of course, which wouldn't start until after the pubs had shut and would only end when everyone had passed out or the local café had started serving breakfast. No, this was a rather more sedate affair where cocktails were mixed, the wine cost more than a fiver a bottle and the food was an improvement on merely emptying some nuts into a bowl. There was even one moment towards the end of the evening when someone was trying to find the corkscrew and we realised, to our shame, that it had already been tidied away and loaded into the dishwasher. We were all becoming terribly middle-aged.

We had all nonetheless managed to get quite drunk and cheerful, except Matthew, who had disappeared off to bed at a rather early hour.

In the morning, we were just stumbling downstairs to make coffee and read the Sunday papers – there was no tidying up to do, of course, as that had been done the night before once everyone had left, in yet another sign that we had all turned into our parents – and he arrived back from the shops laden with breakfast ingredients. He bustled around the kitchen, then disappeared upstairs to Charlotte's bedroom with two fry-ups.

'I just want to make sure that we're on time to go for a walk in the park,' he explained mystifyingly.

All became clear that evening, when they returned from their day out beaming from ear to ear and bearing a bottle of champagne, with Charlotte sporting a rather shiny object on her left hand. The whole day, Matthew explained while wrestling with the cork, had been planned with military precision. After breakfast he'd taken Charlotte out boating on the lake in Battersea Park and then he had taken her off to a secluded corner and proposed on bended knee. He'd allotted a suitable amount of time for phoning families and friends to give them the good news, before they popped back to get changed in time for afternoon tea at the Lanesborough.

It all sounded perfect and not for the first time I marvelled at how men, who generally travel through life happy to take things as they come, more or less handing over vast portions of their lives to mothers, girlfriends and best mates, suddenly became fiercely organised to the nth degree over the matter of a proposal.

Jeff and Alex, sitting on the sofa drinking champagne – Matthew had turned up with a bottle already chilled, such was the degree of his planning – were amazed at my surprise. 'It's the most important question that you're ever going to ask,' said Jeff. 'Of course you're going to be organised about it.'

'I agree that you're going to plan the actual question, whether you get a ring or not and all that sort of stuff,' I said. 'But it's the fact that guys organise so much around it too – such as Matthew factoring in the time it would take to phone the family, get changed and get back to Hyde Park in time for afternoon tea. Or friends of mine who have worked out what view she should be looking at just before the proposal, or how many people will be around, or all that periphery stuff.'

Whatever effort it had taken, it was obviously worth it. Charlotte and Matthew were looking radiant, sitting very close to each other on the arm of the sofa, looking so comfortable and relaxed together and extremely secure in each other's affections.

I was genuinely extremely happy for them. There seems to be an expectation that success in your friends' lives will always make you feel a bit rubbish about your own in comparison, an expectation that I could hear in my mum's and sister's voices when I told them about the engagement.

'Oh that's lovely,' said my mum. Then, in a slightly lower, more serious voice: 'So, how are you feeling?'

It was as if people expected me to feel utterly terrible, not that my friend had got engaged, but that I – still – hadn't.

I accept that sometimes, when you're feeling particularly low, the last thing you want to hear is some fabulous news about someone else's life. I know people who have been desperate to have a baby and who can't hear about someone else's pregnancy without bursting into tears. But, in my opinion, when it comes to love and marriage and all that kind of stuff, the more I hear about it happening to someone else, particularly someone I actually know, the more it gives me hope that it can happen to me too.

A year earlier, Charlotte – who'd moved into the house after splitting up with a previous boyfriend – was only just beginning to venture back into the dating game with a couple of online dates. Then Matthew, a new work colleague, split up with his girlfriend, and they got together just before Christmas. Now just eight months later, and not even living together, they were planning to get married in just a few weeks' time.

I love the fact that life can change so quickly, that in just a year you can go from being sad and single to planning your wedding with the love of your life. The fact it happens to other people makes me think that it's more, not less, likely to happen to me. Charlotte may have been very lucky that Matthew applied to work at the same company and in the same department as her – in fact, she recruited him but for entirely professional reasons (or so she claims) – but the wonderful, life-changing speed of the whole thing just inspires me and gives me hope.

She wasn't the only one. Another friend, Holly, who had spent most of the last decade being completely single, working every hour there was and despairing of ever finding a man, had recently started going on, well, not exactly singles holidays, but holidays for 'independent travellers'. This wasn't a euphemism either, as from her reports from various trips around the world – she had been to Cuba, South Africa, Tunisia, all over the place – her fellow travellers were sometimes single but sometimes couples, or friends travelling together who'd left their boyfriends at home. But I did get the feeling that she was really hoping to meet someone on one of her holidays.

Then one day, she texted me: 'I have news!' This could only mean man news. She'd just spent a week cycling around Vietnam and – drum roll – there had been a very nice single guy on the trip. They had spent the whole week just hanging out together, getting along quite well, and then really well, and then finally, on the very last day of the trip, he had kissed her.

'What took you so long?' her response had been.

'However,' she confided to me over pizza and red wine after work one night, 'I'm really glad that we didn't get together straight away, as then it would just have been a holiday romance, just a fling, and this will hopefully be a lot more than that.'

It wasn't plain sailing from here though – he lived in Wales, hundreds of miles away, and he was widowed with a five-year-old daughter. Holly had been spending the last few weeks trekking there and back on the train. However, I thought that was rather a good sign. With a young daughter, he certainly wouldn't be looking to just mess about, not now that Holly had actually met her – 'She's lovely,' said Holly happily – and this had all the signs of being the relationship that she had been looking for for so long.

'It's just lovely that we got to know each other first, before anything happened,' she said, looking totally in love.

This started me thinking. All the things that I had been doing, such as all the one-off dating events, relied totally on that instant spark, that leap from stranger to potential partner in an instant, which was just so unlikely to happen, particularly in the laboratory-like conditions of a dating event. It was as if the organisers were Dr Frankenstein figures, hoping to create new life by shoving disparate ingredients together in a sleazy-nightclub Petri dish and hoping that their molecules would bond. But a holiday, an actual adventure holiday when you are all thrown together doing something active, such as cycling or climbing or sailing a boat, well, that gave you lots of time to get together. It would be similar to Lundy, but on a slightly more exotic scale. And, hopefully, with lots of single men.

I researched the various holiday companies that did this kind of thing. There seemed to be several, with bold, adventurous names such as Explore, Exodus and Intrepid. I phoned one at random and told them that I was considering going on one of their holidays but that I really wanted to meet a man. I felt a little silly just coming out with it like that, but, well, if I was going to take a week off work and spend hundreds of pounds, as these holidays certainly weren't cheap, I wanted to make sure that I was on the right one.

'Well, we're not a singles holiday company,' the booking agent said, 'but we do find that lots of people do come on their own and a lot of them are single. Many people have met their partners on our holidays, it's true, but that's not the reason that people go on them.'

She had a think about it. 'It is a generalisation but it does seem to be the case that some women book on these types of holidays – not just ours in particular, but the independent, activity-type holidays – because they are hoping to meet a partner, whereas for the men, well, it tends to be that they are interested in the experience itself and want to climb Kilimanjaro or whatever it happens to be, and if they meet a girl in the process, well, that's an added benefit. But it's certainly not the reason why they'd go on the holiday itself, whereas for the women it might well be.'

So the guys were set on climbing a mountain and might end up with a girl as an unexpected bonus, whereas the girls, in order to find men, were prepared to hike up a sodding mountain to do so. 'Sounds about right,' I thought.

'Our boss even met her man on one of the trips,' she said. 'She climbed to Everest base camp and ended up getting married to one of the guys on the trip!'

This seemed like recommendation enough. The holidays themselves also looked pretty good too, but the main thing was it had worked for Holly. I was convinced.

'Great. Which one would you like to go on?' the booking agent asked.

Now this was something I hadn't actually thought about. Something not too expensive, obviously – trekking to Everest base camp cost several thousand pounds – and something that I could do in a week or less, so as not to use up too much holiday allowance. But, other than that, my only criterion was how many men were going on the trip. Call me shallow, or call me single-minded, but that was the most important detail.

'What holidays do men tend to go on?' I asked.

'Well,' the very kind and obliging booking agent said, 'they tend to go on the more active ones, cycling, for example, or climbing.'

'OK, well, that sounds good,' I said, wondering how fit I could get in as short a time as possible. 'What have you got that's coming up soon?'

She clicked around on her computer. 'Well, we've got a week's cycling round Cuba. How does that sound?'

That sounded great. I loved cycling and I'd always wanted to visit Cuba.

'That sounds perfect,' I said. 'How many people are going on it?' Meaning how many men, of course.

She got my meaning. 'Oh,' she said, after clicking about a bit more.

'What?'

'Well, there aren't any men at all booked on that one,' she said apologetically. 'Just women.'

I practically sprang back from the phone. Cycling round Cuba sounded lovely, but the thought of being there with all those women, most of whom would no doubt be terribly disappointed that there were no men going, was not quite what I was looking for. I was very relieved I'd been told now, rather than finding out when I got there. Research, research, research was fast becoming my mantra.

'OK, then, where are all the men going on holiday then?' I asked. Wherever in the world they were going, I was going there too.

'You're going where?' asked my flatmates, who were all in the kitchen in various stages of making dinner.

'Mount Toukbal. Toubkal. Tukball. Something like that

anyway,' I said. 'It's a mountain in Africa, apparently.'

They exchanged bemused glances.

'And that's all you know about it?' said Alex.

'Nope. I know that fourteen strapping young men will be climbing it in precisely two weeks' time and that I will be climbing it with them.'

Jeff looked horrified. 'What in God's name would possess anyone to do anything like that?'

'Very good question,' I replied, retrieving a bottle of wine from the fridge. 'Apparently, it's a boy thing.'

'Well, I'm a boy and I would never consider doing anything like that in a million years.'

Matthew, now the future Mr Charlotte, bounded in. 'What would you never do in a million years?' he asked.

'Climb Mount Tukball or whatever it's called.'

His face lit up. 'Oh, Mount Toubkal!' he exclaimed. 'That's in Morocco, isn't it? It's the highest point in the Atlas Mountains. I'd love to do that!'

Charlotte and I exchanged looks. 'See, a boy thing!'

Matthew whirled round. 'Who's climbing Mount Toubkal? You are? How exciting!'

Exciting wasn't the word I was thinking of. In fact, I was rather alarmed by the whole idea. It was one thing to say that you'd like to go on holiday to meet men, quite another to find yourself having to climb the highest point in northern Africa to do so. The highest mountain I'd ever climbed was Ben Nevis and that was when I was 13.

Matthew went into efficient-traveller mode. 'What jabs are you going to get? And what about anti-altitude sickness pills, they're really good. And what are you going to put all your stuff in? Presumably it's got to be something that'll go on the back of a donkey. And what about . . .'

I fled the kitchen. I needed to do some more research.

The trip itself, I found out when the itinerary came in the

post a few days later, was just five days long. It seemed we were going to pack a lot in though. We were due to arrive on Wednesday afternoon and spend the evening exploring Marrakech. Then at dawn the next day we would head off in a minibus to the village of Imlil, where we would start walking.

We'd spend that night in tents halfway up the mountain, and then early the next morning we would go up and down from the summit. We'd have tea in a villager's house and stay in another house that night. Then back to Marrakech for the afternoon and evening and back home the following day, Sunday.

Still, five days would be more than enough time to decide whether I was going to hit it off with any of the guys. The only thing I knew was that there were fourteen of them and one of me. That in itself was rather terrifying, and it would have been good to have some female back-up, someone to compare notes with. Thankfully, two other girls booked onto the trip at the last minute and were going to meet up with our group in Marrakech.

I suspected that things weren't going quite as smoothly as they could be when I tried to board the plane to Marrakech at Gatwick airport and had to make way for the pilot who was getting off. I was one of the last to board and everyone else was already on the plane.

The pilot began a whispered conversation with the gate attendants. An engineer in a high-visibility vest emerged from the tunnel.

'Is there a problem?' I asked, not entirely convinced of the wisdom of boarding a plane without a pilot.

'Yes, the problem is that this plane isn't going anywhere,' he replied with the cheerful gallows humour of engineers the world over.

I retreated to the waiting area by the gate. Ten minutes

later, so did everyone else, deplaned until further instructions. An hour later, we retreated even further, back to the departures lounge, which involved all sorts of complicated passes and secret routes back through the airport. This wasn't a great start to the holiday. I could see that on our flight there was a largish group of guys who all seemed to know one another. I assumed it was the Explore party. They all seemed quite nice, a fun bunch of blokes in their thirties and forties, laughing and chatting as they made their way back to the bar. I decided not to introduce myself just yet. There would be plenty of time to say hello.

After four hours, I was starting to wonder if my entire holiday would be spent at the airport. I'd explored all the delights that the departures lounge had to offer, won £20 on the fruit machines, read half my holiday books and eaten a lot of Pret a Manger sandwiches out of sheer boredom. Then, thankfully, our plane was called. Something had been fixed. We were off!

Apart from being woken up from a deep sleep by a steward asking if I wanted some food – no, I wanted to sleep, which is why I had been doing it – the flight passed without incident, which was just as well as we were all somewhat nervous after the mysterious delay. Then, we began our descent into Marrakech. Or not.

'We will shortly be landing at Casablanca,' came the announcement. 'We are sorry for the change in destination but due to bad weather we could not land in Marrakech.'

A groan went up. This was getting ridiculous. I had completely gone off the whole idea and just wanted to turn round and go home and back to internet dating. At least I could do that from my own bedroom rather than being carted all over the place.

At Casablanca airport, chaos reigned. No one in charge seemed to have any idea what to do with a planeload of people who had appeared from nowhere. I found the rest of the group, and we tried to find out what we should do from the company in the UK, our guide waiting for us in Marrakech, the officials at the airport and the airline representatives. No one knew.

There were rumours of another plane to take us back to Marrakech, but with a limited number of seats. People crowded round the ticketing desk, imploring those behind it for seats on this mythical plane. There was also talk of a bus back to Marrakech.

Then, there was nothing to do but wait. There was nothing to drink – this was a dry country after all – nothing to eat and nothing to sit on, so we sat on the floor and waited. And waited. The expected plane arrived but it didn't go back to Marrakech. The air got hotter and staler and the floor became more uncomfortable. And then, after another four hours of waiting, we were booted out of the airport.

'Buses are waiting to take you to Marrakech,' an official announced.

First, we had to queue for an hour to go through passport control. Then we had to dig our bags out of a pile of hundreds of them, dumped unceremoniously on the floor at baggage handling, before we finally emerged into the hot night air . . . to find precisely no buses waiting for us.

After we'd waited for another two hours outside the airport in the dark, a bus finally arrived. We piled on, exhausted. Someone in our group started doing a whole round of introductions, which went completely over my head. The driver disappeared for another hour, and when we finally got on the road it was 2 a.m. When he nearly ran off the road, having fallen asleep, we stopped for him to get some coffee at a very shiny service station in the middle of nowhere at 4 a.m.

We should have arrived at our hotel at 4 p.m. the previous

day. We finally arrived at our hotel at six the next morning.

'We leave for Mount Toubkal at 7 a.m.,' said our guide cheerfully.

And so, with barely an hour's sleep, we all set off for Mount Toubkal.

The mountain was steep but we got up and down it in one piece. The views were impressive, the villagers friendly, the food plentiful and the weather warm and sunny. That part was all great. But I wasn't there to admire the views or chat to friendly villagers; I was there to meet a man and, in this regard, the trip was an epic failure.

Firstly, and I should have worked this out beforehand, when you are halfway up a mountain in a Muslim country, there is not exactly a great deal of drinking going on. Drinking usually equals relaxing, flirting, bonding, all that stuff that you have at the end of a long hard day's walking. My Venture Scout days were almost entirely defined by the fact that, wherever we'd descend a mountain, the path would invariably end up at a pub. We'd ease ourselves gradually into a comfy chair and a pint and discuss, in increasing degrees of inebriation, the day's events, the highs, the lows and the comic moments, such as when so and so fell into a bog.

When you are in a tent halfway up a mountain in Morocco, things are slightly different. You finish dinner, and then you go to bed. The next day you walk up the rest of the mountain, walk down it, have dinner and go to bed. The combination of tiredness and the lack of booze meant there was little incentive to stay up and, well, get to know one another. The afternoon back in Marrakech we did – thankfully – find a hotel that served alcohol, but in the Medina in the evening it was Diet Cokes all round.

However, the main drawback, and one that I couldn't have found out about beforehand, was that every single guy on the trip was married, or living with his girlfriend. They were all really nice blokes, very friendly, great fun and up for a laugh and a chat. But they were all clearly absolutely mad about their wives and girlfriends and, in many cases, children, and were all just on a blokes' long weekend away, while their other halves were at home with the kids or having girls' long weekends away of their own.

As a pulling expedition then, the holiday clearly had its drawbacks. All the guys were completely unavailable and all three women were single. Typical.

'Most women come on these holidays to find a bloke,' said one of the girls during our descent of the mountain. 'But it's really hit and miss who you meet. It's best to try not to think about it that way or you'll just have a rubbish time.'

One of the girls had pulled a guy on a previous trek run by the same company – they had done quite a few of these holidays – which had been great fun at the time but lasted no more than a minute after touchdown at Gatwick at the end of the holiday. They now came on these trips for the experience, they said.

And it was certainly an experience. On the final day, me and the three guys whom I'd got on best with during the trip took a walk around the Medina. After a while, I began to wish that I was a bloke too, as I seemed to be a magnet for all of the chaos that the world's largest souk entailed. Street vendors chased after me to try to flog their wares; a terrifying woman grabbed my hand and, in spite of my loud protestations, wouldn't let it go until she had painted a henna tattoo on it, which took ages to disappear; a magician doing some complicated trick rushed into the crowd to grab me and try to make me take part; and finally, out of nowhere, a man thrust two massive hairy monkeys at me, one on each arm. They were huge and heavy and they stank. The boys were constantly having to rescue me and ended up forming a little guard around me to stop me from being hassled.

'It's great having a girl with us, isn't it?' one of them said cheerfully. 'It's like having a lightning rod for all the madness. I haven't been hassled at all.'

I liked being rescued. It was unusual for me to actually have anyone to look after me in that kind of way. I felt all lovely and female and soft and protected. It was a new experience for me.

The next day, we arrived at the airport to fly home to discover that the flight, the only one that day, had been cancelled. Royal Air Maroc was up to its tricks again and it brought back memories of being stuck on Lundy. It would have been great to be stranded with someone you wanted to be with, but it was utterly claustrophobic to be stuck on the wrong continent with nothing to rely on but an utterly unreliable airline. We had no idea how long we'd be stuck there or where we'd end up, assuming it even took off the next day. With no sailors to rescue me this time, I turned to British Airways and my credit card and left the guys to it.

It had been an interesting experiment and one that I'd probably try again. But, as well as time and money, I was going to need a lot more luck on the next trip.

21

What Happens in Greece . . .

It was starting to dawn on me that, while the idea of a holiday away with a group of men was a good one in theory, it was clearly not just a matter of numbers. Going away with 14 fit blokes sounded great on paper but, if they all turned out to be happily married with lovely kids, it was just a waste of time. Similarly, as on the skiing trip, if people were there just to ski, rather than to pull, then frankly I could 'not pull' at home just as easily, and rather more cheaply, even if the skiing was fun.

So I needed to find a holiday that was aimed at singles, while not being a specific 'singles' holiday. I still couldn't believe any bloke I would ever want to be with would sign himself up for a genuine singles holiday, assuming that they still existed. The whole concept of singles holidays to me sounded rather seedy, rather desperate, rather grubby: I had visions of coach trips ending up in roadside hotels with cheap décor and people supping sherries and eating prawn cocktails before sheepishly following one another up to creaky beds in terribly decorated bedrooms. Or maybe I was just getting singles holidays mixed up with the '70s.

A quick Google search proved that singles holidays really

existed, and were called things like Solos or Spice. I even saw one that I quite liked the look of: learning to ski on Sheffield's dry ski slope, staying in a lovely country pub and meeting other 'like-minded folk', as these things always said.

Sport, pubs and singles – it sounded perfect.

I phoned them, and there were places still available. So far, so good, but my recent experiences in booking holidays for which the main purpose was to meet men had taught me that proper research was invaluable.

'Could you tell me who else is going on the weekend?' I asked. 'You know, age, gender, that kind of thing.'

'Sure,' said the booking agent, tapping away at his computer. 'So far, there are three other women, all travelling alone, all in their fifties.'

There was a sympathetic pause, and then: 'Are you still, er . . .?' he asked politely.

I certainly wasn't 'er . . .' at all.

So I needed to find a non-singles 'singles' holiday, where there would be single blokes and not just women over 50. And there needed to be alcohol, lots of it.

It sounded like a Club 18–30 holiday, and I was already some years over the age limit. Not that I wanted to be getting drunk with 18 year olds either. I felt like I was running out of options.

Then a friend suggested one of the main tour operators. I'd heard of them, of course, but thought they were just for families. The resorts were famous for being favoured by middle-class suburbanites who wanted to stay in one place all week with other families, playing tennis and windsurfing and trying not to think about how adventurous and exciting their holidays used to be before they had children.

However, in the spirit of 'Nothing ventured . . .' I phoned them anyway. The booking agent, Susan, was incredibly enthusiastic and I ended up telling her all about my quest for a man.

'This would be perfect for you,' she enthused. 'Loads of people meet on our holidays. Just last week, we were contacted by a couple who met for the first time when their windsurfing boards crashed into each other. Now they're getting married and want to spend part of their honeymoon back at the same resort.'

This sounded beyond perfect. It turned out that the holiday company did three weeks every year that, while not being exclusively single, were single-friendly, with no single supplements and lots of other independent travellers to hang out with.

She clacked away at her keyboard. There was an adult-friendly holiday coming up in two weeks' time in Greece. It sounded too good to be true – all flights, transfers, accommodation, food and, most importantly, alcohol were included for just £570. More than 40 people were already booked on it, guys and girls, and she had even previously recommended it to her sister.

'She's 37 and in the same boat as you,' she said cheerfully (Susan herself had met her husband through the same company, though rather unromantically across an office rather than their windsurfers clashing). 'She went on an adult-friendly week with two girlfriends and had a great time.'

'Did she meet anyone?' I asked.

'Well, not in that way,' Susan admitted. 'But she did meet up with three other girls travelling together and they're all still in touch – they meet up all the time and swap stories about being single.'

Hmm. This didn't sound quite what I had in mind.

Susan sensed my reluctance. 'Honestly, lots of relationships happen, especially at resorts,' she said. 'When you get a hundred British people all in one place, well, anything could happen. You could write a book about it.'

I was sold. Two weeks later, I was at Heathrow.

I surveyed the check-in desk from a safe distance. Presumably everyone who was booked onto the charter flight to Greece would not only be on my plane for the next few hours, but would also be my holiday companions for the next seven days, after which we would all fly home together.

It felt slightly strange being able to size up people before you even said hello – the check-in desk had become the checking-out desk. It was very different from my usual travel experience, which usually started with a cheap flight to Europe followed by backpacking by train, bus and ferry, with no idea whom I would meet on the way. This way certainly had the attraction of knowing that I'd get to meet everyone during the course of the holiday, rather than walking past total strangers who would remain so for ever. And in theory, at least, my Mr Right could be one of the people ambling round the terminal at this very moment, searching for this very desk. There was a kind of romance to it.

My optimistic mood was dented slightly by a distinct lack of Mr Rights in the check-in queue. The immediate signs were not great. There were three bubbly, bottle-blonde girls in their twenties, who looked as if they had walked straight out of a holiday brochure. They were also way more chirpy than people should be at such an early time in the morning. Queuing next to them were two guys at least ten years older than me, sporting tattoos, string vests and skinhead haircuts. And that was it. Where was everybody?

At the boarding gate itself, it was a different, but equally non-ideal, situation. The singletons had completely disappeared and been replaced by harassed families as far as the eye could see. Dads wrestled with buggies, while mums wrestled with wriggling children.

I boarded alone, as usual. I couldn't remember the last time I'd actually got on a plane as part of a couple. Still, that was why I was here, of course, to fix that. Once again, I started to feel that huge weight of expectation. I tried to ignore it.

The plane itself, crammed as it was with fraught family groups, didn't seem to have any room for the 50 singles who were also supposed to be on board. However, as I progressed down the plane, I was increasingly aware of people popping their heads up, like holidaying meerkats, watching who was walking down the aisle. I noticed two guys very obviously checking out the blonde girls who had reappeared behind me, but presumably that happened on all planes, not just singleton ones.

I found my seat, dumped my carry-on bag and then ambled around a bit, doing my own bit of research. I couldn't see any obvious husbands, well, at least not potential ones. There were an awful lot of actual husbands, displaying great 'knackered dad' qualities, trying to organise children and hand luggage into their respective places, and then realising that all the kids were in the wrong seats and they'd just packed the bag with the DVD headphones behind all the other ones in the overhead compartment.

At the very back of the plane, though, there were definite signs of single activity. One guy wearing a baseball cap was making huge efforts to chat up the girl in the window seat near him, completely undeterred by the early hour.

'Do you like tennis?' he was saying, stretching his legs out in front of him. 'I love it. I'm hoping to play a lot of tennis this week. How about you?'

The girl he was addressing seemed nice, my age, quite smart-looking, with big sunglasses perched on the top of her head. She confirmed she did, indeed, quite like tennis.

'I'm Jamie, by the way,' he said, reaching over the empty seat between them to shake hands.

'I'm Kate.'

Jamie, it turned out, had been on several of these holidays before, while Kate had been once before. Jamie looked very much at home.

I went back to my seat. While I'd been away eavesdropping, the two empty seats next to me had been filled by a woman and a bloke, who I assumed were a couple, well, until he said to her, 'So, seen anyone you fancy then?'

She giggled nervously. 'Is that how it works then?'

His reply was drowned out by the roar of the engines firing up, a sound that was the cue for at least five different sets of toddlers up and down the cabin to start yowling as loudly as they could, as they expressed their extreme disapproval of being manhandled onto parents' knees and secured by extension seatbelts. The noise made by the wailing and screaming was immense. The air suddenly became thick with the unspoken thoughts of every single person on the plane: 'We want to be one of *those* people?' Had the parents been aware that there were so many love-seeking people on board, no doubt at least half would at that moment have jumped up and strongly urged the singletons to reconsider.

The yowling of the children continued on the bus to the resort. By the time we arrived at the Beach Scene hotel, everyone was frazzled. Those travelling alone leaped off the bus and away from the children as fast as they could, while those related to the tearful infants looked after the departing crowd with barely concealed envy, sighed and then geared themselves up for the tedious process of finding food and rooms and beds before they could plug themselves into a bottle of wine for the night.

After I'd installed myself in my very nice hotel room – the bed, bathroom, balcony and television were all huge – I wasn't quite sure what to do, so I ambled off in search of people. Everything seemed completely deserted.

I finally bumped into one of my fellow travellers, a white-haired lady called Doris. We sat in the corner of an empty bar and ate Caesar salads. Doris was in her late fifties and an old hand at this type of holiday.

'I didn't really want to go on holiday with my friends and their husbands,' she confided, 'and, although my sister said I could go away with her family, well, the kids . . .' She shuddered.

I was feeling rather the same myself. Doris was lovely but sitting there in the deserted bar with someone 20 years older than me was making me feel rather ancient myself. Where was everyone else? And, in particular, the partying singletons I'd thought this place would be full of?

As if to emphasise the point that I was on completely the wrong holiday, a succession of exhausted parents carting small wailing children came through the bar, all in search of food, all being refused (as by now the bar was officially closed) and told to come back in an hour.

It was all rather depressing, but, ten hours later, I was drinking vodka and being kissed by a nice graphic designer from Southampton called Tom. This was more like it.

I'd found Tom and his travelling companion Kelly in a deserted open-air cluster of cafés and restaurants – rather improbably called Paradise – which were presumably where the evening's entertainment would take place. I'd sat next to them on the plane – Tom was the one who had asked Kelly if she'd seen anyone she fancied yet, but they still looked very much like a couple.

I introduced myself and Tom ordered a round of drinks,

revelling in the freedom of 'all-inclusive'. Tom had done this before, but Kelly was another first-timer and a friend of a friend of his who'd come along in response to a general 'anyone want to come on holiday?' email he'd sent out. They were both friendly, my age and made me feel a whole lot better about the holiday.

Tom courteously invited me to join them for dinner and I accepted on Doris's behalf too, as we'd already promised to sit with each other. There were communal tables where the independent travellers could just turn up and sit down, but first-night nerves meant that everyone was trying to team up in advance. It felt like the first day at school.

At 7 p.m. we trooped down to the beach for the welcome talk. A guy who I'd noticed at the baggage carousel at the airport – he was very fit, very cute, very blonde – turned out to be the sailing coach rather than one of us. Typical. The reps all introduced themselves and, in the special singles-only briefing afterwards, enthused about what a 'fun, crazy time we're going to have together!' That was pretty much the only time we saw them before they were marshalling us onto the coaches on the way back to the airport a week later.

We had dinner – a vast buffet affair – and wine and then trooped back up to Paradise. That seemed to be the place where everyone would congregate after dinner each evening. People seemed fairly sociable, particularly the more they drank, and a guy called Zak latched on to our group when others began calling it a night and drifting off. We ended up in the resort's nightclub, which was completely empty, but, fuelled by Greek beer and rough red wine, our little group danced anyway.

As we were coming back from having a cigarette outside, Zak pulled me to one side away from the others and tried to kiss me. He was nice enough, if completely plastered, but, no, I didn't think so. Although I was glad that the stories about this holiday company at least seemed to be true.

I declined politely.

He was astonished. 'Why not?' he whined. 'Have you got a boyfriend?'

Evidently, other reasons for not getting off with him were unthinkable. He was getting rather persistent even when we were back inside with the others, so I muttered to Tom that maybe we should head somewhere else. So the three of us – Kelly barely seemed to leave Tom's side – trooped off into the night, and eventually convinced Zak, who kept on trying to drag me off somewhere, that we were going to bed.

Instead, we went to Tom's room and sat on his balcony, drinking his bottle of vodka and smoking his cigarettes and exchanging life stories. I was starting to think that the holiday could be quite fun, drinking until way after 3 a.m., talking endlessly and enjoying the freedom of not having anything to do for the next seven days except more of this. I really liked Tom, too, and, had it not been for the continual presence of Kelly, well . . . She was actually very nice, too, but I rather felt that she was ruining her friend's chances of pulling. Unless, of course, that was the point.

When she went to the loo, I asked him, 'So, is there anything going on between you two?'

He vigorously shook his head. 'No, no, not at all.'

I must have looked sceptical.

'No, really,' he insisted. 'We're good friends, but there's definitely nothing like that between us.'

'Then kiss me,' I said.

We kissed and broke apart, then kissed some more. Kelly came back from the loo. We all drank some more. After we had been moved inside by the understandable complaint from the neighbours – we were having a loud debate about exactly what the lyric 'cherry chapstick' meant and it was 5 a.m. – it became clear that Kelly was never going to leave to go to bed, not unless I did, too, of course. I decided that leaving was probably a good idea anyway. It was early days and it did seem a bit extreme to jump into bed with someone on the first night. Although it was nice to know that that was an option, at least.

I announced I was off to bed, and, surprise surprise, Kelly said she was, too. As we all said goodbye at the door, I felt Tom's hand very firmly on my bottom. It was a definite invitation. And, I reasoned, with all the clarity of a full night's drinking, it would be nice to curl up with someone, even if we didn't do anything else.

Kelly and I walked back through the bougainvillea-lined walkways with the birds chirping around us.

'So, you and Tom . . .' I prompted.

As I thought, Kelly totally fancied Tom. Nothing had happened so far, but she was hoping that, by coming on this holiday, something would. Hmmm, I thought. That certainly didn't seem to be Tom's attitude. Maybe I could have a holiday romance with him and then she could take over afterwards.

I had it all worked out. A week of fun and frolicking sounded perfect.

After I'd seen Kelly safely into her room, I made a wide loop back to Tom's block. Cuddling, sleeping and then, who knew what else?

At this point, I realised the flaw in my plan. There were about 100 rooms in each block, and each door looked exactly the same. I wasn't even sure if he was on the upper or lower corridor in his block. It was 5.30 a.m. and I could hardly go banging on doors at random, especially as there were loads of children around presumably on the verge of waking up.

I knocked very softly on a few likely ones, just in case, but no one answered. I wondered if he would have the foresight to hover outside his door for a while, or at least leave it ajar. It seemed not. We hadn't swapped phone numbers either. It was hopeless. I sighed, not altogether disappointed. It would probably have been a bad idea, I reasoned. It was early days after all. I turned round and exhaustedly made my way back to my room. Drunken sex would just have to wait.

22

. . . Stays in Greece

The next morning saw the start of a daily routine. Wake up, hungover, after just a few hours' sleep. Yawn your way down along the winding paths to breakfast by the beach, with possibly a quick swim in the pool beforehand to stop the clanking in your head. Then join the rest of the adults-only gang – who as the week progressed gradually began to emerge as individuals from the general mass with recognisable names and faces – in lying prone on the beach for several hours, tanning and sleeping and cooling off in the sea. The weather was gloriously sunny and the early-season timing meant that the beach was almost empty, with hundreds of sunbeds waiting to be bagged.

Around 11 a.m. people's thoughts would turn to alcohol, and there would be a little procession of people making their way along the beach to the beach bar, and then coming back with cold beers or luminous cocktails. People would always bring an extra drink back with them if they could carry it – it was all-inclusive, so why not? – and the hangovers would subside into a pleasant early-drinking numbness.

Then, as the sun set, it was back to the rooms to shower and change – men into trousers and shirts, women into floaty dresses – for pre-dinner cocktails down at the beach bar.

Then dinner, more wine and a wander up to the outdoor bars, followed by dancing until the early hours.

It was exhausting.

But a lot of fun. Once I had got used to the feeling of being trapped in an admittedly rather nice resort and stopped thinking about the world outside, I started to enjoy it. The concept of pausing to change and dress for dinner was a fairly new one to me – I was more of a 'power-through' girl when it came to drinking and I was clueless about the gradual progression of clothes through a beach holiday.

'Well, you save all your white clothes till the end of the holiday, don't you?' one girl said to me.

'Why?' I asked, completely mystified. 'Is that because otherwise you'll throw red wine down them earlier in the week?' This was, after all, the reason why I had never possessed a white top in my life.

The girl looked at me, equally mystified. 'No,' she said slowly, as if explaining to an idiot. 'It's because white shows off your tan the best.'

Clearly, I had much to learn.

There had been no repeat of the Tom incident, partly because I made no attempt to rekindle it and partly because Kelly stuck to Tom's side like glue. Everyone else thought they were a couple and it made sure that, if they weren't going to pull each other, they weren't going to pull anyone else, either.

On the Monday, the third day of the holiday, I started sailing lessons. The cute blonde coach, Barney, turned out to be a really fun, friendly bloke. He wasn't an actual company employee but had been brought out specially just for the week, so when he wasn't teaching he hung out with us. As the reps had pretty much disappeared, Barney was the only one talking to the guests, finding out if everyone was having a good time, if there were people who were feeling left out, or too shy to join in, and he was one of the most enthusiastic partygoers each night, ordering endless rounds of cocktails, smoking furiously and throwing himself round the dance floor.

He was also extremely good-looking. But he was here to work, and probably too young for me, and way too cute for me so I put the possibility out of my mind.

I hadn't reckoned on tequila.

It was the fourth night, and I was drinking with the usual crowd: Tom and Kelly; Zak who had bounced back from my first-night rejection of him and hooked up with a girl called Sophie; a wide boy from east London called Del; and Jamie, the tennis fan from the plane who was developing a huge crush on me. Jamie was sweet and friendly and great fun to be around but just did nothing for me that way. Still, it was lovely to be adored. It made a change.

We were dancing and drinking and Jamie had made his move. He didn't just lunge in true bloke style, but very sweetly told me how he was falling for me and asked what would happen if he kissed me. I told him that it was a lovely thing to say but I would much rather have him as a friend, and made it clear, as gently as possible, that we were never going to be anything more than that.

He took it well and ambled off to bed. Rather relieved at how well he had taken it, but quite flattered too – three offers in four days! – I threw myself into more drinking and more dancing and even flirting with Tom. I still wasn't sure how I felt about him – I really liked him but wasn't convinced I fancied him – and it did seem a bit unfair to just set out to have a holiday romance with no wish to take it further. It also seemed a bit unkind to Kelly.

With both Tom and Jamie still in close proximity and beginning to compete for the spotlight, it was beginning to get rather awkward. It was time for tequila. I bowled over to the bar, and bumped into Barney. He was sitting at the bar chatting to the barman and looking particularly cute. I put my arm around his shoulder in order to shout drunkenly into his ear, 'Would you like a tequila?'

As he nodded, he put his arm around my waist.

'Well, hello!' I thought. I hadn't even thought that Barney would be a possibility, being so blonde and cute, but things were now looking entirely likely.

'Five tequilas, please,' I said.

When they arrived, Barney helped me carry them back to the table and sat next to me. I didn't need the tequila any more. I could almost feel the crackle between us, that wonderfully charged moment when you know that you are about to kiss someone but before you actually do. It's like a kind of telepathy, that they are thinking exactly what you are thinking, added to that zooming confidence from when you know someone wants you as much as you want them. I had been starved of that feeling for such a long time.

'Right, what you have to do,' Tom was saying, 'is down the tequila and then suck the lemon from the mouth of the person on your right.'

There was a drunken revolt about the lemon-sucking. Half the drinkers complained, while the other half seemed to think it was a great idea. Barney and I both decided we were on the wrong side to be on each other's right so we swapped places, which is drunken logic for you.

'I'm not doing that,' said Kelly.

'Me neither,' said Zak.

'OK, scrap that,' said Tom, defeated.

Barney looked gratifyingly disappointed. 'We should do it anyway,' he said.

'Or just forget the lemon and kiss afterwards,' I said.

'Good idea,' he said.

We downed our drinks, sucked our lemons and dived on

each other. We snogged furiously. I couldn't believe it. He was utterly gorgeous and he was kissing me. I was also aware that poor Tom and Kelly were sitting right opposite us, which is terribly bad manners. But I wasn't going to stop just to be polite. They would just have to look the other way.

We came up for air.

'More tequila?' I suggested.

That night was a lot of fun.

The next morning was pretty good too.

Sex and romance seemed so easy when you just went for it.

Of course, alcohol helped too.

As he lay sleeping next to me, it did all seem rather, well, bonkers. Sleeping with your sailing coach seemed like something out of a daytime soap opera. Although the phrase 'sailing coach' brought to mind an ageing, hairy-chested, tanned lothario with gleaming white teeth and love for cocktails with umbrellas, rather than the Adonis in my bed.

I sent my sister a text: 'I appear to have woken up next to my sailing coach.'

It pinged straight back. 'You're such a cliché!'

It pinged again shortly afterwards. She had obviously thought she should have been more enthusiastic. 'But well done!'

Barney yawned slowly awake and reached for me.

Fifteen minutes before the sailing lesson was due to begin, he thought he'd better go. I decided that not only was I incredibly hungover, or at least I would be if I got out of bed, but also it would be just too weird to be taught by someone I'd been having sex with just minutes before.

I went back to sleep.

I saw him again at lunchtime. He was having a cigarette by the swimming pool with Zak. 'Somebody didn't turn up to sailing this morning?' he said.

He seemed genuinely surprised that I hadn't been there. Maybe even a little offended.

'I know, I'm sorry, I was just completely worn out,' was as honest as I could manage. I escaped the conversation by going into lunch. Kelly and Tom were already there, amused by my antics the night before, but they didn't pry.

Barney came over and chatted, and then when we were on our own queuing for ice creams he put his arm round me and gave me a slightly awkward hug.

'You left something behind last night,' I told him.

'Really?'

'Your boxer shorts,' I said, laughing.

He laughed too. 'Oh dear, when am I going to have a chance to get those?'

And there it was. It was a genuine question. It certainly wasn't a promising 'Well, I'll come round and get those later'-type line. It was a statement from a bloke who obviously couldn't think of a time he might be in my room again.

I tried to ignore it. Girls read far too much into these things. He'd had about two hours' sleep, taught sailing all morning and was certainly not planning the next evening already. And he could be shy, or conscious that he's supposed to be working here. I refused to overanalyse it.

Then he went off, clutching his clipboard, and that seemed to be that. No mention of last night, no 'That was fun, wasn't it?' or 'We should do that again some time' – nothing from either of us. We'd gone straight back to being friends. But the week was still young. There was plenty more time for fun.

That afternoon, I walked back down to the sleeping block with Barney and, as he was walking past my door, suggested he should pick up his pants. I think I put it better than that though.

He came in, and wandered about a bit while I tried to find them.

'Your room smells nice,' he said.

I found the pants.

I wanted him to take me in his arms and kiss me. I wanted him to throw me on the bed and tear my clothes off. I wanted him to whisper in my ear, 'I'm going to have a shower, want to join me?' I wanted him to do something, *anything*, that showed he wanted me.

He took his pants, and said, 'Thanks.'

Then he left.

That night at the club, Barney was in high spirits again. The more I saw him, the more I got to know about him, the more I thought that he was a really nice bloke with a healthy relaxed attitude to life, combined with a bouncy energy that was really refreshing after all my time in London surrounded by men in suits, all of whom were suffering from that terminal London disease – extreme knackeredness.

His parents owned what sounded like an idyllic pub in the countryside and he had four brothers. Four brothers! If you factored in girlfriends and friends, their family get-togethers must have been loud, lively, hectic affairs.

I imagined them all going off in the morning to play golf or tennis or sail the Bristol Channel or something, before coming back hot and sweaty for Bloody Marys and a big Sunday roast, before falling asleep by the fire. It seemed like my ideal existence.

I knew I was projecting a huge amount of wishful thinking onto what had been, after all, just a night of tequila-fuelled sex, but there was something about the hothouse, prison-camp environment of a holiday resort that made such leaps of imagination easier. We were all thrown together for a pretty intense week – sun, sea, late nights and alcohol – and there was nothing else to do but get together and dream.

I met Tom at the bar. He mentioned the first night when

we'd been drinking in his room until 5 a.m., then paused and looked at me. 'And next time, come back to my hotel room.'

I got him to repeat it in case I'd misheard.

He did and I hadn't.

'I'm sorry,' I said, wondering if I should admit to this. 'I did come back. But I'd forgotten your room number.'

He laughed. 'Room 3003,' he said. 'Don't forget.'

But Kelly was close by and, by now, I only had thoughts for Barney.

The hours went by. An older guy whom I'd been talking to on and off throughout the week kept insisting I dance with him. Later, he came up behind me and wrapped his arms round my waist and tried to kiss me. 'What is going on?' I thought. There seemed to be a ridiculous number of people trying to get off with me. This certainly didn't happen in London.

Barney found me on the dance floor and we kissed and kissed. It was towards the end of the night and we stood there kissing for so long that the staff had begun packing up the chairs around us.

Out of nowhere, Del bounded up like an exuberant puppy dog. 'Wow, look at you two!' he said excitedly. 'Give her one from me, mate! Better still, let's have a threesome.'

He clutched the pair of us and we staggered around like a hideous six-legged beast. Thankfully, he then lurched off.

We started to sway back to the room, and stopped on the way to sit in one of the hotel golf buggies.

'Where shall we drive to?' said Barney. 'The King's Road? Italy?'

Fortunately, the hotel staff had removed any chance of Barney being able to actually start the thing. He would probably have driven it into the sea.

The next day – well, a few hours later – we woke up. I revelled in just being there with him, seeing him all cosy and sleepy. And it was fun when he was awake too.

Ten minutes afterwards, he was teaching me how to furl the top sail with Joan and Fiona.

That afternoon, the sun was covered by cloud and there was the occasional drop of rain. We sat around on the grey beach, debating what to do.

From high up above us, Del leaned over the swimming pool balcony. 'Bonsoir, bonsoir,' he shouted cheerfully. He caught sight of me. 'Oi!' he boomed, as loud as a town crier. 'You got lucky last night, didn't you?'

Everyone cracked up.

I blushed, but felt proud. Now everyone knew that I was with the fittest guy here. But I suspected that it might not be that way for long.

Towards the end of the week, the weather turned. Warm rain lashed down for days, turning the beach into a no-go zone. Everyone was spending the time drinking in the resort's bars, and I was spending the time falling deeper and deeper for Barney. And he, well, he was being lovely but it was becoming obvious, even to me, that he just wasn't as interested in me as I was in him.

One afternoon, we were chatting in the bar while drinking rainbow-coloured cocktails.

'This week has been great fun,' he mused, wearing a multi-coloured jumper round his head like a pantomime Lawrence of Arabia. 'But I think the most fun I've had has been out on the boat.'

I wasn't going to let that pass. 'Really?' I said archly. There was no way to say that kind of thing other than archly.

'Well, there have been some fun moments on dry land too,' he said. He smiled cheerfully at me. 'You were involved in those, you know.'

My heart did a little thump.

But here we were again, back at the nightclub bar, me sitting smoking, watching Barney get cocktails for everyone. I was talking to a guy who worked in the industry and who had flown out for a couple of nights to see how things were shaping up for the summer. He was pretty fierce, made it very clear he didn't like journalists in general or me in particular and, just in case I hadn't got the message, had mentioned his wife about four times already.

We were arguing about my assertion that most people came on this type of holiday just to get laid.

'They most certainly do not,' he said angrily. 'You've got it completely wrong.'

'Really?' I said, quite enjoying the novelty of actually having a shouty conversation with someone for once rather than holiday small talk. And he obviously couldn't stand me so there was definitely no flirting going on.

'Absolutely not! These people come for the sports, for the family activities . . .'

'Not the families!' I said. 'The singles. The ones on my holiday.' I gestured around me at the various seduction attempts going on with varying degrees of success. 'I've never had so many people try to sleep with me as on this holiday. You'd have to be an utter lemon not to get laid if you wanted to.'

Light dawned. 'Oh, the singles weeks?' he exclaimed. 'Oh yes, they're all about sex. One hundred per cent.'

We had finally reached an agreement, it seemed. Not that it helped. He glared at me some more and I headed back inside to the club with some relief. Barney was staggering around the dance floor. I decided not to stagger with him.

As the evening was drawing to a close, the scary executive came over to chat, rather to my surprise. What was even more surprising was that, this time, he actually appeared to be flirting with me – there were lots of leading questions, lots of 'I'm not trying to pull you but if I were . . .'-type talk and even an occasional smile. It took a while for this to dawn on me and even then I found it hard to believe.

What, *this guy*? The one who hates me?

We went outside to 'talk'. He said that he couldn't believe it but he really, really fancied me. He'd been married for eight years and had never done or said anything like this before. It may have been a line but he looked genuinely tortured by what he was saying. I was dimly aware of Barney and Del lurching around in the background.

He took my hand and we walked off into the night, through the resort, towards his room.

Suddenly, he stopped, and put his head in his hands. 'I shouldn't be doing this,' he said.

'Then don't,' I said, and turned to walk away.

He caught me. 'Don't,' he said, echoing me but meaning the opposite.

The whole thing was very surreal. He was flying out the next morning – well, within a few hours – to see his wife in another resort. This seemed crazy.

'It's OK,' I said. 'It's really best we don't do this.'

I kissed him and then turned around and walked away.

Barney was sliding along the walls in reception to get to his room. He was beyond plastered. So instead I went back to Del's room for cigarettes and vodka and, as it turned out, some rather persistent attempts to have sex with me. I ended up running out of his room at 4 a.m. with his pleas echoing down the corridor after me.

Why was it that the men you wanted to sleep with and the men who wanted to sleep with you were so rarely the same person?

23

The End of the Affair

Back home, I unlocked the front door and heaved my suitcase into the hall. My flatmate Jeff was in the living room, lying on the sofa watching a film. It seemed, rather improbably, to be *Titanic*.

'Hi, honey, I'm home!' I said, as we always did.

And then I burst into tears.

Poor Jeff. He paused Kate and Leo and looked up, confused. 'Didn't you have a good time?' he asked.

I stood in the middle of the living room and cried. I felt so low, so blue, so miserable. I was also completely surprised at myself. Why was I feeling so awful? A week-long romance, which was after all really only a few days at most, and I was acting as if my heart had been broken.

The fridge was unaccountably free of beer, and it was beer I needed right now. I bought some New York Super Fudge Chunk ice cream in the corner shop too, for habit's sake more than anything else, but that was too girly a comfort blanket in my current state. I sat on the roof terrace back home and drank bottles of Badger ale and smoked cigarettes instead.

I felt terrible. I'd completely forgotten what it felt like to have your heart, if not actually broken, then at least squashed a little bit. I had that horrible sinking feeling in my stomach as if I'd done something wrong, or lost something. Then there was that deep, hungry sadness that made me feel so low and terrible that I had to fight not to just sink to the floor and lie there, wailing. I also had an awful inadequate feeling that made me feel too short, too fat, too boring, too plain to ever be worthy of having someone like Barney look at me the way I'd wanted him to.

The last few days had been great and awful in equal measure. I'd learned a lot about sailing, played some tennis, did a lot of reading, sunbathing and swimming, and generally relaxed.

But I'd also spent the entire time pining over Barney, who, while he was still very much there to have drinks with, chat to and go sailing with, was utterly unapproachable in every other way.

Tom and I had swum out to the pontoon on the last day and talked as we baked in the sun. We talked about sex, relationships and holiday romances.

'The thing about holiday romances is that it's just so abrupt at the baggage carousel,' he said, as the waves splashed around us. 'You see people who get together at the start of the holiday, spend every single waking – and sleeping – moment together and then the moment they get their luggage it's "Goodbye then!" and that's it. They'll never see each other again. It's utterly brutal.'

I agreed, although it felt as if Barney and I had already had our baggage-carousel moment. I may have fallen really deeply for him, but even I could see that there was absolutely no point in thinking there would be a continuation of anything back in London. We hadn't even made it to the end of the holiday.

I had gone to bed straight after dinner on the last night – I couldn't bear the thought of staying up late just for nothing to happen yet again. I later found out that, on the last night, Tom and Kelly had finally got it together. Well, at least that was a result for someone. As for me and Barney, we'd chatted on the plane, we'd walked to the Tube together and we'd sat next to each other all the way to Victoria, me practically bursting with lust, love and unspoken words. A hurried kiss goodbye on the platform, and that was it.

'This is ridiculous,' I told myself on the roof terrace, practically wallowing in beer. 'It was really unlikely that you and Barney would have made it as a couple anyway. He's lovely and cute and energetic and cheerful and all those great things, yes, but could you really see you and him sitting in a restaurant having a proper conversation? Casual chitchat over beers in the sun is one thing, but there wasn't the meeting of minds that you'd hope for in a partner. He showed no signs of wanting to know everything about you, like you wanted to know about him. He chatted to you in exactly the same way he chatted to everyone. He's a sailing coach from Henley who breezes through life with a cheerful confidence and relaxed attitude, while you are a cynical tabloid hack who drives herself mad by her inability to just take life as it comes.'

It seemed that I was mourning far more than the end of a holiday romance. It was as if a door that had briefly opened into a whole new life had suddenly slammed shut. I wanted to have a family pub and four strapping brothers. I wanted to land at Heathrow and have my phone practically explode with messages from friends saying, 'We're in the pub! Come and join us!' I wanted to be part of all that. Seeing Barney's life had suddenly made me feel friendless, boring, lonely and old. I didn't really want Barney. Or at least, if I did, it was because I wanted to *be* Barney. As I couldn't be Barney, then being with him, and part of that set-up, was the next best thing. I wanted to be the girlfriend of someone like that, who had a huge social network and a large interesting family. I love my family, of course, but it's small. And I used to have a huge group of friends who would summon me straight from the airport to the pub, but that had all vanished.

Even putting all that to one side, there was also the fact that it had been ages since I'd actually fancied someone who – however briefly – had fancied me back. Lying next to him and being intimate with him had reawakened all those feelings I used to have, for Scott, for Patrick, even for Daniel. The sheer joy of snuggling up to someone, of feeling their warm skin next to mine, of knowing they were choosing to spend their time with me: I loved all that and missed it, and it felt as if it had been snatched away far too quickly.

It occurred to me that I was extremely vulnerable if I could fall for anyone who showed even the slightest bit of interest in me, which wasn't a healthy place to be in.

And that I had in no way been prepared for the rollercoaster of feelings that this search for a husband would inflict on me.

But the beer was helping.

The next few days were slightly surreal. I went down to my mother's where the rest of the family had congregated for the weekend, and spent the next day crying pathetically. I just couldn't seem to stop. I couldn't believe that I had gone to pieces so catastrophically over a very short-lived affair. How was I going to keep going with the whole dating process if the slightest thing was enough to send me into such a sharp downward spiral? I wanted to get out there, to really go for it, to see who was out there and throw myself wholeheartedly into the dating game. How was I going to do that if I was a blubbing wreck?

I pulled myself together. I went for a long run and long bike rides. Exercise was the only thing that I knew would clear my mind from these squirrelling thoughts. When I was wrenched apart from Daniel after discovering he was sleeping with my flatmate, I crackled with despair and pent-up angry energy, and spent hours marching around the streets in Victoria where I worked, unable to sit still because of the burning pain of what he'd done. I'd race out of the office every lunchtime and walk furiously in any direction, through Pimlico, along the Thames embankment, over the bridges, up towards Buckingham Palace and Green Park, or even on the treadmill at the local gym, pounding away. After 20 minutes, my brain would start to clear slightly, a cooling calm would come over me and some of the sadness and the anger would start to fall away. What with that, and not being able to eat due to the knot clenched in my stomach, I lost a stone in a month. Result. The weight all came back again, though, once the memory of Daniel started to recede – surely it is possible to be thin and happy? Not for me, it seems.

The world did seem a different place after my holiday, though, which sounds dramatic but was actually a nice feeling. Knowing that entirely new people were in the world made it more exciting somehow, more fun. I felt I wanted to do more exciting things myself, knowing that Barney was popping from one party to the next, heading off surfing, just enjoying himself.

It was like those first few weeks when you meet someone, and you fall in love, and all of a sudden it's as if your life is a film set, and even when you're not with them you want to have adventures, be spontaneous, be all the things you know you can be but usually aren't because you're too knackered or just stuck in the routine. The one person who was most thrown into sharp relief by all this was my erstwhile fantasy Will. I looked at him, sitting next to me as usual, and couldn't believe how solid, how unexciting, how leaden he was in comparison. He sat there all week, yawning occasionally, peering at his computer, wearing the same old suit and barely responding to any of my overtures of conversation. How dull, how different from Barney, who fizzed with energy and cheerful optimism.

Even though I knew that Barney and I were over, I was determined to keep up the dating momentum that that holiday had sparked off. It seemed that the whole world – Will excepted, of course – had the flirt dial turned firmly up to 11. Or maybe it was just me. I flirted with one of the staff in the gym over the chest-press machine. In the pub at the end of the week, I rather indistinctly asked a barman for 'some peanuts' and the look of shock and alarm on his face when he'd obviously misheard me set both of us giggling like teenagers. A woman standing next to me at the bar joined in – flirting was infectious. It was getting me nowhere nearer finding a husband, but it was good fun.

24

Playing Away

Midway through my blitz on the dating world, I started to find the whole process both exhilarating and bruising. The more people I met, the more I realised how easy it had been to get stuck into the same old social routine without even realising it. Working as a journalist, it is easy to get sucked into thinking that you are meeting lots of different people all the time, that life is rich and varied, and it is, to some extent. But, if you look more closely at it, it isn't actually that rich or varied. I spent a lot of time in pubs with my colleagues, most of whom I've shared an office with on and off for the last ten years.

Every week, there is something going on in my sectors, which are alcohol and gambling. There are restaurant openings, brewery tours, wine-tastings, beer-tastings, beer awards and beer festivals, as well as countless events in Parliament, where the All-Party Parliamentary Beer Group committee rolls in barrels of ale from around the country and MPs squash in, ten deep around the makeshift bars, as if they had never had a free drink in their lives before, before all decamping to the Westminster Arms or the Red Lion on Whitehall to continue their never-ending discussions on the rise of duty on alcohol.

Then there are the PR parties, the one-to-one PR lunches, the tickets to Wimbledon, Henley, Royal Ascot and Glorious Goodwood or pop concerts – The Killers at The O2, Take That at Wembley.

I have spent years and years attending all these events, usually looking pretty smart, meeting hundreds and hundreds of people – most of whom are men, because the beer and business worlds tend to be fairly male-dominated – and yet, aside from Patrick, whom I met at Wimbledon, I haven't met a single person I either could, or wanted to, be permanently romantically involved with. That doesn't make me feel great, but it also completely baffles me. I think about how utterly unsuccessful I've been in finding a partner – all those parties, all that alcohol sloshing around! – and can't quite believe it.

Of course, there have been guys during that time. There was Patrick, for a start, who took out several – and probably quite crucial – dating years.

There was Henry, a rising star in print who went on to become a rising star in broadcasting; we spent the night flirting and then snogging at a PR party near Liverpool Street station and then crashed our way into the members' private bar so that we could keep on drinking and kissing. (We were soon rumbled and rather abruptly thrown out.)

Then there was Nigel, a broadsheet business journalist whom I met over vodka luges at a PR party and kissed in a taxi all the way home. Halfway to Balham, he confessed he was married. 'That's it,' I said, furious. 'You should just get out now.'

He kissed me again and, well . . . 'So much for my willpower,' I thought the next morning, as he asked me the way to the Tube.

Now that I was actually opening myself up to the whole idea of dating, of meeting new people, having new experiences, I was finding that the experience was actually starting to change me. From thinking that the world – or, at least, my corner of it – was short of decent men, I was finding that they were everywhere. OK, I still hadn't found the guy for me, but it was heartening to know that there were people out there who liked being with me. It wasn't just lovers either, but friends too. By being more open to meeting new people and being more proactive about talking to them, as well as making sure I kept in contact afterwards, I was finding that I was adding many new friends to my social circle, which made up for the ones who were still my friends but who I now never saw from one year to the next.

In my more positive moments, I felt as if I was discovering a whole new world. It was refreshing and inspiring to find all these new people out there. I knew that I was very unlikely to see Barney again, but that was OK – I'd got over my brief but very intense feelings for him and now, rather than feeling loss, I wanted to have some of his energy and attitude towards life for myself.

When things were getting hectic, I no longer wanted to get off the treadmill of late nights and small talk; I'd learned to love the fact that I was busy and out all the time and meeting new people, and instead tried to curb the unnecessary drinking, the sloping mindlessly to the pub with work colleagues that I'd known for a decade, or arranging meetings with friends whom I hadn't seen for a while out of a sense of duty or 'not wanting to lose touch'. It was going to be new experiences only from now on, and I was revelling in it.

While I was enjoying this sense of renewed optimism, I was sent on a press trip – the kind that journalists fight over: three days in the Caribbean courtesy of a hotel chain, all expenses paid. There was some work to do – I was going to interview the chief executive of the hotel company – but maximum pampering. The flights were first class, the hotels had improbable numbers of stars next to their names and, in between bouts of lying next to the pool, there were various trips and activities laid on. What better way to meet someone lovely? There were journalists, there was booze and there was sunshine.

And so I met Ian. He was in PR and from London. He was gorgeous, not in an obvious way, but in a sweet, friendly, chirpy way. He looked like Anthony Andrews in *Brideshead Revisited* and was a lot of fun. I had the vague idea that he was married and so I didn't actually think of him that way at all. We just bumped into each other at various points throughout the trip – during the morning press conference, at the bar for cocktails and on the dance floor during the big evening parties.

The last night was particularly full on – a cocktail party for 300 press and VIPs. There were the loudest fireworks I'd ever heard, an ancient Spanish guy hand-rolling cigars, and 10ft-tall stilt walkers and acrobats. And there was me and Ian going bonkers on the dance floor to the rather brilliant band. We danced like people in their thirties – far too exuberantly, wanting to savour every moment, as we knew we far too rarely did this kind of thing any more.

Afterwards, we grabbed some other people from our group and headed off to find a nearby nightclub. Ian and I drank, chatted and flirted so much that I did say, just to double-check, 'You are married, aren't you?'

I hoped I'd got it wrong, that he wasn't, that I had found the one guy in the whole world who was both lovely and not married. But no, he was married. He beamed when he said it, and was obviously very happily married. Maybe the flirting was all in my head.

At 2 a.m. the club was starting to get a little wild – people were dancing on tables, a couple was making out next to us and clothes were being removed. Four of us smuggled some drink out and decided to go to the beach. It was a lovely balmy night, the sand was soft and smooth, and we lay in the moonlight, sharing the beers around.

With the other two almost asleep, Ian decided that it was time for a swim, stripped down to his boxers and hurled himself in the water. I took off my sandals but left everything else on, and jumped into the ocean. The sea was beautifully warm, like being in an enormous bath. My dress was floating up around me. Ian came over and, without a word being spoken, we moved straight for each other. It felt like something out of a film. We rolled in the waves, kissing as if we were drowning. We were grabbing, clutching at each other, going under the waves and coming up for air before plunging down again. I stripped off in a watery striptease, looping each item round my arm in case the current caught them and took them off to Cuba.

'This is how much I want you,' he said, as we whirled around in the sea.

'I want you too,' I said, rising and falling with the waves. We were out there so long our friends woke up from their impromptu snooze and thought we'd drowned. They were composing headlines in their minds before they caught sight of us and hallooed us back into land.

Back at the hotel and with the others gone to their rooms, we fell into each other's arms in the lift, clutching at each other, kissing the life out of each other while the lift, unnoticed, rode up and down between floors. We were soaking wet. Sand was everywhere.

Halfway to my room, he stopped. 'I can't do this,' he said.

'I know,' I said.

We clung to each other again and then wrenched ourselves apart. He went to his room and I went to mine. I got in the shower and took my dress off.

He was still lovely the next day, but muted by a hangover. We lay on the beach next to each other and pretended to sleep. We caught ourselves peeping at each other and shared a shy smile.

He wiggled closer. 'I'm sorry for pouncing on you last night,' he said.

'It's OK,' I said. 'It was fun.'

He sighed. 'I've been married for seven years,' he said. 'And I've never, ever done anything like that before.' He looked so pained and ashamed I believed him.

'It's all right,' I said. 'It was just drunken tomfoolery.'

And it was, but it was also one of the most romantic experiences I'd ever had. And he was just so perfect that it broke my heart that I hadn't met him eight years ago.

We spent the day on the beach together and drank cocktails on the flight back. There was no question of anything ever happening again between us, but it was lovely being with him, chatting and laughing, not in a flirty way but just enjoying spending time together. With Barney, I had quivered with desire just being next to him, but the conversations were never more than superficial. With Ian, I could see how, had things been different, we could very easily have ended up together. It would have been nice to think we could be friends, but a married man from Highbury suddenly, randomly making friends with a single 38-year-old woman with whom he'd been making out the night before? Not a chance. It was sad but I wasn't going to try to pretend to myself that it could be any different.

We chastely kissed each other goodbye at Heathrow. I sent him a text saying it had been lovely to meet him. And that was that.

Until he called me that evening. I'd just got off the train at the station near my dad's house in Sussex. The joys of first-class flying and an overnight flight meant that, once I'd dropped my luggage off at home, I was still wide awake and headed down to meet up with the rest of the family.

When I saw Ian's name come up on my phone, I just knew what he was going to say. I knew that there was going to be *something*. There always is, with married men. (I say that, having slept with only one of them, the vodka-luge guy. It's something you just know.)

We had a very nice relaxed chat for five minutes or so. We talked about the trip, the flight, which in-flight films we'd watched and what we'd thought of them.

The preliminary small talk over, there came the inevitable pause and clearing of throat.

'I think I've turned into a bit of a cliché,' he said dolefully. 'Not only because of what happened the other night, but . . .'

I waited for it, thinking, 'I can't believe he's told her.'

'. . . I've told my wife.'

There was a pause.

'Oh dear,' I said, because that's what I felt. 'And how is she?'

'Not great,' he said. 'I've being trying to tell her that, well, we were drunk, and that I hadn't eaten anything all evening, but she didn't seem to think much of that.'

I wasn't quite sure why he'd rung. I think he just wanted to talk to the only person in the world he could talk to about it. I wasn't there to make him feel better, which I couldn't, or to tell him he was an idiot for telling her, which he was, but it wouldn't have helped much for me to point that out. I think it was just to help him try to get through all this in his own mind.

To his credit, he didn't try to pull some hurtful 'I was just *so* drunk I didn't know what I was doing' routine, or, even worse, 'I so regret it – what a stupid thing to have done, what was I thinking?' number, which isn't the greatest thing to have someone say to you.

In return, I told him that it was just spontaneous drunken nonsense and we got carried away, but we didn't sleep together and he shouldn't beat himself up about it. But I didn't ask, 'Why tell your wife when it will hurt her, and make her think about it for every second of every day for ages and every time you go away and every time she sees you being friendly with another woman at a party?'

We parted on good terms. He later sent me a text. 'Sorry for getting heavy before,' it said. 'All fine here. Had fun time. Was great to meet you. Must keep in touch. Ian x'

I wrote back saying that I understood, and that I didn't want to have been the cause of trouble in his household. I told him that he was utterly lovely, because I think he is, but didn't tell him that he was hopelessly naive when it came to relationships, but that that in itself was quite endearing. I also didn't say that we'd keep in touch, because we won't. Eight years too late means there's just no point.

25

Lessons in Love

I knew that it was coming but it was still a shock when it did: the 20-year school reunion. There can be few more chilling phrases in the English language.

Firstly, there is the awful sense that life has just zoomed by without your really noticing. Twenty years! You have to be joking. Twenty years is such a long time . . . I instantly felt ancient and creaky. I must be really, really old.

Then, the panic sets in. What have I done in 20 years? I don't seem to have done anything. I remember going to university, and then spending a year travelling round Australia before getting my first reporting job . . . and then it's all a total blur until the moment when the invitation arrived. I must have done something more than that, surely?

There is nothing quite like a school reunion to make you look back over your life and wonder what happened. Some people must feel pretty good about their progress over a couple of decades – great careers, houses and, of course, the most obvious signs of achievement: a husband and children. But I hadn't got a husband or children and, against that utter failure to achieve even the most basic domestic situation, everything just faded away. I couldn't think of anything I'd done, anything I'd achieved. It seemed as if I had spent the years between 18 and 38 doing absolutely sod all except moving my books around between addresses. A lot of movement, maybe, but not a lot of progress. If any. I felt entirely pointless. And the last thing I wanted was to go somewhere where everyone else would be parading their dashing husbands and beautiful wives and leading a whole bus queue of adorable golden-haired high-achieving children behind them. I decided not to go.

Even though I wasn't going to go, my sheer nosiness still lured me to the Facebook page that Camilla, ex-head girl and ultra-efficient organiser of the whole ghastly business, had set up. Just looking at some of the names and faces felt like going back in time, but to someone else's life.

I had spent two years at the school, just there for the sixth form, and the culture clash between my life in London – a lot of freedom, a fair amount of boozing and typical teenage rebelling against authority – and a boarding school in Somerset, where there were curfews and chapel and all the hidden rules of the school society, was quite considerable. I was nothing if not adaptable, though, and did enjoy my time there, much to the surprise of all my friends back home.

However, after two years I was off to university and, while I had vaguely kept in touch with some friends, it was no longer part of my life. After 20 years' separation it felt as if the entire school was a mythical building, a figment of my imagination, and the fact it still existed and that other people shared the same memories of such a place felt surreal.

It wasn't just the lack of partner and children that was holding me back, though. It was the fact that all the boys I had been out with at school – apart from Scott, there had been Dan, Pete, Evan and Lucas, in varying degrees of seriousness (I went out with Dan for half a year, but Evan a mere three days) – all seemed to be utterly festooned with wives and offspring. Each of them was married and had at least two children. Scott, one of the loves of my life, had three, while football-mad Dan was obviously trying to start his own league side and already had four.

I was going to turn up with, what? The square root of fuck all, evidently.

'But you've got a great job and have travelled the world!' said my mum supportively, in the way that mums are contractually obliged to be in these sorts of situations. 'That must count for something, surely?'

I suppose it should have done, but it didn't. It just seemed as if I'd had 20 years to get married and have children and I had completely failed on both fronts. Nothing else seemed to matter.

Friends had varying opinions on the subject. 'A reunion? Never!' shuddered my flatmate Jeff, declining to elaborate further.

'A reunion sounds like great fun!' said my other flatmate Alex, ever the optimist.

'How exactly?'

'Well, umm . . .' he floundered.

My friend Adrian volunteered to come as my fake husband. 'I promise not to be too gay,' he said.

Various people kindly said that they'd lend me their children.

'Do you want young and therefore unable to speak and give you away?' asked one of my friends, with a variety of infants on offer. 'Or do you want older and therefore more bribable?'

I just couldn't decide whether to go. I was torn between the feeling that my ego really didn't need another battering just now – I was feeling single enough without a crowd of people rushing up and saying things like: 'I've got a lovely husband and some lovely children, how about you?' or 'So what went wrong? Why are you such a marital failure?' – and feeling very curious about what the weekend would be like. It would be fascinating seeing everyone again, as if we'd all jumped forward 20 years, and the event was unlikely to be repeated again on such a grand scale.

It was my sister who came up with the clincher. 'Look, remember my college reunion a few years ago?' she said, one evening when I'd popped round for a glass of wine and a good moan about the whole thing. 'Well, my friend Helen really didn't want to go. She was feeling incredibly single, incredibly ancient and really unhappy that she couldn't see herself ever getting married and having children. But she put on an amazing dress and some fabulous heels, got her hair done so she looked stunning, and everyone there was talking for ages afterwards about how brilliant she looked and how happy she seemed. And all the married couples there were obviously completely bored with each other and had all gone to seed and were completely envious of Helen. And within a year she had met a bloke, got married and now they're having a baby.'

It was an appealing picture, not least because it was also true. I liked the idea of turning up, happy and confident, showing that life wasn't a complete disaster even if I hadn't quite achieved the husband and kids part of it yet, if indeed I ever do. My sense of self was becoming rather skewed by all this emphasis on finding a man and yet there was obviously so much more to life than happy domesticity.

'Look,' I said to myself, while running round Clapham Common in an attempt to get into some semblance of shape just in case I ended up going, 'you've got a great job, you have lots of nice friends, you've lived in some amazing places, you have even run a few marathons and climbed some stupidly high Moroccan mountain recently. It's hardly as if you have sat around and done nothing for the past 20 years, is it?'

Brave talk and, even if I didn't quite believe it, the thought of missing out on what promised to be quite an interesting weekend – my inherent journalistic nosiness – was enough to make me finally say yes. I still couldn't quite shake off the feeling that, if I hadn't got a husband, then I should have, perhaps, an Oscar or the Booker Prize instead, but I tried to ignore it.

Even when one of my (short-lived) boyfriends from school emailed me on Facebook, saying, 'Bridgie! Why haven't you got married yet? You're leaving it a bit late, aren't you?' I refused to be deflated. Presumably everyone else would be feeling similarly nervous about the whole thing too – you'd need the ego of Piers Morgan not to be slightly intimidated by meeting up with all the ghosts from schooldays past – and so I decided that it was best to look upon it as a fun weekend in the country and not take it too seriously.

The day arrived, and I drove off to Bath in the pouring rain. Dan, bless him, had invited me to come along for pre-reunion drinks in town with him and some of the other guys, which would be a perfect way of easing into what could be quite an alarming evening.

Walking across Bath Abbey courtyard to Browns was one of the more terrifying journeys of my life. I was astonished by how nervous I was. I felt sick, my head was spinning and my heart was thumping so badly I thought I might have some kind of seizure.

'You are going to a pub to have drinks with old friends,' I told myself, forcing myself to continue forward when my legs wanted to run in completely the opposite direction. 'It is going to be fine.'

I walked in, and, of course, it was completely fine. There was Dan, Pete, Evan and lovely Scott, four out of the five people I'd kissed at school, plus their friend Kyle. They rose as one to embrace me with huge hugs and then fell over themselves to order me a drink and to share whatever food they were scoffing.

Everyone looked surprisingly similar: older, of course, some slightly rounder or with less hair, but generally we all looked pretty great. Meeting them beforehand was a perfect way of slowly sliding into the past; everyone confessed how nervous they'd been and it turned out we had all been checking one another out on Facebook. Girls proved to be a problem as many had changed their names: 'Which Nicola is that, then?' was a common refrain, but the joy of Facebook was that, not just in the pub but for the entire evening, there was no 'so are you married, have you got any children'-type interrogation at all. Everyone had obviously worked out everyone else's domestic situation already, so all the nightmares I'd had of arriving and people shouting across the room at me: 'So, you haven't got married or had any children then? What have you been doing with your life?' never materialised.

I knew there were at least two other girls there in a similar situation but it never came up, not even once. A minor miracle but proof that whatever was obsessing me was certainly not bothering anyone else.

The boys headed on up to school while I nipped back to my hotel to change into something slightly more glamorous than a pair of jeans. A chorus of genuine-sounding 'but you look great as you are' compliments buoyed me all the way back to the hotel and brought me out again in quite a different mood from when I'd arrived.

'These are lovely people,' I thought happily. I'd been a fool to wonder even for a second whether I should come or not.

We were all meeting in a beautiful old country pub just next to the school. Outside on the terrace, as the sun was setting, was my past. There must have been around 50 school friends all chattering away at high speed and even higher volume. It was an utterly bizarre sight. It seemed hardly any time at all since we were all at school together and now, here we were, looking the same but not quite, all wearing grown-up clothes and trying to work out who had changed the most. Some hadn't changed at all, but one guy was completely unrecognisable to me, until someone helpfully pointed out that he had left school before I'd even arrived.

Fortified by gin and tonics and pints of lager, we traipsed across the road to the school and managed to remember our way to the sixth-form block, with its long-forgotten but instantly familiar smell.

My study partner Heather dragged me along the corridors and dramatically threw open the door to one of the rooms. She stood in the middle. 'Can you believe we used to do our homework in here?'

'We didn't,' I said. 'We were in the one downstairs, weren't we?'

Neither of us could remember.

The drink flowed, the conversation never stopped and there was even a cluster of smokers outside, just like in the old days, although this time round we didn't have to go down the path to the fag-bush and keep an eye out for teachers. We posed for a picture, which probably horrified the current members of the sixth form, who no doubt thought we looked ancient, whereas we all thought we looked pretty fabulous.

At 11 p.m. when we got booted out of the school grounds, we hit the nightclubs of Bath – almost exactly the reverse of what used to happen 20 years ago – and engaged in some seriously embarrassing dancing. The young trendies of Bath were no doubt utterly appalled by this influx of late-30-somethings totally lacking in any credibility whatsoever.

The next day, we all reconvened at the pub by the school, sharing hangovers and a fair amount of gossip from the night before: a few people had been refused entry into various clubs and taxis due to being extremely plastered, and some other people had even ended up together, 20 years later than expected but no less fun for that. The sensible ones who hadn't partied until 3.30 a.m. had gone on a school tour that morning, some dragging their families with them. One child likened the school to Hogwarts, and I suppose it bore a passing resemblance, but it also echoed my feeling that school was a figment of my imagination that only came back into existence when I came to visit.

Along with the Bloody Marys and Sunday lunches out came the photographs – impossibly young-looking versions of ourselves, dressing up for school plays, hanging out in the dormitories, looking proud and grown up before the Leavers' Ball. There was one of me and Scott, me in my green ball gown and him in the black-tie get-up that I remembered so clearly. He would be walking down the misty path in the dead of night towards me waiting for him just a few hours later. I showed it to him: if it meant anything to him, he certainly didn't show it but it made me feel incredibly sad – sad to think of how in love we were then and how it had all gone. So much happiness and so much love, all vanished.

Scott was no doubt thinking of his wife and three children and how he had to go home and tidy the house before they returned from their weekend away, while I was thinking of how happy I had been with him and whether he was the one who got away. Could we have been happy together? There was a poignancy about our young love, how I had thought it would always be there and yet it was gone for ever. I felt as if our lives, having been so intertwined, had gone on totally different routes and I wasn't sure how or why that had happened. How had he and so many of my school friends ended up with partners and children, proper families of their own, while I had ended up with nothing?

Real life was starting to seep back in: people had trains and even planes to catch and families to be reunited with. I didn't have any of those things. I had a drive back to London but decided to stop off along the M4 and spend the night in a cosy pub deep in the Hertfordshire countryside. I felt the need to hibernate, to look after myself and prepare against the deep feeling of loss I could feel coming. I drew the curtains, wrapped myself up in the warm duvet and made hot chocolate. I hunkered down, waiting for the clouds to pass.

26

Matchmaker, Matchmaker

Back at work, word had obviously got around about my dating quest, and Timothy, one of my colleagues, arrived unprompted at my desk to offer some words of wisdom.

'You know, if I were single, I wouldn't do online dating,' he announced, with all the smug certainty of someone who'd married his childhood sweetheart 20 years earlier and lived with her and their lovely children in a house in the suburbs.

'Oh, really,' I said, with little enthusiasm.

'Yes,' he chattered on, regardless. 'All that internet stuff is just rubbish. I'd go to an agency and they'd sort it all out for me.'

Timothy, like me, a business journalist, had obviously been writing about outsourcing so much that he'd decided that it was possible to outsource one's love life. Now, I was already pretty fed up with people telling me about how I just needed to 'get out there', so I was even less prepared to listen to dating advice from someone who had most likely been on only one date in his whole life.

I pushed my chair back from my desk and looked up at him. 'You mean that, if your wife ran off with the milkman tomorrow, you wouldn't go to an online dating site, where you can browse hundreds of people's pictures and details for free, but you'd rather go to an agency where they charge you thousands of pounds and don't even tell you if they've got someone even vaguely suitable for you on their books?'

He looked aghast. 'Thousands of pounds?' He suddenly backed away from his imaginary role as the cuckolded husband who would simply order a replacement wife. 'That's insane!'

'Timothy, what's insane is you telling me about dating when you haven't been on a date yourself since you were 15.'

He acknowledged the point and retreated to his own desk and happy domesticity. He was presumably also relieved not to have to fork out two grand. As for me, I started to wonder whether he might actually have a point. Maybe it was time to consider signing up with a dating agency.

I had pretty much dismissed all of them out of hand, seeing them as rather antiquated institutions that had been completely superseded by the internet, but I had to admit I didn't know much about them. None of the images that immediately leaped to mind was particularly encouraging: Sid James and Hattie Jacques running some highly implausible love-matching bureau in a *Carry On* film I remembered watching one hungover Saturday afternoon; or adverts in the back of Sunday newspapers featuring earnest-looking people sitting around at '70s-style dinner parties. Did that type of organisation really exist any more?

A quick search online revealed that the dating-agency industry was, in appearance at least, still alive and thriving. Just Googling 'introduction agencies' revealed a whole host of companies promising 'personal' and 'exclusive' and even 'professional' services in this field. They all had rather posh names and repeated the word 'professional' many times. They were all clearly keen to give the impression that both they, and their members, were thoroughly professional. No amateur daters here.

There was even a trade body, the Association of British Introduction Agencies, whose website assured potential clients: 'Although each has its own unique selling points, the one thing all member dating agencies have in common is a strong commitment to providing professional singles with the best possible service.'

There you go again, all very professional. It sounded as if they had an awful lot of men in suits on their books. I began to wonder if this emphasis on 'professional' would be rather at the expense of 'fun'.

I started checking out what each one had to offer, besides a thoroughly professional service, of course. One claimed itself to be 'the introduction agency for thinking people', which sounded rather grammatically clumsy and implied there was a very real possibility that, if I signed up with someone else, I would end up dating a load of brainless zombies.

Several had pictures on their homepages of people sporting the whitest sets of gleaming teeth I had seen this side of Simon Cowell, which seemed more appropriate for a Hollywood dentist's website. Another proclaimed itself to offer 'global head-hunting for the super-busy', which seemed wrong on so many levels, not least because, if you were too busy to even look for someone, it implied that you weren't going to be around all that much for the relationship either.

One claimed to have a 100 per cent 'exclusive bespoke search service', whatever that was, and offered introductions from 'the upper end of the single market only'. The upper end? Did this mean money? Or attractiveness? I was itching to find out but I suspected that, as I was several rungs below the upper end of the single market, they might not even take my call.

The general idea, though, that someone would take you in hand and deal with the whole dating thing was actually quite appealing. Rather than the brutal snap judgements of the online world, where you can click on and off people at random in the blink of an eye, maybe I needed someone to get to know me first, and then go out and find someone suitable for me, based on the judgement of someone who knew both of us.

I imagined going in for an interview and some matronly figure being able to spot the 'inner me' after an hour of soul-searching questions, and her saying, 'You know, Sarah, you would be simply perfect for . . .' well, would it be David, the entrepreneur, Simon, the writer, James, the executive, or possibly even Paul, the company director? And then I would go off on some lovely posh dates and be engaged by Christmas.

I may have been getting ahead of myself though, as there were several major flaws in this lovely scenario. Firstly, it all looked, well, a bit grown up. All the people in the pictures were very good-looking but more in their fifties than in their thirties. Reading through the blurb on the websites, I was beginning to get the impression that this was all an older person's game.

'We cater for 30+ through to 70+,' proclaimed one. This was the first time in a while that I had felt like the baby in the group but I wasn't sure that a company that catered for 70 year olds would be able to find what I was looking for.

Secondly, what kind of man would sign up to something like this? A very busy, rich, professional executive type, maybe someone who had made his millions and now wanted someone to share it with. Or maybe a workaholic who couldn't find the time to date and yet wanted a relationship. He would probably be absent for much of the time and we'd have to schedule times for sex via BlackBerry Messenger.

Perhaps they were well-preserved divorcés, globe-trotting executives who lived in hotels and out of suitcases, dotcom millionaires who had only met women in cyberspace and lonely aristocrats who needed a woman's touch for their crumbling country homes rather than for themselves – I had a whole list of people I suspected would be on the books of agencies like these and it rather put me off.

However, those concerns were secondary compared to the price. I simply couldn't afford to pay the membership fees, and, more importantly, certainly didn't want to. I had been guessing about the thousands of pounds when I was talking to Timothy, but it turned out to be rather more accurate than I'd hoped. One agency quoted me £6,000 for the standard membership and a whopping £10,000 for the executive package, which included a minimum of 18 introductions and other perks, such as your own personal matchmaker. Ten thousand quid! For that, I would need to be actually guaranteed a husband. And not just any old husband, but the actual man of my dreams. I could put it on my credit card but only if a return on my investment was guaranteed.

In true journalist fashion, I tried to see if I could get a few dates for free, just as a 'taster', if you like. If I was going to hand over thousands of pounds, I wanted to be sure that I was doing the right thing.

Unfortunately, none of the agencies I contacted was up for that.

'Our members are very private people,' I was told frostily by one.

'I'd change the names,' I pleaded. 'I'd be very discreet.'

'Sorry,' said another. 'You simply can't be a journalist and single. People will never trust you.'

I thought that seemed a little harsh. Did being a journalist and single mean that I was completely undateable?

'You did it for *The Sunday Times*,' I pointed out to one of them, who had the article on their website.

'That was different,' I was told. 'There happened to be

some gentlemen who didn't mind being written about. But we'd never do it again.'

I wasn't getting very far and, to be honest, I was feeling rather intimidated. All these agencies seemed to be run by very posh women who had a way of speaking to me as if I was rather inferior to them. Maybe this was just my own insecurities coming out – Eleanor Roosevelt was supposed to have said: 'No one can make you feel inferior without your consent.' However, I didn't believe that sentiment for a second. I was certainly not consenting to anything but they were definitely making me feel particularly insignificant and pathetic.

Some of them weren't even on my wavelength. I asked one particularly Sloaney woman, who was suggesting that I entrust my future happiness to her in exchange for several months' salary, where she would recommend that people of my age and situation could go to find suitable partners.

'Oh, you know, art galleries, museums, that kind of thing,' she said airily.

Now that may work in American romcoms, but I was somewhat sceptical that this could actually work in real life.

'Are you actually recommending that I go on my own to a museum or hang out at art galleries trying to pick up men?' I asked rather suspiciously.

She let out a shocked laugh. 'Oh, Lord, no!' she said in horror. 'I thought you meant on a date.'

'So where should I go to actually meet people?' I repeated.

She laughed again. 'Oh, meeting people is simply impossible in London!' she tittered. And this was the person who was supposed to be a dating expert.

If it was indeed impossible to meet people in one of the most vibrant, cosmopolitan cities on the planet, then it meant that the millions of single people living here were completely screwed. Or not, as the case might be.

I declined to take up her offer of membership.

I was beginning to feel that the whole thing was deliberately rather opaque. It seemed a massive gamble and quite a leap of faith to hand over such a large sum of money to an agency when you had no idea at all how many people they had on their books, or how many of them were suitable for you. At least with internet dating you could see everyone who was on the site for free, so, if you did a search on, say, *Guardian* Soulmates for 41-year-old single men who lived within five miles of Clapham, you could find out exactly how many there were (with a picture: 172). I could sign up for Mrs Snooty's Exclusive and Professional Agency to find that the only man they had on their books was over seventy and had been married four times already.

The following week, at a friend's party, I did actually meet a woman who had joined a dating agency a few months earlier. We clicked immediately. Tara was fun, friendly and had an engaging manner and openness about her, which made her great to talk to. She was also pretty, intelligent and entertaining, and, in spite of really wanting to find a long-term partner for marriage and babies, she hadn't got that sad, resigned or desperate air that I was terrified I would get before long.

Tara had spent the last ten years in relationships that hadn't worked out for one reason or another, watching her body clock tick down and her fears of being single and childless for ever rocket up.

When it came to online dating, she was an expert. She'd done all of them and had been on hundreds of dates. She was still optimistic that it would all one day work out for her – she has friends who met on *Guardian* Soulmates and got married three months later – but earlier this year she hit a particularly low patch. So she signed up to a dating agency.

'So, how much did it cost and what do you get for that?' I

asked, getting straight to the point like a typically nosy journalist.

Tara looked a bit depressed at this point. 'I paid £1,500 up front,' she said.

'Blimey,' I said.

'I could have paid monthly but it would have been £1,700,' she said. 'So I thought . . .' She trailed off, obviously trying to work out what had possessed her to fork out such a large sum of money. 'I think I was at a particularly low ebb,' she said uncertainly.

'Well, look, if it works, it's a complete bargain,' I offered. 'If they find you a husband, they could charge double and it would still be worth it.'

She drooped even further. The signs were not great. When she'd gone for her initial interview, they had asked her what her top age range was for a prospective match. At the age of 38, she wanted to meet someone around her age but was realistic to know that that might not be possible, so she said that up to 50 years old would be fine.

They looked at her doubtfully. 'What about 60?' they said hopefully.

It turns out she'd had to compromise on height too. Apparently, they didn't think she should specify how tall someone should be, so Tara at five feet nine was now terrified she was going to be set up with someone barely over five feet. A 60–year-old short person.

'Anyway,' said Tara, rushing on, 'they promise to set you up with fifteen dates over two years . . .'

'Fifteen dates over two years!' I repeated, shocked. 'But you want them all as soon as possible, don't you?'

The thing with getting stuck into this dating game is that, after a while, you become so used to sharing the intimate details of your life and listening to other people's that the social niceties no longer seem to apply. I have become like one of those old ladies who loudly discuss bodily functions in the queue at Boots. I had met Tara for all of five minutes and here I was implying very obviously that, because of her age, she was about to run out of eggs and so she really needed to get all her paid-for dates as quickly as possible. Two years was just far too long for her to wait.

Thankfully, she took my outburst in the spirit of sisterhood in which it was intended.

'I know,' she said. 'But they said it takes them six weeks to fix you up with the next date. It doesn't really, of course, they could look at their list and do it in half an hour but for some reason they don't.'

I had my own theories about why they didn't, namely that they were so short of men that they were buying themselves time to find suitable candidates. This wasn't just me being nasty and suspicious, I hasten to add. Before meeting Tara, I had been doing some research of my own.

One guy I spoke to said that he was offered free membership to an upmarket dating agency because there were so few men on their books. He was happy to go along to dates but had a certain type of woman in mind – tall, skinny, blonde, the usual. He was honest with the company and said that he didn't particularly fancy larger women. The first four dates they set him up with were all fairly, well, fat.

By the fifth, he had to say something, and he told the woman, 'You are perfectly lovely and let's have a great evening. But you should really demand your money back. You are being set up with people who have specified that they are looking for something different and, if they are charging you money to set you up with me, then you are being completely ripped off.'

Another woman I spoke to said that the agency she'd signed up to admitted that they were so short of men they trawled through the online dating sites to find blokes to sign up, again for free. This seemed astonishing to me. Surely the women who were signing up to dating agencies had already been doing the rounds of the online dating sites themselves and still were? So they were essentially being charged thousands of pounds to meet up with people they had probably already seen online and passed on.

As for Tara, she had been on two dates so far. The first was a guy in his late forties who was in a terrible mood because he had just flown in from a business trip and was tired from the plane journey. (The timing of the date had been his idea, incidentally.) He didn't drink, which unnerved Tara, and the entire date, in which he talked about himself and didn't ask a single question about her, was over in 50 minutes. Amazingly, at the end of the evening – well, the end of the date at least – he suggested that they go on a second date. Tara politely declined.

She then had to wait six weeks for her second date.

'Now, I've been on hundreds of dates and dating sites and read articles about it and I know all about matching people up,' said Tara. 'I know it's not necessarily about having exactly the same interests but about having the same outlook on life, or shared values – those kinds of things in common. I also know that there is no way in a million years I would have chosen my second date if I'd seen him online, and the agency certainly didn't spend six weeks trying to set me up with an appropriate person for me. They basically went, she's a solicitor, he's a solicitor, they'll have loads in common. If I'd seen him online I wouldn't have clicked on him, and if he'd contacted me online I wouldn't have replied. Frankly, I'm so fed up with them that the third date had better be a vast improvement or I'm going to sue.'

It turned out the second date was with a guy in his fifties who lived with his mother in a village near Brighton and had never been to London before. Tara has lived in London all her life and gets panicky whenever she ventures beyond the M25. It was never going to be a great match.

She wasn't the only one who was feeling rather let down by dating agencies. Another friend of mine had signed up with an agency and had been on just one date but was so depressed by it that she was thinking of never going back and just writing off the £2,000 she'd just handed over.

'He was too old, too set in his ways, too rude, too bossy,' she said. 'I thought, "If that's the best they can do, then I'd rather not be here at all."'

Another friend who signed up had specified that she definitely didn't want to go out with a man who already had children. She was sent on two dates and both men had children. She complained and managed to get a small refund, but remains angry about it.

'These people are promising things that they just can't deliver,' she said. 'If they really haven't got any men who are suitable for you – and I wasn't being choosy but the question of children was quite a fundamental one to me – then they should just say so.'

The next day, I found that, in fact, they could be rather too honest.

I was walking back across Clapham Common after a catch-up drink with my only single male friend, Damien, when the owner of a dating agency rang me. She was very friendly and chatty and within about two seconds had made me want to shoot myself.

'How old are you?' she said briskly. 'Thirty-eight? Men will run an absolute mile from you. An absolute mile. They want someone who is fertile, but who doesn't want children yet, so someone in their late twenties or early thirties. Why would they want someone who may not be able to have children but, if she can still have them, would want to have them straight away? No, men will run a mile. Sorry, dear.'

She paused for breath, while I sat down on a bench on the side of the common and tried not to cry, or rush out into the traffic. I felt as if I was being punished for being so ancient. But 38 wasn't that old, was it? And surely she couldn't be saying that no 38 year old in the history of the world has ever found someone who will go out with them?

'Well, I can't really help being 38,' I said rather crossly. 'So are you saying that it's completely impossible for me to find anyone and I should just give up now?'

'Don't give up!' said the woman cheerfully. 'But what you need to do is juggle.'

The conversation had gone from suicidal to surreal.

'I beg your pardon?'

'Juggle men,' she said, as if such a thing were an entirely normal concept. 'No man wants to think that you've latched on to him because you are desperate for babies, even if you are. So you have to show him that you aren't just seeing him, you are also seeing lots of other men, and that will pique his interest as well as reassuring him that you are not just targeting him.'

But how could I juggle *no* men? It sounded like an Eastern philosophical conundrum. Hadn't she just pointed out that men would flee from me as if I had a particularly virulent form of the Black Death? Now I was supposed to somehow persuade more than one of them to go out with me so I could juggle them.

'So is there no hope for me then?' I asked rather pathetically.

She thought for a moment. 'You should go for men in their late forties,' she said. 'Men who suddenly decide that they do want children after all but also realise that the women they are most interested in – the young, fertile ones – are not going to be interested in them, so they will actually go for the older women who might still be able to have children.'

Great. It all sounded a really appealing prospect. So, given all this, why would I want to sign up to a dating agency?

'Let me tell you,' the woman said, 'frankly, men in their thirties are deserting agencies likes ours in their droves. They really are. They are going online instead, when you can see everyone and take your pick.'

So there it was. A moment of honesty and one that didn't surprise me at all.

I told Tara.

'Gosh, I wish I'd known that before,' she said sadly.

I was feeling pretty depressed by this time too. Not depressed to the tune of £1,500, but really quite low. It was one thing knowing that you were not at the most attractive age for men – I know that single women in their late thirties are seen merely as walking, ticking clocks to most men – but to have it confirmed by a dating expert was another. It felt as if the whole thing were a complete waste of time, a fantasy that I would ever meet someone. Now I was so miserable I could barely put one foot in front of the other, let alone summon up the energy and willpower to get out there again, especially as this time I would feel as though I should be ringing a large bell and shouting, 'Unclean! Thirty-eight-year-old woman coming through!'

I could feel that terrifying sad look starting to settle on my face. It was time for a massive confidence boost, or at least a second opinion. It was time for some tarot.

27

Consulting the Cards

There is a little fishing village on the Hampshire/Sussex borders that is rightly proud of its annual show. Every August bank holiday, come sun or, more usually, rain, the recreation ground would be taken over by tombolas, a bouncy castle, stalls selling homemade cakes and second-hand books and CDs, a miniature railway and a huge marquee where local farmers and gardening enthusiasts competed for various prizes – the prettiest fuchsia, the largest carrot, the finest cabbage, and so on.

Wandering around there this August bank holiday, past the clog dancers and the dog acrobatics display, I spotted a plain white tent. A sign on the side read simply 'Tarot'. It seemed a strange thing to have at a village fair, next to the lifeboat charities and the 'splat the rat' challenge, and I wasn't sure that I'd ever seen it before, but it called out to me like a siren.

Just the previous week, in one of those conversations where I was banging on about my search for a man and the other person felt obliged to actually come up with some useful advice, one of the girls at work had said to me, 'You should get your fortune told. You know, like with tarot cards.'

I looked at her to check whether she was joking but, no, it

appeared that she was completely serious. Mind you, this was the same person who had previously suggested surfing and mountain-climbing, so she was obviously trying her best to come up with something other than the by now tedious 'Have you tried online dating?' line.

'I think you should do it!' she insisted. 'Honestly, it could be fun.'

She started frantically Googling 'tarot card readers' and printed out a whole list of them. They looked completely wacky to me. I knew nothing at all about tarot apart from what I'd gleaned by watching Roger Moore trying to seduce Jane Seymour in *Live and Let Die*. Not only had I been brought up in a C of E household, which certainly had no time for all this mystical nonsense, but also I was now a cynical journalist and viewed anything from horoscopes to fortune-telling as a complete waste of time.

There was a self-styled 'Gypsy Rose Lee' who told fortunes next to the public toilets across the road from Bognor Regis pier. I liked to think that there would never be a time in my life when I would need to seek advice from someone who practically lived in a toilet.

On the other hand, what had I got to lose?

Well, my sanity, apparently. When my sister heard that I was going to have my tarot cards read, she told me that she had just heard about a friend of a friend who, equally single and desperate, had consulted a fortune-teller. He had told her that she would never find love in this country and would have to move overseas. What's more, the woman was actually taking this advice seriously and was preparing to up sticks and head off abroad. Unfortunately, the oh-so-helpful fortune-teller hadn't even told her where she should go to find that elusive man (even after writing off every one of the millions of single men in Britain) so she was just flying blind. This only served to convince me even more that both those who practised tarot and those who were stupid enough to believe in it were numpties who deserved everything they got.

However, in the spirit of opening my mind to new experiences and doing things that people suggested to me rather than just dismissing them out of hand, I'd told my colleague that I would at least check it out, then completely forgot all about it. So, when I walked past the sign saying 'Tarot', I thought that there was really no excuse for me not to give it a try.

Unlike most fortune-telling booths I'd seen (in films of course, except for the Bognor pier-toilet woman), this was an open tent so you could see the guy inside sitting across a table from his customers. This comforted me. I realised that I hadn't been looking forward to going behind a curtain and being trapped in a darkened room smelling of incense and lit by red candles and being greeted by a mad old woman in a veil. In the middle of a village fair next to a field where a group of middle-aged couples from the local dance class were currently dancing rather sedately to Lady Gaga's 'Bad Romance' over a crackly tannoy system, it all seemed very normal and unthreatening.

A notice on a table next to the tent offered 'starter' readings of ten minutes for a fiver and a twenty-minute, more detailed, six-month reading or answers to specific questions for a tenner. It seemed like a bargain. So, telling myself to be open-minded and not at all sniffy about it – nor to leave the country if the reading wasn't great news – I signed up for a 20-minute session. What surprised me was that even though it was fairly early in the day – the fair had only been open for an hour or so – so many people had already signed up. He was almost already fully booked for the day. All the names seemed to be female, too. I bagged one of the few remaining slots, which was in an hour's time, and headed off to mooch around the rest of the show.

At my allotted time I was back, now clutching various cakes, tombola prizes, books and all the other stuff I can never resist acquiring from fairs. The previous woman was just leaving – smiling, I was glad to see – and the whole thing seemed to be run extremely smoothly for a one-man band. According to the leaflet I'd picked up when I was booking my reading, Tim Bagshaw had been practising tarot for more than twenty years, having had 'a chance meeting with a medium' in 1989, and had given up his job in the IT industry six years earlier to go full-time in the tarot world.

He was into all sorts of things that good Anglicans were unlikely to have much contact with, including numerology, astrology, spiritual healing and crystals, but tarot seemed to be his main thing. The picture in the leaflet showed a friendly, smiley man who looked far too nice to tell me that I was utterly undateable in the UK. If I was going to get involved with fortune-telling at all, this seemed as good a place to start as any.

Tim waved me in and gestured to the chair opposite him on the other side of the table. In person, I realised that he was the spitting image of my flatmate Jeff, which made me instantly and quite irrationally warm to him. While he didn't have Jeff's New Zealand accent – that would have been just too weird – he had all his mannerisms: a friendly smile, a welcoming demeanour, and he was as unthreatening and non-Gypsy Rose Lee as you could wish for.

'Is there anything specific you'd like to know?' he asked. 'Or are you just wanting to find out more about the immediate future?'

'I know absolutely nothing about tarot at all,' I said, thinking it best not to mention *Live and Let Die*. 'But I was going to ask what the next year held for me, both professionally and in my personal life.'

I also thought it best not to hit him straight away with: 'When on earth am I ever going to find a flipping husband?'

He nodded. 'OK,' he said. 'Well, we can either do a general outlook over the next few years, or I can give you a detailed idea of what's going to happen in the next six months.'

Six months seemed awfully precise, but as it was August bank holiday this would take me well into the next year. And a forecast covering a few years would probably be very vague. Having been hugely cynical about the whole thing until roughly two minutes earlier, I was now counting on the cards to, well, if not actually provide my future husband's phone number, at least give me some idea as to when he might actually show up.

I decided on the six-month forecast. Tim shuffled his pack of cards while I sipped nervously from my can of Diet Coke. I did feel quite apprehensive, which was surprising as I wasn't expecting to believe a word of it. He split the pack and handed me half to shuffle – which I did with difficulty, as they were much bigger than ordinary cards – and then did the same with the other half.

'I first shuffle them to clean them of the last person,' he explained, 'and then you shuffle them so they are your cards, personal to you.'

He then dealt out twelve cards, in two rows of six. The Lovers – which I recognised as being wielded by James Bond – was the first card out. This could only be a good sign, surely? Unless it was all some kind of code in which the Lovers actually mean, I don't know, a new haircut or a forthcoming purchase of garden furniture.

He peered at the cards. 'These are laid out so they represent six months, from September to February,' he said. 'This line here relates to work, and this line relates to your personal life.'

He had another look. 'Well, from this, I would say that it's looking very good for your love life. It's looking pretty good for your work life too.'

I felt – how did I feel? – as if a weight had been lifted off me.

'Very good for your love life!' I knew it was daft and they were just cards, and words uttered by a complete stranger, but I felt such a feeling of relief, when I hadn't actually expected to feel anything at all. It was the fact that someone had said, with confidence, that something good was going to happen.

I had been trying to convince myself for such a long time now that it was all going to turn out well but it was getting harder and harder to believe. Throughout this search, I had always said that it would be so much more bearable to do if only I knew it was actually going to work.

The awful thought that kept me awake at night was that, in spite of all my efforts and all my hopes and those of my family and friends, nothing was going to happen and I was never going to meet anyone. That was so depressing, so dispiriting, so terrible to contemplate, and yet here was someone saying, with confidence and even an air of certainty, that this was not the case and there was someone waiting, out there, for me. My massive overreaction made me realise how much I had been hoping for someone to tell me that it was going to be OK. It was astonishing how much comfort I got just from someone saying it.

Tim was talking about the first card in my work row: the Page of Wands. Apparently, this didn't mean a new career or a dramatic change like that, which was just as well, but a new challenge within my current job. The Lovers card – which, yes, did mean a romantic interest, thankfully – could be linked with my new project in some way apparently, not necessarily meeting someone actually at work (which was just as well, considering my previous Will fixation), but maybe through a trip or a new contact.

So that was September sorted.

October, said Tim gravely, was the most difficult month of the six. A nameless card with people fighting on it and the Hermit: this meant that, when it came to the relationship, if it felt right and people around me were generally supportive of it, great, but if it was too much effort to get people behind it, it was best to leave it.

However, after the battles of October came sunny November – not only a good time to take a holiday, which I wasn't doing, but the Page of Cups, which signalled a new relationship or the flourishing of the September one.

Tim had asked me if I was single once the cards had been laid out and he now told me why. 'If you had been in a relationship already, I would have said that this would be fertility,' he said. 'But I'm assuming this is more the flourishing of the relationship instead.'

'Oh, I dunno,' I thought happily. 'New man in September, pregnant by November, that would mean it would be born in . . .'

I gave up calculating the maths to listen to Tim tell me that there was a contract to be signed in December, and the High Priestess was there to tell me to trust my gut instinct on whether it was right or not. I was rather enjoying all this. Not only did he seem to have the utmost confidence in my love life springing back into existence, but it was also rather reassuring to have someone pointing out the future pitfalls and what to do about them in advance.

In January, the King of Cups with the Strength card told Tim that the relationship signalled by the Page of Cups, or possibly the Lovers, was growing and it was time for another holiday. There seemed to be a lot of emphasis on holidays here – was that what a lot of people consulted the cards about? Tim said the combination of holidays and romance, coupled with the gap in December, meant that maybe my lover didn't live near me, and we had to do our separate family thing over Christmas but would travel to be with each other before and after. I was beginning to like this narrative logic.

In the final month February, Justice and the Page of Pentacles, whatever they were, showed the culmination of an exam or a qualification – I couldn't think what that might be all about – but that wasn't all. Over the first three and the last three cards, Tim laid two more cards – the Devil for the first month and the Fool for the last. The Devil card didn't look so good – the jolly naked Lovers who had started off my reading so well were now in Hell looking rather less cheerful.

'That's a warning of what will happen unless you sort out the potential problems with your relationship that I mention,' said Tim. 'Not to force it if it doesn't feel right.'

This made a lot of sense – not just because it makes sense anyway – but because my experience with Barney had taught me that I was utterly bloody desperate for a relationship and therefore probably completely wide open to all sorts of nonsense. However, it seemed all was not lost: even if I did end up in Hell, I still had my holiday in November to look forward to. So that was all right then.

The Fool, which I'd naively assumed to be a bit of a duff card, turned out to be the top card. All was well when he was around, apparently, because he was the overlooked everyman in mythology who was sent off on all the quests and would get the girl and the kingdom, against all the odds. All would go well where he was looking, said Tim, fiddling the card around a bit, claiming that he was looking at the contract or even, rather improbably, November's new relationship.

Three more cards were dealt out – all sunny positive signs apparently, though I heard barely more than that, with my head completely full from taking it all in. There were the

Star, the Wheel of Fortune and the Hierophant – which I'd first read as a Heffalump – and then we were done.

I stood up, my head spinning.

'So does it mean that I'm going to meet someone?' I asked again, rather pathetically wanting a firm confirmation of this miraculous news.

Yes, he said, it did. And most likely next month. But I had to keep my head.

'But it was a really positive reading,' he said, beaming. 'A great first reading.'

I wondered what would have happened if I'd had a bad set of cards. 'Do you tell people if it's not looking great?' I asked. 'You know, "Brace yourself, I've got some bad news"?'

Tim nodded gravely. 'Yes,' he said. 'I do tell them. But –' he leaned forward conspiratorially '– they usually already know.'

I paid my ten pounds and practically levitated out of the tent. I felt amazing: happy, confident, able to take anything on, invincible. I felt ten feet tall and super-attractive. It was as though I was surrounded by a force field that made me feel as if I was radiating gorgeousness. I could see how people might get addicted to this feeling, or want to go back time and time again to get that boost of security, of knowing what was going to happen in the future and already know how to deal with it. I still didn't rationally believe in it but, for the next few hours, I loved the feeling it had given me. I felt able to take anything on.

I felt as if I could walk into any pub and be the centre of attention.

I walked into a pub. There was no one there. I ordered a beer anyway.

I phoned my sister and babbled incoherently down the phone at her, high on beer and tarot. I'd worked out that, if I was to meet someone in September, away from home but related to work, it would have to be in either Panama or

Liverpool, where I was scheduled to head off on work trips.

'I'm going to meet someone next month! In Panama or Liverpool!'

My sister was impressed. 'Blimey, they're very accurate these people, aren't they? How do they know it's one of those two places?'

My mum was more to the point. 'Well, he sounds lovely, darling! Is he single?'

He wasn't and that would have been just too weird. But, while the feeling of absolute invincibility didn't last beyond that evening, the feeling that the future held something pretty special certainly did. The whole dating game had started to take its toll on me recently. I had felt jaded, exhausted, cynical and despairing – hardly the best position from which to find the man of my dreams. Now, just for a while, I had got my mojo back.

28

Lust for Life

After months of complete non-activity in the dating department, it seemed that I was finally back in the game. A week's flirting, shagging and having my heart very briefly broken in Greece, followed by my midnight plunge into the ocean and the married man's arms, made me feel as if the world was once again full of possibilities. When you are single for such a long time, it can feel as if you are so shut off from that part of life that you are never going to get back there again. Sometimes you forget it even exists, and that kissing, cuddling and making love, or just being with a guy, are things that other people do. It almost comes as a shock when you remember that you also used to do all those things.

When I was 18 and in love with Scott and just discovering how wonderful sex could be, it was pretty much all we did. The idea that 20 years later I would spend months and months without being with someone, that I would have sex once in a blue moon and then retreat, or be forced, into celibacy, would have seemed unthinkable. Looking at it from this side of 30, I found it utterly depressing that my teenage self would be having so much more sex than I was. I was jealous of the younger me.

Now, it was as if a whole neglected part of me had started to wake up again. Greece had definitely started it, and it wasn't just Barney. Simply being in an environment where people were flirty and horny made me realise that it had been way too long since I'd been flirty and horny. It had somehow carried through to the Caribbean, when, even after that wet and wild night, there was still enough unspoken sexual tension in the air for me to feel very sexy again. Of course, it was frustrating that someone as lovely and sparkly as Ian was married, but that's the way it was. I wasn't going to pine over him but I was going to use the way he made me feel to get back out there again.

Now, like buses, the men who had been absent for so long were arriving in threes.

There was David, an old friend, who I jumped on after a night's binge-drinking. Well, I didn't physically jump on him, but I might as well have done. We'd spent from 6 p.m. till midnight drinking red wine and, after despatching the rest of our party into various taxis, we decided that we could do with some more booze. So we hit the casinos. David took out £200 and gave me half. It didn't last too long – I crashed out at the blackjack table, while the roulette took his money. We were debating getting some more drinks in when, drunk and horny, I said, pretty much out of the blue, 'We could get a room instead?'

He looked at me. 'You what?'

I was rather astonished about how brazen I was being. 'You know, a hotel room. For the night.'

We hadn't so much as kissed at this point. Or at any point over the ten years that we'd known each other.

David looked incredulous, and, thankfully, also rather delighted. 'Are you being serious?'

I gave him what was my most winsome, drunk, flirty smile. 'Totally.'

He bounded up from his chair. 'OK then – I'll be back in a minute. Don't go away.'

I was left marvelling, not for the first time, about how easy it was to chat up a guy you're not in love with. It really could be this easy. It wasn't as if, at this particular moment, I didn't fancy him – I did. Because he was there, I was drunk and fancied spending the night with him – not just anyone, but *him*. I knew him and liked him and had never fancied him before or even thought of him in that way before, but it seemed, that night, I did. He was single and I was single, so what did it matter?

However, had it been someone I fancied, or wanted to go out with, or had any of those sorts of feelings about at all, I simply wouldn't have been able to casually proposition him like that. I suppose I'd spent so long flirting pointlessly and one-sidedly with Will, who had utterly failed to react to any of my overtures, such as they were, that I was in shock that anyone actually reacted positively to my advances.

It certainly seemed that men were not as likely to turn down a horny woman as I'd thought. Silly, naive me. Why hadn't I learned that years ago? I'm not saying that I would have had more sex, but I would have maybe been a bit more blatant about going up to guys I'd really liked, and shown that I was keen on them. But, of course, if you are interested in someone, there's much more to lose if you get knocked back. It seemed very unfair that if you cared about someone it meant you were far less likely to be able to approach them and let them know. I suppose that that's what alcohol was invented for.

I had another drink and lost some more money at a ridiculous game called three-card poker, which wasn't really at all like poker. I started to wonder whether David was ever coming back and whether it would be a good or bad thing if he didn't. I had decided that I wasn't particularly bothered either way, and turned to go.

At that moment, David appeared, somewhat out of breath.

'I've been to four different hotels and they're all completely full,' he said.

'Really? What on earth is happening in Kensington tonight?'

'I dunno,' he said. 'But there's the one the other side of the Tube station left if you want to check that one out?'

So, feeling a little daft, we set off for the hotel. It was also closed. We sat on a wall and looked at each other.

He could tell I was about to say that we should call it a night and was having none of it. 'I'm not going to let you bail out on me now,' he said.

It did seem a little unfair to start the whole idea running and then disappear before anything had actually happened. And I was rather curious after all.

We kissed, for the first time. And went back to mine, instead.

The week after I got back from the Caribbean trip, one of the companies in my sector was holding its annual pub quiz for journalists. The only other time I'd attended was the first year, in its head office, and it was a pretty soul-destroying experience. Fresh back from New York, I'd gone on my own and been dumped into a team of also-rans, the rejects from the *Times* and *Telegraph* teams who'd had too many people turn up and had to ditch one of their number. We'd had four people when everyone else had eight, and had called ourselves something like 'The Also-Rans' just to ram the point home. We inevitably came last. I went home vowing never to go again.

However, two years on, I was trying to keep my resolve not to turn down any invitation that might involve meeting new people, particularly journalists and particularly where there was alcohol involved. Of course, I ended up going on my own once again, the only two colleagues I had managed to persuade to come with me having bailed at the last minute, and so I was foisted on the Dow Jones team, who seemed like a nice enough bunch.

The pub was packed and round every table was a cluster of hacks. All the national newspapers and broadcasters were there – BBC, Sky, *The Times*, *The Telegraph* – and the industry journalists such as Drinks International and JustDrinks. com. It was a free bar all night and the quizmaster was adept at whipping the crowd up into a state of cheerful competitiveness.

In spite of a heroic effect on my part, we managed, inexplicably, to come last and my team drifted off into the night. However, fuelled by the best the bar had to offer, I table-hopped quite cheerfully, bumping into old friends and colleagues and joining in the prevailing debate, which was how much the winners, Sky, had cheated by having at least four people above the maximum number allowed.

The evening became a cheerfully chaotic melee of gossip and alcohol. I put my newfound confidence to good use, not by obviously or even deliberately flirting, but just by being interesting and interested, by chatting to people I hadn't met before rather than sticking with my good friends. When the pub finally shut, it seemed perfectly sensible for me to be whisked away with a group of assorted hacks who thought that midnight on a work night was way too early to go home, especially when we were still capable of standing and there was alcohol in the world waiting to be drunk.

We wandered off in no particular direction but happily found a pub that was still open and willing to serve us. There was a rather nice bloke called Jake in our group who had a flat near mine and we bonded over our mutual love of cigarettes – I was in my 'I'll smoke when there are nice boys also smoking' phase – and so, when the lights went out in that pub, it seemed logical that I would share a taxi back with him. The other girl in our group, who had also been chatting with Jake, lived in north London, totally the opposite direction; such are the small levers that direct our fate.

His flat was gorgeous – a little haven of calm just round the corner from the hubbub of Clapham Junction – and we sat out in the large garden smoking and drinking champagne. I was in one of those moods – which I had permanently been in when I was younger, and so rarely am now – of being completely in the moment and fully enjoying it, not thinking about what I had to do tomorrow, or should have done today, or how this moment would be really great if only I'd eaten less/drunk less/had more sleep the night before/worn something different/didn't have to work the next day.

I felt completely comfortable in my own skin, fairly buzzy from the alcohol but not too much so. I wasn't thinking at all about the next day – I knew I'd suffer for this night, but I was prepared to deal with that later – and I was just having a really nice time doing something completely different with a perfectly nice guy I'd never met before but who I knew was a colleague of one of my best friends (and therefore not an axe-murderer, I had assumed).

We drank some more. I discovered his old record collection and went through it, playing each one. We danced and danced like idiots to lots of '80s music. It was a lot of fun.

Then we started kissing and spent much of the night and the next morning having fun in his bedroom. I felt young, thin, confident and happy, and even the sober part of my brain – the bit that tells you when to stop drinking, when to go home, how to be sensible – was just standing back and saying, 'OK, I see that you're having fun and pretending to be young again, just go for it.'

At about 8 a.m. it seemed that the new day had finally arrived, and so, after a quick shower and some more fun, I said a cheerful goodbye. I ambled home across the common, cycled into work and settled down for a quiet day in the office, wondering where my hangover was hiding and still rather surprised about how debauched a pub quiz could be. Jake had been great fun and, while there was part of me that thought it would have been nice to do it again some time, I wasn't bothered enough to actually do anything to make it happen, such as contact him.

Suddenly, the world seemed to be full of opportunities and possibilities and I was quite keen to go off and explore some more. While I didn't plan on making a habit of sleeping with people quite so quickly – my newfound confidence may have temporarily turned me into a bit of a tart, but even I knew that that wasn't the best way to find a husband – it was certainly more fun than speed-dating.

29

On the Shelf

It did seem that life was moving on, for other people if not for me. Holly, who had met her boyfriend while cycling round Vietnam just 18 months earlier, emailed me to let me know that she was pregnant. Charlotte returned from honeymoon glowing with rather more than just newly-wed bliss and announced that she was pregnant too.

And at a former colleague's leaving party in the City, Will got a round of drinks in and then announced, 'Oh by the way, Michelle is . . .'

He didn't need to finish the sentence. We all leaped in with congratulations and clinked our glasses.

I was very happy for all of them. I really was. I wasn't one of those people who got depressed at other people's happiness or success, and didn't subscribe to the notion that, if good things happened to other people, they were less likely to happen to me. Holly's and Charlotte's stories in particular filled me with hope, as they were proof that life could change so quickly, that this kind of thing did happen to people, and so there was no reason why it shouldn't happen to me.

But there was still the fact that it hadn't yet happened. The more I looked, the harder it seemed to find. Having been so open about being single and wanting a husband and babies,

I was starting to worry about becoming typecast as a single person, the modern equivalent of a maiden aunt. It seemed, in retrospect of course, incredibly simple for everyone except me to achieve all that I was looking for. Go to Vietnam and come back with the father of your child. Say hello to a new colleague at work and at the same time say hello to your new husband. I'd gone to Morocco and come back with nothing except blisters and some nice photographs. I'd gone to work and come back with heartache and a deep sense of embarrassment about the whole Will thing.

Now, everyone else's good news just threw into sharp relief the fact that they were moving on and I wasn't.

The whole dating thing was starting to feel like a rather bad and tedious homework assignment. There was absolutely no fun in it any more. I would sign up to things, go along to them with less than zero expectations, which would usually be met, and then I'd go home feeling glad that the evening was over. The idea that this was supposed to be enjoyable had long gone. I started to look upon nights when I wasn't going out as my 'evenings off' – I'd go out with friends, go for drinks with colleagues after work or just head straight home for an evening with my flatmates, luxuriating in the freedom but at the same time feeling rather guilty that I wasn't trying to pick up men in the supermarket on my way home.

I was definitely becoming jaded. I needed some time out from the whole process, not just to recharge my batteries and to clear my head from the monotonous grind it had become, but also because I couldn't imagine that I would be a very attractive prospect if I started turning up to dating events exhausted, pissed off and desperate to leave.

When my friend Lucy emailed me to ask if I fancied staying for the weekend, it seemed like a perfect chance for a break. Lucy is one of those really good friends whom you hardly ever see but when you do meet up again it feels as if time hasn't passed at all. We knew each other from school and, while we had gone our separate ways afterwards, we had always kept in touch and had seen each other about once a year ever since. Now she was living in a lovely little cottage not far from Reading and was engaged to a guy called Robert.

News of my dating project must have reached her as she wrote in her email: 'I've got loads of opinions about how to find a man, as I think I must have bought every single book on the subject. I was going to throw them all away but wondered if you'd like them instead.'

This seemed an interesting prospect at least. So far I hadn't gone down the self-help-book route because, as I saw it, the only problem was the fact that I didn't know any man I wanted to marry and I didn't think they'd be literally hiding in the pages of a book, although that would be a great idea if anyone wants to run with that one. But I was more than happy to read them if it was the secret to Lucy's success. I duly got in my car and drove west, discovering to my surprise that Lucy lived only about half an hour outside London, whereas she had seemed a million miles away.

After I'd met her man, and her cat, and we'd opened a bottle of fizz, we decamped upstairs, leaving Robert to do the cooking. There was an astonishing number of books on the shelves of her spare room that seemed to be entirely dedicated to the subject of men. She threw them down to me as I sat on the floor drinking, reading each title as she pulled them off the shelves. Books about how to find a man, how to know if he's the right one, how to get away from the wrong one, how to have sex, how to say no to sex, when to say yes to sex, how to look after your man, how to enrich your life without a man, how to admire men, how to find intimacy, how to respect your man, how to be feminine, how to make him desperate for you, how to flirt, how to spot time-wasters, how to spot the one and how to attract good men.

I was exhausted just reading the titles.

'So, which one worked for you?' I asked Lucy. 'And how did you ever meet a man if you were reading these all the time?'

Lucy threw the last of the books over to me with a huge sigh. It sounded like a sigh of relief. She was also looking quite angry. 'These books are awful,' she said. 'These books did absolutely nothing for me apart from tell me how I needed to suppress or change every part of me in order to find a man.'

I sipped my wine. This wasn't what I had expected to hear. 'So why did you buy them then?'

It turned out that Lucy had spent months feeling at a very low ebb. She felt utterly single, completely worthless as a woman and as a human being, and not worthy of love or happiness. So she started buying books to fix that.

'I read these religiously,' she said, sitting down on the floor amid the pile of books. 'I read them, I believed them, I did everything they said to do and it just ended up making me feel a million times worse.'

'What kind of things did you do?' I asked, curious.

'Well,' said Lucy, looking even angrier, 'one of the books said that you shouldn't have sex for six months.'

'Six months?' I repeated. I couldn't work out if that was a long time or not. I supposed it was a long time if you were going out with someone, and not so much if you weren't. I was fairly sure there had been times when I hadn't had sex for six months but that was because I wasn't going out with anyone at the time. I couldn't imagine actually meeting someone and just watching telly for the first six months though.

'And not just sex,' said Lucy. 'But you know, anything. No masturbation, nothing.'

This seemed a bit steep.

'I'm a very sexual person,' said Lucy earnestly, 'but I went along with it, and it made me go completely mad. You weren't supposed to do anything sexual, so I didn't, but it was just awful.'

'But what's the point of not even being able to sort yourself out?'

It didn't seem to make any sense to me. If you were in a state of frustrated sexual arousal all the time, was that supposed to attract men? Especially if they couldn't do anything to, erm, ease the situation.

I flicked through some of the books on the floor.

'When you try to corner a man into commitment, you drive him away,' said one.

'Don't call him,' said another.

'The things that we women admire in each other are rarely attractive to men,' said a third.

I read on, appalled.

'A man cannot derive any joy or satisfaction from protecting a woman who can obviously do very well without him. He only delights in protecting and sheltering a woman who needs his manly care and protection, or at least appears to need it.'

I read it out to Lucy, who nodded.

'These types of books are all about denying who you really are, as a woman, as a person – they are all about hiding all the parts of you that make you who you are, so in the end you have no idea who you are. I spent months trying to act a certain way, dress a certain way, and I was completely lost. And any man I met never got to know me at all.'

'So how did you get out of it?'

'I finally realised it was making me completely unhappy,' she said. 'And not only was I denying lots of things about myself – the fact I am a sexual person for example – but I was also wearing different clothes, making sure I was looking, saying, thinking and doing everything I could to find a man while not paying any attention to how I was feeling or whether I was happy or not – it just got too much. So I went on a workshop about how to find myself as a woman, how to reclaim my sense of self, myself as a feminine person rather than trying to hide who I was as a woman, and stopped thinking about myself solely in terms of needing a man.'

It sounded slightly too touchy-feely for me but then I am a cynical hack and Lucy has always been into things like yoga and herbal remedies. Mainly, though, I completely agreed with her. I wondered whether in my attempt to find a man I had also completely lost sight of who I was and what I wanted in life.

'I then started to focus on me and what I wanted,' said Lucy, echoing my thoughts. 'I realised that there were loads of things that I had been putting off, or waiting to do until I had found a man. All of a sudden, I realised that I didn't have to put my life on hold. It was just little things mainly, but I painted my bedroom, and planted a herb garden, and went on holidays on my own instead of waiting for a man to do them with. And I think that I was much more open to meeting Robert when I actually did.'

Emboldened by her newfound womanhood, Lucy joined a local drama group and, when some of them invited her to come with them to a fancy-dress ball in Vienna, although she would usually have said no, she said yes and met Robert on the dance floor. They are getting married next year.

'I really believe that, if I hadn't been content within myself, I wouldn't have met Robert,' Lucy said, as he called up the stairs to say that dinner was ready. 'Either I wouldn't have gone to Vienna, or joined the drama club, or been feeling confident and attractive when we met, but I do believe you have got to love yourself before anyone else can love you, and most of these self-help books do the exact opposite.'

I pondered all this over dinner. The self-help books looked

so hideous in every way I was quite happy to take Lucy's word for it. I agree that, if you are happy, confident and content, you are bound to look and feel more attractive, and have the confidence to go out and do interesting things, and naturally be more likely to meet someone.

But I also know heaps of girls who are completely neurotic basket-cases with no self-confidence at all who have found husbands. I know married women who wouldn't dream in a million years of walking into a pub or restaurant on their own and the thought of going on holiday by themselves would induce a nervous breakdown, whereas I've always been happy in my own company and love heading off on my own. So I think I'm already pretty content with myself and who I am. But maybe I'm too self-reliant. Being completely confident and not looking like you need a man at all is apparently not a very attractive quality, according to the books I was now leafing through.

There's a real chicken and egg debate here. I may be confident enough to walk into bars on my own and eat alone in restaurants but that's because I've had to be, not necessarily because I want to be. I could never see the point of not watching a film at the cinema or not trying out a gorgeous new pub I'd just discovered just because I didn't necessarily have someone to go with, but now it seemed I was being punished for being able to stand on my own two feet.

I discussed this with my sister later.

'But that's exactly our problem,' she said. 'We've always been too good at being on our own. We've been on holidays on our own, bought houses on our own, done the whole lot on our own.'

'But that's not by choice!' I wailed. 'We've done lots of this stuff on our own because we've had to. Or we wouldn't have bought houses or gone on holiday at all. What else were we supposed to do?'

'Well, maybe we should have given the impression that we were helpless, even when we weren't,' she suggested. 'Remember Ellie from school? She's not particularly good-looking, or amazingly charismatic, but she's never been without a bloke, because she makes them feel needed. She's as capable and intelligent as the rest of us, but she never lets guys know that and it's totally worked for her.'

There was a thoughtful pause.

'I blame our mother,' we said simultaneously.

We had been brought up to believe that showing an interest in boys was 'chasing' them, that we should make our own way in life and not have to rely on a man for anything, that we were quite capable of doing anything a man could and that to grow up with the dream of marrying a nice man and looking after his children was a massive betrayal of everything that women had been fighting for. And where had it got us? On the shelf.

So much for feminism.

I talked to Lucy about how tired and fed up I was feeling about the whole process.

'It's not surprising,' she said. 'You are so totally focused on finding a man that you have completely forgotten who you are.'

I wasn't entirely convinced by this but I listened anyway.

'You don't need a man to complete you,' she said. 'You need to be happy in yourself before you find someone.'

'I thought the reason that I hadn't found someone was that I'm too happy in myself?'

'Well, I don't think you are, right now, are you?'

'No, because I'm trying to find a man. If I could find one, I'd be happy, surely? And the problem is that I haven't found one yet, so I'm not happy. But before I was trying to find a man, I was happy.'

I thought about what I'd just said. I couldn't honestly work out what I felt. Was I happy being single or not? Either way, it was obvious that I was totally confused. I didn't seem to know what I thought any more.

I sighed.

'Look, I don't think this search is doing you any good at all,' said Lucy. 'You need to take time out, to rediscover what you want, to be happy within yourself. Do what I did, and get back your sense of yourself as a woman.'

'And how did you do that?'

And that was how I found myself dancing without any pants on in south London the following Saturday.

30

Earth Mother

The workshop Lucy had recommended was run by a woman called Star Anise. 'Discover your femininity,' said her website, which promised:

> A journey towards finding the potential of womankind
> to change the world. Get back in touch with what it
> means to be a whole woman in the new Millennium.

I was very aware that, as a journalist – the adjective 'cynical' seems tautologous here – and as a woman who didn't think she was particularly unconnected with what it meant to be a woman, I was probably not the most obvious participant. However, there was clearly something that was going slightly awry within me, and, as this seemed like a million miles away from what I would usually do if I was feeling a bit discombobulated with life generally – my usual coping mechanism is to hibernate for a day or two, with lots of sleep, steak and spinach – I thought that it seemed worth exploring.

In addition, I believed that it really had worked for Lucy and therefore there was no reason why it couldn't do something for me too. I was definitely going to go with an open mind, and not a Fleet Street one. I hated journalists who were intent on being cynical and sniffy about anything out of their usual field of experience and who would rather be standing outside feeling superior than getting stuck in and actually learning something.

Lucy, quite understandably, had her doubts too. 'Please don't go unless it's something you really want to do,' she wrote in an email. 'I feel like you should decide whether or not you want to do it for yourself first and foremost, rather than it being something to tick off a list.'

I assured her that I was going with no preconceptions but with a willingness to explore something completely different. I had no idea what my reaction would be, but I hoped that I would be open to the whole experience.

In fact, just getting there had been a measure of my commitment. To make it to the assigned venue on the day of the workshops, I had had to be in Morden by 9 a.m. on a Saturday, which meant I had to get up at a time more usually associated with having to get on a Ryanair flight, and, to make matters worse, England were playing France in the Rugby World Cup at the same time that the workshop started.

I walked to catch the Northern line, thinking, 'Open mind, open mind,' while I tried not to be diverted into any of the pubs I was passing, invitingly full of men and huge TV screens. I sat on the Tube with my special bag of things that all participants were asked to bring: a blanket, a cushion and some pens and paper. I was also, as instructed, wearing something loose and floaty I could dance in. I felt as though I were off to playgroup and had forgotten to take a toddler with me.

The place itself seemed pleasant enough, a leafy courtyard and dance studio tucked round the back of the high street. I paid my £75 to the bubbly 20-something on the door, finished my espresso, tried not to think about the rugby and went inside. My first impression was, blimey, that's a lot of incense – the large room was hot and fuggy with the smell, not unpleasant but fairly overpowering. My second was that there were an awful lot of women there, all prepared to pay a sizeable amount of money and spend the entire day in this room getting in touch with their womanhood. There were about 25 of us, ranging from mid-twenties to mid-fifties, but most of them were my age or younger. It was a whole new world to me.

Star, a friendly, slim woman with long dark hair and a welcoming smile, called us to sit round in a large circle. We sat there, waiting expectantly. It felt like a prayer circle. Star introduced us to her helpers, one of whom was the bubbly woman from registration. She seemed in an incredibly good mood and straight away told us why. 'I've just spent the entire week in a yurt with this really gorgeous guy,' she giggled.

I was slightly taken aback. I'd thought the whole point of this workshop was to be self-empowered, rather than rely on a man for happiness. Or maybe I was overanalysing.

Star began to speak. She talked at some length about what it means to be a woman, how powerful femininity can be, but how it has all been lost in our male-dominated, patriarchal society.

She described how women used to be connected to the earth, to the plants and the trees in the forest, but that we had lost all that. She spoke of the disconnect between who we are now and who we used to be, and can be again, of the value our male-dominated society places on facts, decisions, competitiveness and power, and physical wealth and strength, and how little value it puts on more female traits such as emotion, intuition, empathy and instinct.

She told us that women who showed signs of intuition and instinct were denounced in days gone by as witches and in more recent years as mad, or hysterical. She also talked about how female sexuality was either ignored or misunderstood or was seen as a threat and therefore suppressed or denounced. There was a lot of talk about bleeding, wombs, cycles and the sacred feminine. There was none at all about the rugby score, but that was OK. The real world had simply faded away.

After Star's talk, it was our turn. We all stood up and had to say our names and what we were feeling and why we were here. Some people simply said they were nervous, or excited, or looking forward to the day, while others spoke longer about how they needed to get their confidence back, or to be able to deal with issues facing them.

Several people were already quite emotional and were already crying – we were clearly all coming from very different places. Some mentioned that they were currently 'bleeding' and how centred this made them feel.

When it came to my turn, I said, very honestly, that I was completely new to all this, I felt quite secure in who I was but most of my close friends were men. I worked in a mainly male-dominated profession that valued male characteristics and maybe it was about time I explored my feminine side. This was all true and I meant it sincerely. However, I was feeling rather disconcerted about so much emphasis on wombs and bleeding. It wasn't that I was especially squeamish, but surely women were much more than wombs and bleeding? Or maybe that was me completely missing the point.

We then spent some time walking around the room, approaching people individually and saying a number of phrases. 'I am a woman'; 'I am a powerful woman'; 'I am a sexual woman'; 'I am an emotional woman' and, for a change, 'I am a man'. It felt like acting class again.

I was finding the intimacy a bit of a challenge already, looking into someone's eyes, speaking directly to them, and after each affirmation I wanted to bow or smile or do something to acknowledge that we had spoken. I had no problem at all saying 'I am a powerful woman' as that seemed perfectly natural, but saying 'I am an emotional woman' I found rather, well, embarrassing to say. I was certainly learning about where my own boundaries were, to use the accepted lingo. Sometimes we had to say the phrase while clutching between our legs. When it came to saying 'I am a man', people stood taller, adopted manly characteristics and spoke louder.

'Well, they would, wouldn't they?' said my inner voice. I squashed it back down.

We lay on the floor together, wrapped round each other. We paired off and talked to each other about what we liked about being a woman. We sat down and imagined a whole line of women going back behind us, from our mothers, to our grandmothers, to their mothers and all the way back through history. I liked this exercise best of all. I imagined a whole line of woman stretching back behind me, like one of those effects when you stand in between mirrors and see images snaking back into the deep distance. All those women, and I was right at the head of the line, being supported and loved by all of them. This was powerful stuff.

'Now think of how many of those women were assaulted, raped, physically, mentally and emotionally abused,' intoned Star into the meditative silence. 'Think how many were oppressed, silenced, had no power, had no say over their lives and their bodies.'

My reverie was ruined. Rather than a line of powerful, supporting women, I was supposed to think of them as victims, raped and abused by those perpetrators of a patriarchal society. I was starting to get annoyed.

'Now look into the eyes of the woman opposite,' said Star. 'And tell her of your deepest hurt.'

I thought. I couldn't think of anything. I know that makes me very, very fortunate, but I simply couldn't think of something that would not seem completely pathetic after hearing about the mass rape of my grandmothers' grandmothers.

I hadn't been raped, or abused, or seriously attacked – the only things that would come close were a couple of times when I'd been attacked by various men while on my travels but I'd punched and yelled my way out of those situations – and my heartbreaks on discovering that first Daniel and then Patrick were cheating on me. But they were trivial in comparison.

'I'm sorry, but I really haven't anything to say,' I confessed. I felt very lucky to feel such a fraud.

Thankfully, it was time for lunch.

I marched round the block for most of the break, ranting at my mum on the phone. 'Why is it all about abuse and unhappiness?' I said. 'Why are women being told that their history is full of unhappiness? Why is this workshop so intent on making us all feel like victims?'

My mum got nostalgic down the end of the phone. 'Aah, it reminds me of the '70s,' she said.

Jesus. And there was still half a day to go of this.

The only saving grace had been that, by hearing all about what bastards men were for raping my ancestors, I'd missed seeing England be completely humiliated by the French at the rugby. There was a silver lining after all.

I went back in and talked to my fellow attendees. Quite a lot of them had been to these events before, I was quite surprised to learn, or had gone on the longer residential courses. Everyone spoke very highly of Star in the same way that Lucy had done.

'She is amazing' was a phrase I heard a lot, as well as 'She has really helped me'.

I began to suspect that this kind of workshop was meant for people who were unhappy, who had been damaged in some way. I didn't feel as if I had a great hurt that needed healing, or addressing, and I was obviously very glad of that. I could be in denial, of course, but how would I know?

The afternoon was the dancing session and seemed to be the high point of the day for many of the women. Star showed us first. She planted her feet shoulder-width apart, then started swaying and moving her hands.

'It's a mixture of the feminine and the masculine,' she said, 'and will connect you back to the earth through your womb space and your yoni.'

Talking of yonis . . . apparently, it was much better to not have any obstacles in the way of this transmission of life-force. There wasn't much we could do about the plastic floor covering but, well, we could take our tights and pants off. Thus attired, well, actually rather less attired, we began.

I was a knot of tension at this point. I felt stupid, draughty and in urgent need of a strong drink. But I did it. Along with the rest of the women, I danced, swayed, shouted and yelled. For ages. Much to my surprise, the dance came quite naturally – there did seem to be a rhythmic force coming through me that bent my knees, bowed my head, moved my hips and set my whole body in motion. Some of the others were old hands at this and were stomping their feet, shrieking and moaning, eyes wild and shining and hair swaying.

There was high emotion in the room – we had to shout 'NO' very loudly many times, thinking of all the times when we wanted to but hadn't been able to, and one woman collapsed in tears. A lot of hurt was being addressed; a lot of pain was being relived and hopefully removed.

After an hour or so of that – we had done away with clocks and watches earlier, as time, said Star, was a 'linear construct of a patriarchal society' – we calmed down in groups of threes, holding on to one another's chakras (near the womb space, aka one's tummy) and breathing in step with one another.

Then it was time for discussion. I found this the most interesting and useful part of the day, which might be reflective of the fact that, at heart, I'm a words person. Women, taking turns to hold the stone of speech, rather like Piggy's conch, talked about their hurts, their bad experiences, the times when they hadn't been able to say no and the times when they had, but it had been ignored.

Some women had harrowing tales of child abuse and marital rape, others spoke of boyfriend troubles or being too scared to date, but they were very real areas of pain for these women and they saw this as a fulfilling and productive part of their healing process.

I met up with Adrian in the pub opposite for a pint immediately afterwards. Maybe after so much concentrated femininity I needed a dose of male behaviour to rebalance me, or maybe I just always fancy a drink after a tough day.

I'm not quite sure how or if the workshop helped me regain my womanhood, or even work out if I'd lost it. The link between being a woman and being oppressed or abused really annoyed me, although considering a lot of the women in the room had been hurt in some way, who am I to deny such a link?

'The thing is,' said Adrian thoughtfully, sipping his drink, 'you are probably way more masculine than I am.'

I nodded. 'I think you're right,' I said, not sure whether to be glad or sad about that.

'And it's not a gay thing,' he added.

I agreed. 'I know,' I said. 'It's nothing to do with that. But I probably do have lots of typically masculine traits. Maybe it would be good for me to temper them with some more female ones. But I'm not sure that taking my pants off and talking about wombs and bleeding is the way to do it.'

Poor Adrian. No guy, straight or gay, really wants to hear that.

'Did you hear about the rugby?' he said.

31

It Pays to Advertise

As the months went by, I was beginning to wonder if anything would work at all. I felt completely exhausted, demoralised and generally downhearted about the whole process. I wondered if the whole thing might be a self-defeating exercise in which the harder I tried, the less I would actually be successful. Far better, surely, to relax and let things just happen naturally? Maybe the fact that I was so focused on dating, so focused on finding the right man, was in itself ruining the whole thing anyway. There can be few sights more off-putting than a woman who is desperate for love and is charging through the male population discarding men in the same way she rummages through a pile of discounted cardigans in the Gap sale.

'Just relax and take it easy,' my friends would say, as I dragged myself out of the house once more in my man-hunting uniform, while they lounged on the sofa watching *Downton Abbey*. 'If it's no fun, then it's just not going to work anyway. If it's destined to happen, it will happen.'

This wasn't just something they believed for me, but also for themselves. At Charlotte's wedding, Jeff and I were sitting out in the courtyard, while various relatives were risking life and limb in the ceilidh inside. Small children were threatening to hurl themselves into one of Chatsworth's many fountains and Jeff kept on popping up to prevent disaster and shepherd them back into the arms of their exhausted parents. As he returned to his seat, chuckling indulgently over other people's children, it occurred to me that he was incredibly broody.

'Oh, I'd love to have kids,' he said instantly when I mentioned it. 'Absolutely love to.'

I was slightly surprised too, as I wondered how this would ever happen, given what seemed to be his total lack of interest in actually pulling. I mean, we were at a wedding at that very moment, a wedding at which there were several very nice-looking single girls (no other single men at all, it will be unnecessary to point out), and he had spent most of it smoking outside on his own. Even now, when the dancing demanded that he pair off with some young lady and manhandle her around the dance floor, he was very much opting out of the proceedings.

'Well, that's lovely, but how is that actually going to happen?' I asked, probably undiplomatically but then we were both rather drunk.

He smiled, relaxed and contented. 'Fate,' he said. 'I would love to meet someone, and if it's meant to happen, it will happen. I don't know where or when, but it will happen.'

As I sat there in the evening coolness, sipping my champagne and watching the newly-weds swirl around on the dance floor, I wondered whether I should be taking a more relaxed approach. Maybe it was all down to fate and I was ruining it by working too hard at it.

However, I argued with myself in typical Libran style, one could say that I've been leaving it up to fate for the last 20 years. If I were a bloke, or 20 years younger, then maybe I'd be more than happy to leave it all up to fate. But I can't afford to do that any more.

In ten years' time, Jeff will no doubt be sitting smoking in his own back garden, while his own adorable children are being read bedtime stories by his lovely wife, whom he happened to bump into one evening on the night bus, or queuing up for cigarettes at the 24-hour window of the BP garage at the end of our road. I could very probably still be single, having spent my fast-dwindling patience, energy and financial resources on trying whatever it takes to make up for fate's inadequacy, but in fact inadvertently buggering up whatever great plan fate had been storing up for my 40th birthday surprise treat. Great.

It was the not knowing that killed me. If I knew that fate had it all under control and that there was nothing for me to worry about, then I could have sat back, stolen one of Jeff's cigarettes and been as relaxed as he was. But I didn't know that, and so I couldn't relax, and by not relaxing I was probably as attractive to the average guy as a coiled rattlesnake or a primed hand grenade.

Bugger fate. I decided to go all out for this. No messing about, no fudging the issue, no feigned nonchalance and no 'I'm just going to play the field for a while and see what happens'.

I was 38 and I wanted a husband and babies, in that order and as soon as possible, please. So I took out an advert saying just that.

I've read the satirical magazine *Private Eye* since before I really understood what it was. My dad has had a subscription for decades now, and every other Wednesday morning the thin black and white edition would arrive with the rest of the morning post. At first, I used to ignore it because it looked so boring, and then later I read it just for the cartoons. But, as my interest in politics and the media grew in my teens, so did my appreciation of what *Private Eye* was all about – rude, irreverent, iconoclastic and, above all, funny. Now I was a newspaper journalist, I would devour it word by word every fortnight, turning first to the 'Street of Shame' section to see what scandals were occurring in my own profession.

There had always been a classified adverts section at the back of the magazine, where adverts for holiday cottages jostled with pleas for financial assistance. There was also what used to be a thriving 'Eye to Eye' section in which people advertised for love but that had pretty much disappeared with the internet. However, I thought it might be worth a try. Moving away from the numbers theory and towards the 'you only need to attract one guy, the one who's right for you' approach, I thought, might attract the type of guy I was looking for – a bloke in the media who has a sense of fun, is confident enough to reply and, oh, I dunno, it seemed like it was worth a shot.

I also decided that, instead of the usual pretence about 'just wanting to meet someone', I would lay it right on the line. I wanted a husband and a family – well, why not say so? This would also avoid all the inadvertent phrases with double meanings – 'friendly' means 'into threesomes' or other such confusion.

My advert read:

> Fun, attractive female journalist, 38, seeks romantic, sporty, intelligent guy, 30s/40s for adventures and hopefully LTR/marriage/babies/the lot!

Well, I thought, if that isn't clear and direct, I don't know what is.

I paid my £50 (fifty quid! No wonder classified ads were dying out) and waited for the ad to appear. It did within a few weeks and looked, well, exactly how I expected it to. I decided that maybe it would have been better to put writer rather than journalist though. Journalist seemed a bit, well, scary.

I showed it to people at work – like I say, I had lost any sense of embarrassment about this by now – who thought it looked, well, fine. Though no one had an idea what LTR meant.

'London Transport?' said one, looking confused.

I snatched the copy back. 'It's long-term relationship,' I sniffed. At least, I hoped it was.

I'd set up a new email account for replies, which had London in the address so hopefully people could work out where I was.

I logged in. To my surprise there was already one email there, which had been sent at seven that very morning. That was speedy! It sounded promising too:

Hi Sarah. I saw your ad in PE, and thought it was worth giving replying a shot! It is beautifully to the point. I am in my late(ish) thirties, relatively sane, and 6'2". I am public school educated (don't hold that against me!) For work . . . I'm afraid I work for a bank. Would be great to know a little bit more about you.

All the best, Chris.

I was rather surprised, I have to admit. I had practically no expectations at all, apart from the fact that I was probably going to get emails from all sorts of perverts and lunatics, but this guy not only seemed sane but actually rather perfect. A good job, tall, posh – I belatedly realised how utterly shallow I was. Still, he sounded great, funny and he could punctuate.

I replied back in suitably interested fashion and we started off a whole email conversation. He turned out to be interested in books and wine, and travelled a lot for his work. He admitted to being a born and bred Tory – well, I couldn't afford to be too choosy – and sounded like a really nice, genuine guy.

We even discussed what we were looking for:

> I think, without reflecting your answer back, someone
> to do different things with – I like doing different
> things, and it's more interesting when you have
> someone to do it with. I think the most important
> thing is to meet someone where both of your lives get
> enriched. I thought your ad was very straightforward
> and honest, which was why I replied.

I was halfway to being smitten. I couldn't wait to meet him.
Emails are fine up to a point, but you only really know
whether you can stand each other when you're actually face
to face.

Then he emailed: 'Shallow question I know, but what do
you look like?'

Fair enough, I thought. We were moving along the
acceptable stages of email courtship. I'd send him a picture,
he'd send me one, we'd meet up for a drink and then, who
knows? I pictured our wedding invitations done in the style
of a *Private Eye* cover, complete with speech bubbles. I duly
emailed him a picture – not a particularly fabulous one, but
one in which I looked perfectly fine, all laughing and
cheerful.

Chris promptly died. Or emigrated to an island that has
yet to discover broadband. Maybe he had been electrocuted
by his computer and had developed an acute phobia to
emails.

Or just couldn't stand the sight of me.

I think the odds are that it was the last one.

Either way, I never heard from him again. After all our
friendly emails in which, I'd thought at least, we were
developing some kind of rapport, at the first sight of my
hideous face he dropped me like a stone.

'Maybe he didn't get your email,' my sister said hopefully.

'Yes, he got all the other emails, but the one that happened to have a photograph of me attached, that got lost in cyberspace,' I said, trying not to sound too bitter.

I was pretty pissed off, I have to admit. It seemed pretty bloody rude behaviour. I wasn't that bad-looking, was I? I was no supermodel but really . . . He must have known that by not replying he would have left me feeling completely rubbish. He could have at least written something polite, along the lines of: 'You look great, but I'm afraid I've just met someone/turned gay/entered the priesthood.' You know, a diplomatic lie. Instead – nothing.

Urged on by my sister, I emailed him one more time:

> Hi Chris, I hope all is well with you. I'm assuming you haven't replied because your situation/thoughts might have changed but just wanted to make sure that you're deliberately not replying rather than waiting for an email from me that might not have arrived! I'm assuming the former, but it would be nice to receive a closing 'good luck on your search' kind of email, which at least makes it clear, rather than me always wondering . . . All the best, Sarah

To which appeal, there came no reply.

Oh, well. Onwards and upwards. It seemed that, if I wanted to be made to feel pointless and unattractive, I could do that any day of the week rather than pay good money for the privilege, but that wasn't the right attitude. Besides, there was, if not exactly a flurry, then a certain amount of activity in my inbox. If that doesn't sound too rude.

They ranged from the surreal to the improbable. One guy wrote:

> Hi Sarah, I've just read your innovative advert in 2
> September edition of Private Eye and just thought I'd
> send you a message and to give me something to do.
>
> Best wishes and I hope you are well.
>
> Alan x

I wasn't quite sure what to make of that. He appeared to have
sent me a message without any content.

Another guy sounded promising but worked in Namibia
and only made it back home to London once every blue
moon.

Another one sounded very keen and not at all put off by
the fact that he lived a hundred miles north of Sydney. 'Shall
we Skype?' he wrote.

'Why?' I thought.

Another sounded – well, possibly a little bit dull.

> Hi, I'm just responding to the ad. I'm a 30 yr old
> man. I fit your description and I'm looking for
> similar. Dave.

My age didn't seem to have put some people off. Another
email read:

> Hi fun attractive female journalist. I'm romantic, sporty,
> intelligent and looking for LTR, and the lot. Not quite
> at 30 yet but don't hold it against me – almost there!

Tempting but . . .

One guy sounded like a rather secretive professor:

> Would describe myself as intelligent. More on that
> later.

One guy gave little information, but sounded supportive at least.

> Sarah, you are going to be inundated!! Good luck with marriage, babies etc. Choose wisely. Dom

I wrote back: 'Thanks for your interest but you didn't say why you were writing?' to which he replied: 'Sorry, but I'm married, so don't meet your requirements. Just wanted to say good luck!'

Which was sweet. But it was a little strange when he emailed again: 'How goes the shortlisting?'

I began to wonder about Dom's intentions. I sent another email: 'Your interest is touching but intriguing . . .?' to which he replied: 'I suspect that intrigue piques your journalistic mind? Touching can be good . . .'

Great. My first sleazebag.

I didn't email again.

Over the next few weeks, I received a succession of plaintive emails from him: 'Did my reply fail to elicit a smile?' asked one.

Later, 'A reflective silence?' he asked.

I wanted to write back and tell him that my love life might be a hilarious source of entertainment to him or at least a vicarious escape from his evidently mundane life if he took such an interest in mine, but I didn't. Life is definitely too short.

Some men who started off promisingly ended up rather less so. One guy wrote that he loved history, geography, travel and was a keen skier. All perfect, then he asked: 'What's your favourite dish?'

Before I had a chance to reply, he had written again. 'I mentioned I enjoy cooking. Anything really from the traditional roast to stir fries. I do like to do a salmon en croute. Do you like it?'

I was considering what my favourite dish might be when another email arrived. It detailed at great length his long walk along a canal that weekend. When yet another one arrived asking if I'd been up to anything interesting, and adding, 'I had a walk along the canal towpath for about an hour. Otherwise just chores really,' I decided that we probably didn't have a great deal in common. I wrote him a nice email saying as much.

Some were probably rather too frank:

> Just thought better be honest I'm getting close to 50, never been married, running out of time and looks, though not my sense of humour.

Reading through these and, to echo the Beatles, thinking of all those lonely people out there, was starting to get depressing. One bloke, a fireman from North London, sounded nice and we exchanged emails for a while, but every time I left more than a day between emails he would get very stressed and would write:

> Is all ok? Have I pissed you off? Please let me know if I have and please give me a chance to make it up to you. You sound interesting and someone who is worth getting to know. I have not tried to upset or deceive you in any way.

I reassured him that all was fine but the next time the same thing happened:

> Are you OK? Please email! Whatever I've done I apologise and I'll make it up to you.

After a third one, it was clear we were not destined for great things.

Oh well, I thought, when the emails finally dried up. It's been an interesting experiment at least. I was reading out some of the more choice ones to my flatmates one lazy afternoon, when I found one I didn't even remember reading. Simon's email was funny, interesting, had just the right amount of detail – he was into cycling, running, lived in south London – and said he was 'looking for someone who can hold up their end of a conversation, enjoys sport or even just being outdoors and prefers people to the internet'.

I looked up from my computer to find my flatmates looking very excited, like lots of little meerkats.

'He sounds lovely!' Alex said. 'Really nice. You should meet!'

He seemed to be up for meeting too, which was always a good sign, I thought – I was getting fed up of exchanging endless emails only for it to go nowhere.

> I'm currently on gardening leave so if you fancy doing lunch near where you work, then that would be great and neatly offers you a 1 hour get out clause should I make a hash of things. Attached is a photo taken this summer.

'Gardening leave! He's rich! He has a good job!' Jeff said, sounding like a male Mrs Bennet.

I wrote back and Simon replied straight away, inadvertently ticking many more boxes. He'd just cycled from Land's End to John O'Groats and he was about to head off to a beer festival in Germany.

'Beer and cycling!' Charlotte said approvingly. 'You guys are a perfect match.'

We arranged to meet for lunch in a nice foodie pub down the road. He was friendly, chatty and we got along fine. Lunch started at 1 p.m. and finished at 5 p.m., which can't be a bad thing, and we were both cheerfully merry when we finally rolled out into late-afternoon Clapham. There was no instant chemistry as such, but I've come to think that there really is no such thing in these circumstances. Chemistry when you're plastered and spy some cute guy across the bar at midnight, yes, chemistry when you're in a pub on Tuesday lunchtime talking to a virtual stranger, no. But it was a very nice lunch indeed.

The day after, Simon flew off to study the Galapagos turtles for three months. And then, who knew?

I reported back the good news to my flatmates.

'See,' said Jeff, nodding wisely. 'The power of the press.'

32

Enough Is Enough

I was starting to feel completely and utterly run down – emotionally, physically, mentally – the whole lot was going. I was going out too much, drinking too much, eating either lots of rich, posh food or nothing at all, and not getting anywhere near enough sleep.

Every morning, I would wake up with a grimy, sandpaper mouth, peel my gummy eyelids open, do a big, bear-like stretch and yowl, and then reach for the Nurofen before turning over and trying to get an extra 20 minutes' sleep. I would start to wake up on the bike ride into work, overtaking cars on the inside with inches to spare as they queued over Battersea Bridge.

The adrenalin from that – plus a hot shower at work, followed by toast and several espressos – would keep me going until lunchtime, when my hangover and general tiredness could be fought no longer, and then I would stagger, thankfully, to the gym. No workout kit needed here, though – I would swim a couple of lengths in the tiny pool, have a quick pummel from the hot jets in the jacuzzi, and then wrap myself up in a cocoon of white fluffy towels and lie on one of the deckchairs next to the pool. Entirely cut off from the world with an eye mask and ear plugs, I would have a straight 40 minutes' sleep, motionless, dreamless, a mini-coma from which I would emerge to find that a whole load of children had been shrieking and splashing near my prone figure without disturbing me in the slightest.

I would still be bleary but after a brisk shower would be back at my desk, eating my lunchtime sandwich and feeling at least a hundred times more able to face the rest of the day. Straight from work, I'd head off to a date, or a work do, or some horrific singles function, and then the whole process would start again, leading inexorably to a crippling headache and the Nurofen breakfast the following day.

One Friday, I woke up and decided that I'd had enough. I just didn't want to do this any more. I had been more or less permanently drunk or hungover for months now. My body had lost any attempt at having a shape, my hair was dry and scratchy, my face was getting lined and old, and I dreaded to think what my liver looked like. It wasn't just the exhausting schedule that seemed to be almost entirely reliant on alcohol, though, but the emotional strain it was having on me. Frankly, I was turning into a complete basket-case.

I felt incapable of relaxing, feeling that every hour of every day I should be on the hunt for that elusive husband. The fact I was completely failing to find him was also on my mind, ruining my sleep and any sense of equilibrium or contentedness in my life. Having been very happy with my life before – happy with my friends, my social life, my single status – I was now resenting the fact I was still – after all this bloody time and hard work – single, and I was beginning to believe that this was actually it. I was never going to find someone, never going to have children, or a family, never be important to someone, never have someone looking out for me. The thought was so utterly devastatingly depressing that, even if I had not been head-crushingly hungover each morning, I would still have wanted to turn over and pull the duvet over my head.

The night before this revelation had been a particularly bad one. I had a book launch and then a date to go to, and I had felt so terrible all day that even my life-saving sleep at lunchtime hadn't really had its full effect. I had to have another shower at work before setting off just to wake myself up, and had to strongly resist the urge to simply lie down on the tiled floor and close my eyes for a few minutes. That way lay disaster, I knew, so I showered and dried my hair and generally made myself look as beautiful as possible before hurtling out of the office and onto the Piccadilly line.

The book launch was for the *Aphrodisiac Encyclopaedia*, written by the chap who made the Bloody Mary vodka I had been drinking at the Harvest Festival all those months ago. I wanted to go along and show my support, but I also thought – in one of my more optimistic moments – that it might be a good way to meet people, nice posh blokes who did something creative for a living and who would be put in a romantic mood by all this talk of love. And the aphrodisiac food that was being served. Or something.

As I say, it was a long shot, but when you are trying to cover all options, you have to, well, cover all options. Having a date immediately afterwards was a slight flaw in the plan – both had been rearranged and now unhelpfully clashed with each other – and it meant that I had about 45 minutes to scour the room for food-horny husbands before dashing off, but this was becoming typical of my life at the moment.

Due to an incorrect postcode on the invitation and my over-reliance on my BlackBerry, I went to the wrong Tube station and so I made it to the party with just ten minutes to spare. This didn't give me much time. I congratulated the author, bought his book and got him to sign it. I chatted to some nice posh blokes who looked like they worked in literary circles but who were all clutching their women in front of them like shields in case the aphrodisiac canapés were so powerful it would cause them to lose all reason and run amok amid the waiting staff. Finally, I drank two dirty martinis like they were water and ate oysters and quails eggs like a starving man at the Ritz. Then, mouth crammed full of some raunchy delicacy, I threw myself out into the street once more, into a cab and into a traffic jam.

Thankfully, unlike the lizard-suited date from hell, my date had taken his phone out with him, so when I arrived – just ten minutes late, not bad, I thought – he hadn't already eaten two courses without me.

Eric had emailed me via eHarmony.

> You're the first person that I've been sent who mentions triathlons. The rest of your profile seemed great too, so if you want to chat or meet up that would be great. I haven't got much time for all those questions and answers though.

This sounded very promising indeed. Apart from a flurry of activity when I'd just joined, hardly anyone had emailed me through eHarmony. I'd no idea whether my picture was just way too hideous for any man in the entire world, or whether I'd inadvertently written 'allergic to sex' when I'd meant to write 'likes classic films' on my profile, but the whole thing was turning out to be an entire waste of whatever it was I was forking out each month. After the last guy had died of exhaustion having actually made it through to 'non-guided communication' – after getting through a seemingly endless number of rounds in which we established that neither of us was racist or mean, I never heard from him again – I'd pretty much written the whole thing off.

So for me to actually get an email was a pretty big deal – not least because it showed that the guy was proactive and capable of making decisions. If you subscribed to the theory that men are only interested in the chase – no hang on, that's just the guys I've been out with – that men want to make the first move, Eric certainly ticked that box.

His profile seemed great too: he was good looking, 41, had the requisite 'action man' pictures that most men seemed to have on their profiles – him hiking, him running, him skiing, etc. – but had indeed done several triathlons including a half-Ironman, which I thought was pretty impressive.

He also had four daughters. When I mentioned this to my sister, she whooped and said, 'That's great – you can overtake everyone else!'

While I didn't exactly subscribe to her theory of having children as some kind of 100-metre race, the idea of him having children certainly didn't put me off, which it might have done in the past. I talked it over with my ever-supportive flatmates, who very sweetly were showing no signs of getting bored with my constant blether about men, and even seemed to be finding the whole thing extremely entertaining, no doubt because it meant that they didn't have to get out there themselves, but could just listen to tales from the frontline while watching *Spooks* from the comfort of the sofa.

'Four daughters?' said Alex. 'That's pretty heavy duty . . .'

'I know, but I thought it could actually be a good thing,' I said, wandering round the kitchen in search of food. 'It means that he's not afraid of commitment, he's taken on responsibilities, you know, that kind of stuff.'

'You mean he's a grown-up,' observed Jeff from the back door where he was smoking a cigarette.

'Exactly. And he can share all the parenting duties with his ex-wife while I get to have him when he's into doing more adult stuff,' I said, hastily clarifying before the boys started sniggering, 'I mean, pubs rather than playgrounds.'

'If he's got kids, he's going to be less likely to just be

messing around,' said Alex. 'He's going to be giving it a lot more thought than the rest of the guys out there.'

I thought about it a bit more myself. 'And you know, having four daughters, he might be quite keen to have a son . . .'

Jeff choked on his cigarette. 'Not that you're thinking too far ahead,' he said, once he'd stopped coughing.

'Well,' I said defensively, 'there's no harm in thinking about all the possibilities.' I didn't mention that my mum was so excited about Eric she was practically ordering a hat.

We had exchanged about six messages in rapid succession – Eric wrote interesting, chatty, well-punctuated emails – and he had suggested meeting for a drink.

The place he'd chosen, just off Carnaby Street, was nice but seemed rather on the restaurant side for a first date. It was pleasant enough, though, a little French bistro in the heart of London. Eric was sitting upstairs and when he turned round as I walked into the room I had the feeling of relief rather than the feeling of 'oh no' that usually happened at these moments. He was not at all bad-looking, exactly as in his photos, if a bit smaller than I'd imagined, but friendly and cheerful and only the slightest hint of sad eyes.

We got a bottle of wine and some starters to share, and chatted away fairly cheerfully about marathons and triathlons and all that kind of stuff. I wasn't sensing any particular chemistry between us but it was fun enough.

It was when we went to the pub next door that it got both better and worse. He visibly relaxed when we walked in – well, we probably both did – as standing at the bar ordering drinks just felt just like a normal night out rather than a rather forced interview sitting across a table from each other. When I came back from the loo, he'd got me a pint – I'd just asked for a beer – so he got full marks for that. However, halfway through the second pint, he opened up about his divorce – how they'd been married for 12 years but all the passion had died and then he'd fallen in love with a work colleague, and his wife had thrown him out and had taken all his money – and the whole thing began to feel less like a date and more like a therapy session. While there may be people who would find a guy more attractive after he'd admitted to having an affair that broke up his marriage, I don't think I'm one of them. I mean, I'm sure there was fault on both sides and so on, but as a first-date conversation it had limited appeal.

We ended the evening quite amicably and parted promising to do it again soon – I'm not sure either of us meant it, but it seems to be an accepted convention that it's OK to politely lie at this point – and then we went our separate ways, him to north London and me down south, by way of another pub to have a much needed post-date, pre-Tube restorative.

I arrived home feeling quite cheerful about the whole evening. Or so I thought. It had been hectic but pleasant enough, and I was home by midnight, which was becoming my definition of a good evening, hopefully signifying a decent night's sleep.

The boys were hanging out in the kitchen.

'So, how was your date?' Jeff asked cheerfully.

I dumped my bag and coat and joined them. 'It was OK, I think,' I started off. 'He was quite nice and we had a good time . . .'

Suddenly, I realised I was going to cry. And not just cry quietly, but weep and snivel and sob, and generally be overcome by a whole variety of rather unattractive ways of crying. I put my head down on the table and howled.

The boys didn't quite know what to make of such a massive disconnection between what I was saying and what I was doing, and so continued to chat away as if one of us didn't seem to have completely fallen apart mid-conversation.

'Oh, that's great,' said Alex, no doubt looking at me in horror. 'You see, there are lots of really nice men out there. It's just a case of getting out there and finding them.'

I continued weeping rather pathetically into the table.

'So, erm,' Alex went on, 'are you going to see this guy again? Or, er . . .' He fizzled to a halt.

Jeff dived for the safety of the back door and a Marlboro Light.

I got up, blew my nose, poured myself a large whisky and lit one of Jeff's cigarettes. This was not my usual behaviour at all and the boys started to look alarmed. I was rather surprised at myself too, to be honest. The evening hadn't been that bad, had it? The date had gone fairly well for a first date, revelations about his ex-wife notwithstanding. So why did I feel so utterly depressed?

I think it was the realisation that in spite of all the good early signs – the interests in common, the friendly email exchange – he just wasn't the guy for me. I'd built the whole thing up so much that it had suddenly hit me that he wasn't the man I was going to marry. Not only that, but he was the best of a really bad bunch. If he was the best out there, there really was no hope for me. It really was all just a torturous waste of time. I was going to end up pathetic, alone, sad and lonely, while the rest of the world went about the normal process of meeting people and falling in love.

I was so tired, so fed up of the whole thing now. I never wanted to go out ever again on a blind date. Or a singles evening. Or do anything that involved trying to meet a guy. It was just never going to happen.

'But you said he was nice?' said Alex, having listened to everything pour out between hiccups and puffs on the cigarette. (It surely goes without saying that I was looking particularly attractive at this moment.)

'He *was* nice!' I wailed. 'But, you know, he had that look, that sad look . . . I don't want someone with a sad look. I was someone loud and cheerful and optimistic and bouncy and . . .'

'And Patrick,' said Jeff meaningfully from the patio. They had seen him around.

'Not everyone is going to be loud and bouncy and Patrick-like,' Alex pointed out.

'I know, I know, I know,' I said miserably, pouring myself some more of Alex's whisky. 'But I don't want quiet and sad and ground down by life.'

The boys looked at me.

'Yes, I know I'm weeping and sad at this moment,' I said. 'But, when I go out, I'm not. I may feel knackered and shit and want nothing more than to come home and watch whatever rubbish you guys are watching that night –' I waved away their yelps of protest with my cigarette '– but when I go out on a date I really get myself together. I do all the millions of things that girls do to make themselves look as beautiful as possible and I wear a little dress and vertiginous heels, and make-up and earrings and all that kind of stuff, and I go out and I sparkle. I fucking well sparkle. I'm chatty, I'm friendly, I'm fun, I'm witty, I make people laugh and I shine. And it's all so much hard work. But I do all that and then I come home and burst into tears because it's all so pointless, it's such a huge effort for nothing and I'm just fed up. I'm fed up and tired with the whole thing. I sparkle and shine and all I ever meet is people with sad eyes and ex-wives when all the bouncy, interesting guys are in the pub with their mates or off pulling girls ten years younger than me.'

I was on a roll now. I was whining and I didn't care. I was drunk and maudlin and self-pitying and pathetic.

'Come on,' said Alex, making frankly heroic efforts to cheer me up. 'You are gorgeous, you will find someone, no one said it was going to be easy but, trust me, it will happen.'

He was so American and optimistic. It broke my heart to bring him down to my level. But I was British and depressed and I had to.

'You know, I don't think it will,' I said, tears falling into my whisky. 'I really don't. And I just don't want to put myself through this any more. I feel as if this whole process is in danger of making me very, very sad indeed. So I'm going to stop. I have to, for the sake of my soul. It's just killing me.'

I drained the last of my drink and, rather wobbly, got to my feet. 'I am never, ever going on another dating thing in my life,' I declared to the room.

'OK, then,' said Alex. 'That's your decision.'

'It is,' I said, feeling a great weight suddenly lift from my shoulders.

'Except for the fact that you have wine-dating tomorrow and a singles ball on Saturday,' said Jeff, returning from the garden.

'Oh fuck,' I said.

33

Grape Expectations

Knowing that I was only going to go on two more dating events in my entire life, or at least for the foreseeable future, somehow made the whole thing a lot better. I felt I could cope with both of them much better knowing that there was an actual end in sight. The process had begun to seem like a never-ending series of torture sessions, stretching on and on throughout the rest of my life. Just two more nights, though. I could do that! And then I was going to sleep for a month. No drinking, no going out – it was going to be bliss.

I ignored the fact that whenever I stayed in more than two nights in a row I would usually go out of my mind with boredom and instantly be on the phone making all sorts of plans. I could barely wait to finish all this.

I woke up the next day, feeling as rubbish as usual, and rather embarrassed that I'd been such a weepy blob in front of my flatmates and had probably ruined their perfectly pleasant evening, but, on the positive side, it felt like the end of a prison sentence. I even emerged from my lunchtime snooze feeling rather cheerful. No, I still didn't want to go out tonight but at least I was ready for the final push.

It was in the shower that I realised how daft my attitude had become, or how daft the dating process had made it. I was viewing the end of it all as a wonderful event, but dating was supposed to be fun, right? I was meeting new people and doing all sorts of things I would never normally have considered doing. But it was like working in a chocolate factory: it might sound great fun but after a while, it was just another day in the office. Especially when the chocolates weren't that great anyway.

That evening, I rushed out of work the moment my editor said I could leave and jumped in a cab. It was already half past seven, when the event was due to begin, but I figured that there would be a fair amount of arriving and pre-event drinking going on before they got down to business.

In spite of my moaning, I was actually looking forward to this night, and not just because it was the penultimate event on my list. I had signed up to wine-tasting dating, organised by a company called Grapevine Social, and had wanted to try it out for ages. The website proclaimed that it offered 'the perfect alternative to speed-dating – the chance to taste six wines and meet twenty dates after work'. Even better, it split its evening between two age categories: 24–38 year olds and 36–49 year olds. I fitted into both categories but, not wanting to be the oldest in a room full of 20-somethings, had opted for the 36–49 year olds' one.

As usual, girls' places had sold out weeks earlier, while the guys not only were able to decide to come along at the last minute but were also offered all sorts of half-price ticket enticements to come along. Still, that was the nature of the beast and would at least mean – in theory – that there would be a fairly equal number of guys and girls there.

The venue itself, a subterranean bar in Chelsea, was rather nice, as was the fact that we had the whole place to ourselves, rather than being cordoned off in a corner somewhere, while normal people did normal Friday-night flirting without having to be shown how to do it by paid professionals. I arrived just before 8 p.m. while the pre-dating drinking was still going on, so I was in perfect time.

Soon we were all signed in and shown to our respective tables. Our hosts for the evening turned out to be a part-time actor from Liverpool, who was rather self-conscious about the fact that he'd had a front tooth knocked out in a cycling accident, and a skinny blonde woman who had an astonishingly loud voice.

'Hellooooo!' she sang out to the six tables of people that were dotted around the room. 'Let's get ready to PAAAARTYYYY!!'

There was much embarrassed shuffling of feet. Most of the men were in their forties and wearing suits. They seemed to have come straight from work, and were therefore in the mood to be ordered to party by loud blonde girls.

Looking around the room at everyone perched on ridiculously tiny stools at their respective tables, it seemed that there was a near 50/50 split between guys and girls, which was definitely a tick for the organisers. They all seemed to be of a suitable age too, unlike the cocktail dating that had made me feel geriatric. On our tables were one quiz sheet per person and a laminated page giving descriptions of six wines. It all looked pleasingly well organised. Instantly, I felt rather worried. I was now of an age and disposition to want my love life to be 'pleasingly well organised'. God, I needed to get a life.

The rules of the evening were run through loudly and rapidly: guys moved tables with each new wine, girls stayed put. Guys got the drinks from the bar, girls stayed put. The girls all looked very pleased at this. Fuck equality. We want men to bring us drinks. We had to guess each wine and answer a wine-related question per round; the winner would get a bottle of wine. It was all very straightforward.

'Guys, get to the bar and get the girls a drink!' shrieked the blonde.

They duly did so, giving the girls a chance to have a quick introduction. On my table was Annie, from Scotland, mid-forties I guessed, with dark hair and sharp eyes, and Maureen, who had just moved to Guildford and looked about 25, with a mane of stunning auburn hair.

The men returned with the drinks and the dating began. I actually began to enjoy myself. The wine was pretty terrible, to be honest, and there wasn't enough of it – she said, sounding like Woody Allen – but having six people round a table with something to discuss took away a lot of the usual 'interview' feel that most blind dates have. The men were chatty and friendly, and once the wine had been guessed at – 'We're doing the wine-tasting together and writing the same thing down,' Annie said bossily – we all informally paired off and made small talk about where we lived and what we did. Well, we were British. Every 15 minutes, the shrieky blonde (who was really starting to get on everyone's nerves) would scream for silence and then order us to move on. The guys would get the wine to take with them to their next table, and the girls would have a quick 'anyone you liked?' discussion before the next set of men arrived. At the end of the evening, you wrote down the ones you liked and your details would be passed on to your prospective suitors.

Six wines and about fifteen men later, we were done. I had enjoyed chatting to all the blokes but couldn't really picture myself on a second date with any of them, but I didn't mind too much. I'd accepted I would never meet anyone at these kinds of events so tonight was no surprise.

The nicest guy of the evening, a tall, blond Canadian called Paul, won the quiz and dutifully opened his prize of a bottle of wine to share with the group.

'Right, we're off, enjoy yourselves!' said the blonde, her quietest comment of the night, and our hosts disappeared into the Chelsea night, while the rest of the crowd hurled themselves at the buffet that had just been laid out.

I popped out to get some money from a nearby cash machine.

'Hello, Sarah, how are you?' said the guy next to me in the queue.

Momentarily baffled and with that 'do I know him?' mild panic that sets in at these moments, I belatedly realised that I was still wearing my name badge. What a good way to pull, I thought, as I headed back to the bar. Had he been any cuter, I might have stayed. Had I known what was waiting for me back at the bar, I definitely would have done.

The conversations were continuing in earnest. The hosts would have been proud, had they stayed to see us all getting along. But what was everyone talking about? I joined a conversation at random. Oh, it appeared that we were talking about . . . dating. Wine-dating, quiz-dating, online dating, holiday dating . . . It seemed that no one was actually having a proper, normal type of conversation that people have when they are actually dating. We were just all talking about it. It made me want to throw myself to the floor and start howling. However, given that I've often reached that stage far earlier in the evening, this wasn't too bad.

But dating is something that people usually *do*, rather than discuss; wasn't it all just going to make us feel incredibly sad and pathetic standing here comparing notes about what things we'd done and how none of them had obviously worked?

Apparently not. The group of people standing immediately next to me were talking about holidays. You know, the 'independent traveller' holidays such as Explore and Exodus. I realised to my horror that they were talking about the type of holiday that I'd gone on, mountain trekking in Morocco. I knew exactly what they were talking about, whereas a few months ago I wouldn't have had the faintest idea: this meant I was actually one of them. I was, officially, a tragic dater.

'I went on a ten-day trip to Cambodia,' said the tall woman standing next to me. 'It was great fun, really,' she assured us, not that we'd asked.

'What were the people like?' asked another woman, which is single-person code for: 'Were there any single men of the right age there that I could have copped off with had I been on that holiday?'

The first woman looked slightly mournful. 'Well, it turned out that there were seven other couples on the trip, and a French-Canadian woman travelling on her own,' she said. There was a sad little pause while we all tried not to gasp in horror. 'But she was really nice,' she added quickly.

'I'm off to India for three weeks in a fortnight's time,' volunteered the only guy in our little group. 'I've already checked and most people are travelling on their own.'

The Cambodia-trip woman looked most put out. 'You can check?' she said, almost crossly.

'Oh, yes, I always check,' said the guy very seriously. 'So it looks good for this trip . . . not that you go with the idea of meeting someone in mind, of course.'

It was as if an inaudible bell had rung, a cue for the whole group to suddenly start reassuring ourselves: 'Oh, no, of course not, you don't go for that reason.'

'You go for the experience, don't you? The fantastic experience . . .'

'Oh, yes, I mean, you're probably going to make lots of friends and meet interesting people but probably not, you know . . .'

'Oh, yes, I've made lots of friends on these types of holidays, we still all keep in touch . . .'

I'm not entirely sure whether we all succeeded in kidding ourselves.

'Still,' said the guy, giving the game away a bit, 'you never know.'

I moved on, snaffling some food from the buffet as I did so. There was a group clustered around the chicken wings who were talking about . . . surprise, surprise, online dating.

'It's just so depressing,' a woman was saying. 'You spend so much time, and so much money and where does it get you?'

'I've given up entirely with online dating,' said another. 'You know what I'm doing now?'

We all leaned in to hear her magic formula.

'Delectable Dinners,' she said.

I felt cold, and needed to leave. I was going to a Delectable Dinners ball the very next day. I was truly one of these people. I fitted in. I could talk the talk. I had dating stories of my own. It was time to get out of there.

Safely in a cab, I had what could be called an epiphany. A revelation. A something, anyway.

I realised that there was a whole parallel dating universe that most people, particularly coupled-up and married people, would never know about. It was almost like a secret society.

Most people would pass through life without having to sit in an underground bar on a Friday night in winter guessing whether their glass of red wine was a merlot or a malbec in the hope that the complete stranger sitting next to them might turn out to be the man they wanted to spend the rest of their lives with. Most people were lucky. They met someone, fell in love, got married, had babies, not necessarily all of those or in that order, but that was the general idea.

If you weren't fortunate in that respect, you had to make your own luck, or at least give luck a helping hand – or a hefty kick, depending on how well disposed you were feeling towards luck at the time. But joining the single underworld in which the same people did the same merry-go-round of single events didn't seem to be the answer.

It seemed to me that there were many single people, all doing the same thing, meeting each other but not pairing off at all. They were remaining single and becoming sadder and more desperate and angry, and prone to saying things like: 'I really enjoyed going on holiday with a load of couples,' when they really meant: 'I'm utterly furious that I forked out two thousand quid for the holiday and I never felt so lonely.'

Meanwhile, out in the real world, people were getting on with having fun and meeting people and dating and getting married and having babies. It seemed that the more single things I did, the more likely I was to remain single. It just confirmed my decision to stop. Just one more event and that was it. For ever. I was going to go back to how I was before: single and happy and content and loving life.

34

The Hunt Is Over

I had met Rebecca at Jo's party in the summer. We hadn't talked a great deal, but she seemed nice and friendly. A few months later, Jo emailed me. 'I bumped into Rebecca the other day and she mentioned that she was a member of something called Delectable Dinners. Maybe that's something you should check out.'

Still game at that stage, I clicked on the website. Delectable Dinners described itself as 'social events for busy people'. The website looked pretty old-fashioned and the whole thing felt rather grown up.

The introductory blurb on the website said that every month:

> We arrange up to a dozen opportunities for like-minded people to meet and make friends. Our events range from dining to dancing, from theatre to travel, from galleries to golf and much more besides.

From galleries to golf didn't suggest a particularly large range of activities, and, frankly, the whole thing sounded like something my mother would like. Delectable Dinners offered late-night dinners in posh restaurants in the City of

London, or guided Dickensian walks, or concerts at the Royal Albert Hall, all something that appealed more to 60 year olds than to 30 year olds. However, I was still prepared to try anything – once – and this seemed grown up enough to attract only well-off gentlemen who were serious about trying to find someone. The recommendations on the website seemed glowing enough, although 'I have even made friends with a psychiatrist whom I have seen a couple of times since' hardly filled me with anticipation.

I spoke to Jo.

'Rebecca says that she didn't particularly recommend the dinners but there is a Halloween Ball coming up,' she said. 'It's supposed to be a pretty fun evening and Rebecca's thinking of going. Maybe you could go together.'

A singles ball! This sounded even more archaic than a Dickensian walk around Aldwych. My favourite film as a pre-teenager – which I'd watched on average twice a day for about two years, I reckon – had been *The Slipper and the Rose*, a musical version of *Cinderella*. The extremely handsome Prince Charming, played by Richard Chamberlain – yes, it was quite a long time ago – is being forced by his parents, the King and Queen, to marry and produce an heir.

He, on the other hand, wants to marry for love, leading to one of the more lively scenes in the film in which the Prince objects to his royal parents throwing a ball in which he is supposed to choose a suitable bride.

'A bride-finding ball!' exclaims the Prince in an all-singing, all-dancing number, and the singles Halloween Ball was incredibly reminiscent of that. I suspected my dress might not be as grand as Cinderella's – more High Street than Fairy Godmother designer chic – and I would be arriving by Tube rather than glass coach, but the concept was the same.

I phoned the organisers. They seemed delighted to hear from me – and who wouldn't love to hear someone call to give them £107, which was the ticket price for the evening – and took down my details.

'I hope you don't mind me asking, but how old are you?' the lady on the end of the phone asked.

'I'm 38,' I replied.

'Thirty-eight!' she exclaimed. 'Well, you're just a baby!'

Loud alarm bells started clanking in my head. 'Well, it's been some time since I was called that,' I said cautiously, and sadly realised that was indeed true. 'How old will everyone else be?'

'Well, there's a wide age range of people there,' she said. 'It starts off from, well, late thirties and forties, and it goes up to people in their sixties and even seventies.'

Goodness. I was really marching through the decades with this one. I started to go off the whole idea and the woman probably sensed that because she rushed in with: 'But don't worry, we'll sit you on the younger persons table. You won't be sitting next to 60 year olds, of course not, ha ha.' There was a pause. 'Unless, of course, you'd like to?'

'No, no, that's fine,' I rushed in hastily. 'The 30-something table would be fine. Otherwise, well, it would be just like having dinner with my parents, wouldn't it?'

'If we all wore ball gowns for dinner, that is,' I thought.

I filled out the guest details form that Delectable Dinners later emailed over. As well as date of birth, address and so on, the form also bizarrely demanded my height and weight. I have no idea why but it seemed unnecessarily personal – rather than the young persons table, would they seat me at the fat persons table if I weighed over a certain amount? – so I let them know my height and deleted the weight question entirely. Cheeky sods.

My card debited, it only remained for me to decide what to wear, which I did precisely half an hour before I had to set off. Thankfully, my only choice – a long black silk dress – was still presentable, and a quick iron and I was off. Our invitations had specified 'formal dress' – dresses used to have to be ankle length but they had relaxed the code for ladies now – and a 'token of Halloween'. My sister had given me a pink and white fairy wand for my birthday – for you to conjure up your own Prince Charming, she said, admitting that it wasn't entirely guaranteed to work – and so I took that with me. It turned out to be extremely useful for hailing a cab – it had started to rain so I decided not to walk to the Tube – and I arrived in good time for dinner, which was scheduled to start at 8.15 p.m. on the dot.

There was already a large chattering throng of smartly dressed people clustered round the bar when I walked into the conservatory at the top of the hotel. The room did look very impressive, I had to admit: a high glass ceiling displaying the pitch black night sky, and enclosing towering palm trees that were lit up with fairy lights for the occasion. More than a dozen tables circled round a central podium, each bearing flickering candles that illuminated the various Halloween decorations.

The two women at the desk were very friendly. 'Sarah, is it? Of course it is. You're with Rebecca, aren't you? She's at the bar.'

They handed me a couple of gold cards and beamed at me cheerfully. I had no idea what the cards were for but I took them and my wand and headed towards the bar. There was no chance of finding Rebecca: she was completely hidden by the crowd. I managed to find a route in and order a drink, discovering that the cards were wine tokens. Armed with a glass of white wine, I took myself off to a corner of the room and started grazing on a dish of peanuts while surveying the scene.

The general theme seemed to be posh and formal. There were a lot of ladies in their fifties who were very smartly done up in tight ball gowns with a fair amount of cleavage on display and a lot of very bright make-up, and quite a few elderly gentlemen with black cummerbunds wrapped tightly round their midriffs. However, there were also a lot of fairly normal-looking men and women in their forties, so my fears were allayed somewhat. And the rather grand attire was somewhat softened by the various Halloween tokens – devil's horns, pumpkin brooches, spider earrings – that people were wearing.

Many guests seemed to know one another from previous events – plenty of 'Peter! How delightful to see you again!' and 'Clarissa! You're looking more beautiful than ever' – and generally the whole thing felt like a rather reserved affair for grown-ups. Which I suppose it was. I had never really felt like I fitted in at any of the dating events I'd been to and I still didn't here, but for different reasons – this was definitely more my mother's territory than mine. I struck up conversations with several people – mainly by offering them a peanut – and found that most people had been to a Delectable Dinners ball before and preferred them to the other events.

'The great thing is that you know all the men here are single,' said one woman who rather improbably claimed to be called Clytemnestra. ('After the tragedy, you know.') 'There's no chance of you chatting away to a man and then him suddenly saying "we" instead of "I", or, even worse, his wife coming over and dragging him away.'

I could see her point. The men too seemed to be very friendly in an attentive rather than a sleazy way. There was an undercurrent of flirting, but in a courtly, gentlemanly manner, and certainly no one was so ill-bred as to be caught checking out other women when they were talking to you. It was a definite improvement on hanging out in a nightclub.

A bell was rung, some welcome speeches were made and

we made our way to our tables. I was at table number one, 'Werewolf', where I finally found Rebecca and her two friends, Vanessa and Susan. We were all on the same table, which was rather nice – I got the feeling that we could rescue one another if we were sat next to a complete horror – and beside each of us was seated a dinner-suited man.

I started talking to the guy on my right, first, who was called Robin. My opening line wasn't particularly imaginative, but at least it wasn't 'So, how was your journey here?'

'Where's your Halloween token?' I asked.

He looked blank.

'You know, your little Halloween thingy . . .' I gestured around at the various items being displayed by people on our table, including one guy who was wearing a deeley-bopper headband with little spiders on springs.

He sneered. 'I didn't bring one,' he said. 'I couldn't be bothered.'

He peered at me in return. 'Where's yours then?'

I waved my pretty wand at him.

He sneered some more. 'That!' he exclaimed. 'That's rubbish! That's not a Halloween thing at all.'

I was beginning to get slightly annoyed. The starters hadn't even been served yet and the guy had already run out of small talk.

'Hey,' I said, not particularly caring whether this went against the general tenor of the evening, 'people are supposed to be chatting each other up or at least making polite conversation and instead your opening line to me is how rubbish my Halloween thing is when you haven't even got one yourself.'

He got the message and apologised. We then talked about what our journeys there had been like.

The guy on my left was called Laurence, youngish-looking but made older by a receding hairline (he was not the only young oldie on our table) and was thankfully much more pleasant to chat to. It turned out he didn't know he was coming until the night before.

'I got invited by the woman who runs these events, you know, the one who made the speeches earlier?'

I hadn't been paying attention then, but nodded as if I knew whom he was talking about. 'Well, she phoned me last night and asked if I would come along.'

My heart sank. It was the same old story – too few men and others being roped in just to make up the numbers. He must have read my expression as he added quickly, 'No, I am actually "here" –' I correctly interpreted this as meaning single '– it's just that I was invited at the last minute. Look, I had to pay and everything.'

That seemed rather unfair on him but I let it go. Talking about why we were here was bringing the evening down somehow. We might all know that we were there because we had paid a hundred quid in the hope of meeting someone but it seemed a bit 'bad form' to mention it.

We chatted away and then it was time for the men to swap places. Instead of Robin and Laurence, I got Toby and Alistair, both friendly, both old fogeyish, both well versed in the art of small talk. I discussed shooting with Toby – he and Robin turned out to be best pals who went shooting every weekend, which makes them sound a lot posher than they actually were – and I discussed, well, a whole lot of nothing with Alistair.

'You have very small hands,' he said, staring at mine.

This was news to me. I had thought that my fingers were actually quite fat and chubby (I had always wanted lean, tapering piano player's fingers). I also don't think that I've ever heard anyone comment on the size of someone's hands before.

'Yes, they're incredibly small,' he repeated, looking closely at them, but, thankfully, not trying to grab one to measure.

He laughed. 'It's quite ironic really, isn't it, considering you come from Clapham?'

I still can't think of a suitable reply to that.

I was saved, in a manner of speaking, by Vanessa, who suddenly decided to include me in the conversation she and Toby were having.

'How old do you think everyone here is?' she asked me.

I looked round. 'Well, anything from 30 to 70 I would say,' I answered.

'No, not here generally, at our table,' she said. 'I assumed that everyone would be in their forties but now I'm not so sure. I'm 40 myself – how old are you, Sarah?'

I almost wished I was back in the small-hand conversation. It seemed to be an extremely odd topic of conversation to have when there was a whole table of guys you were supposed to be dating just inches away. Declaring how old you were seemed a trait more suited to 90 year olds and, unless you were particularly old or particularly young, I couldn't see the point. Thankfully, the rather dishy waiter arrived to top up our glasses and provide a rather useful diversion.

The plates were soon cleared away and the coffees poured, which was a signal for the general free-for-all table-hopping to start. Little groups were gathering here and there, and presumably all the people who knew one another were comparing notes. The woman with the improbable Greek name whom I had spoken to earlier had said that the only negative thing she could say about the previous Delectable Dinners ball she had attended was that everyone leaped up after the meal and rushed back to the friends they had come with, leaving all the people who had come here on their own still on their own, and I could see her point. It seemed a bit daft to me too – surely the time to compare notes was in the cab on the way home or over brunch the next day? Anyway, it seemed like a good time to escape to the loo.

The Ladies, it turned out, was the place to be. Women were not only clustering round the mirror and re-trowelling on their make-up but also sharing all manner of intimate secrets with complete strangers.

'My husband ran off with a woman half his age,' one woman was announcing to the world as she put her lipstick on. 'My son refused to speak to him afterwards – he was ten years older than his father's mistress, for heaven's sake. It didn't last long anyway, and when they split up she took him to the cleaners, the silly bugger. Last year, he dropped dead of a heart attack – she had completely worn him out.'

This was greeted with a whole host of sympathetic murmurs from inside and outside the cubicles.

Two women with platinum-blonde highlights and brightly clashing dresses were having an animated discussion, even though they had gone into two adjacent loos.

'It's the same as last year,' one was saying loudly. 'The men are just so old! Why can't we have men who are the right age?'

'I completely agree,' shouted the other invisible woman from the end cubicle. 'It's the same old story, not enough young men.'

They flushed and emerged to convene at the sink.

'So how old are you then?' asked one.

'I'm 59,' she said, looking pretty good, it has to be said, for a 59 year old. 'I just want a man who's 43, that's surely not too much to ask?'

I didn't say, 'Join the queue, lady. And stick to your own pool!'

We emerged from the Ladies serene, calm, repainted and rejuvenated, and without the slightest hint to the men that they had been picked over, discussed and dissected in such detail.

It was time for the dancing. I had expected a sedate

'shuffling round the dance floor in couples' affair, accompanied by some light jazz. Instead, we were blasted by what seemed to be the theme of 'the very best and worst of the '80s' – Wham!, Abba, Nik Kershaw – they were all there. Women were hurling themselves enthusiastically around the dance floor, while the men, in time-honoured fashion, stood around the edges with a drink in their hand. The music was so loud that, even if you wanted to chat or flirt, you had to do it in the traditional nightclub manner of shouting into someone's ear while the other person said, 'Sorry, what?'

I had a quick chat with the girls who seemed to be quite content to talk to one another, and then struck out on my own, reasoning that, as I was paying over a hundred quid for this, I should make sure I talked to as many men as possible – except the really old ones. Laurence from dinner seemed quite keen on me, as did another bloke called Tim, who was a good laugh – as cynical and acerbic as I was, not (to me) fanciable, but a great partner in crime to have at these events.

I met two guys who hadn't come together but who seemed to be content to talk to no one else and stand next to each other in quiet solidarity. 'What is the point?' I thought.

One very distinguished-looking old gentleman came up to me and very politely introduced himself, then ran his hand from the back of my head all the way down to my bottom, where he had a good feel.

I jumped back. 'You dirty old man!' I exclaimed, and retreated sharply to safer climes.

By now, there was that rather nice feeling of familiarity with a lot of the people there, so, even if you struck out with someone or, more likely, just ran out of conversation, you could always retreat to the bar and find a familiar face.

Some people had already pulled – Robin from dinner was having a vigorous game of tonsil hockey with a lady who was a good ten years older than he was. I found his friend Toby sitting on his own rather disconsolately in the corner. 'Robin's got my house keys,' he said, watching them grapple with each other. 'That was a mistake.'

'Maybe you could join in?' I suggested. Well, I had been drinking a fair amount by this time.

Toby shuddered. 'Last time I came here, I slept with a woman who turned out to be 60. I only found out in the morning.'

Goodness. I made a mental note to come back here in 20 years' time. No wonder the ladies in the loo were put out that they were seated with men their own age.

While everyone was friendly and chatty and perfectly amiable, I hadn't seen anyone that made my heart go thump. Then, I saw him. He was gorgeous. He had dark hair, the right amount of stubble, and he was Scottish. Obviously so, I mean, as in he was dressed in the whole Scottish get-up – the kilt, socks, sporran, belt, wee little jacket. The outfit was an absolute girl magnet. There are few women who can resist.

Now I'm not saying that it is the sexiest outfit in the world – it's not bad, but there's something about a man in cricket whites that makes me go wobbly every time, and due to Scott I cannot resist anyone in black tie whose unknotted bow tie is hanging around his neck – but, as far as flirting goes, it is a winner. There are so many things to discuss, for a start. You can charge straight up to a guy in the full regalia and ask him where his dirk is and you're away; you can get up close and personal without being arrested, he gets to show off all his trinkets and you do it all with an undertone of sexual innuendo, which is just a gift to the underflirted.

Within seconds of introducing myself to the very lovely-looking Scottish gentleman, we were straight into discussing what was in his sporran and we hadn't even got down to the fundamental question of what was under his kilt.

It turned out he was actually genuinely Scottish – in that he had a Scottish accent, not the underkilt situation – and he knew the organiser. 'So I'm here to help out,' he said.

'Like Laurence?' I said, and he agreed. So far so good. The whole evening was looking up.

We finally exhausted the Scottish-dress theme and moved on to all sorts – what we did, where we were from, what we thought of this evening. It was going well.

Or so you'd think, given that I was at a singles ball and talking to a handsome Scot. I was already thinking about how handsome he'd look at our wedding and whether his family owned a castle, when he got called away by a rather pushy-looking lady in a red dress. 'No matter,' I thought happily, 'he'll be back.'

Laurence sidled over. 'Are you having fun?' he asked.

'Yes,' I said cheerfully. 'It's a good bash, isn't it?'

'Yes, really great,' he agreed. 'I noticed you've been talking to my brother-in-law.'

He nodded to where my Scottish dreamboat was, now sitting down rather glumly next to the red-dress lady who seemed to be rather cross with him.

'Brother-in-law?' I echoed. 'How does that work then?'

Laurence laughed. 'Well, he's married to my sister. That's her sitting next to him, in the red dress.'

I couldn't fucking believe it. The one guy in the entire room who was married and I had to make a beeline for him, and spend all that time flirting with him! How embarrassing. And how utterly rubbish of him! He should have a sign on his forehead: 'Married man masquerading as single guy at a singles ball. Women beware.'

My mood plunged as low as some of the dresses on display. Thankfully, the disco reached a top '80s climax (Jennifer Rush, 'The Power of Love') and it was the end of the evening.

The lights came on abruptly, causing many couples who were sitting rather close together to spring apart in alarm and horror under the unflattering glare.

I needed a strong drink.

A couple of dirty martinis later at the hotel bar, I was feeling much better. A succession of perfectly nice men from the ball had drifted through in search of cabs and a nightcap and had all been rather charming. The general consensus was that the evening had been rather nice but nothing special.

'It wasn't as good as usual,' said one distinguished gentleman, who was having a coffee in the very optimistic hope of counteracting all the wine he'd had before driving home to Surrey. 'But it was not a bad way to spend the evening.'

At the other side of the room, Toby and Robin glared at each other, while Robin's new girlfriend perched awkwardly in between them.

Finally, it was just me and my partner in crime for the evening, Tim.

He looked at me rather forlornly. 'So you didn't fancy anyone there tonight then?'

I fished my olive out of my drink. 'Nope.'

'Well, I fancy you.'

'Thanks, honey, that's very nice of you.'

'But you don't fancy me.'

'No, sorry. But thanks again.'

'No problem. Shame though. Here's my card in case you change your mind.'

We kissed farewell and he got in his taxi.

That was it. I was done, through, finished with this dating lark. I felt dizzy with vodka and relief. I would never again go to anything so contrived as a dating event, a singles evening, or anything in which the whole reason was to find a husband. It was bad for the soul, bad for the ego and bad for your general sense of who you were and what was important.

It was time to celebrate. Happily, there was a casino next door. I ordered a quadruple Baileys, lost £20 on the slot machines and was in bed at 5 a.m. I slept well.

35

Brave New World

A week later, I was up at 7 a.m. walking a dog around Battersea Park, throwing sticks for him to chase and hoping that he'd retrieve some of the good-looking men walking their dogs at the same time.

Later that day, I met an important work contact at a very posh restaurant and halfway through lunch a guy texted me a picture of an intimate part of his body at its most cheerful.

I think it's fair to say that neither of those things would have happened if I hadn't taken a conscious decision to actually start looking for a man.

Dating, someone once told me, is just a numbers game. Get the quantity and the quality will follow. Juggle men, advised that dating-agency woman. The more the merrier. Well, it had seemed an impossible task at the time, but I was, slowly and tentatively, actually starting a bit of juggling of my own.

I've started seeing quite a lot of one of the men I met on my travels and, well, while it's still early days, I think we could have a lot of fun.

Then there is Barney. Lovely, gorgeous, cute, fun-loving Barney. Greece turned out to be the beginning of something, rather than the end. In real life, he is every bit as cute and fun-loving as I remembered. I have tempered my completely irrational, out-of-all-proportion feelings I had for him and he, in turn, has become rather more keen on me.

He has also been rather keen on sending me pictures of his, um, amiability, hence the rather unexpected picture on my phone while I was waiting for dessert. He had texted earlier saying that he was still in bed, hungover and horny, and would I like a picture. I didn't really know how to say, very politely and diplomatically, of course: 'No, never in a million years.' None of the etiquette books had much to say on the subject. So there it was, in its full glory, on my phone. I was terrified I might accidentally show it to my lunch date, or even forward it on to my entire address book. It wasn't just a one-off either. Our relationship seems to have gone down a wholly unexpected path, and I still don't really understand why he would want to send me a picture of something I actually encounter in the real world. Still, it certainly makes for a heightened sense of drama every time my phone beeps.

My single friends, both existing and the new ones I've made during my quest, have become much more proactive too. There is now quite a group of us who are making the effort to introduce new people into the circle, so, as one part of my social life disappears off to the suburbs, another part of it is expanding. Next week, I have two dinner parties to go to, both where everyone has to bring a single friend, and, while it might not yield my perfect guy, it will no doubt introduce me to new friends. The world is becoming more interesting, more exciting. There are a lot of people to meet out there.

And there is Simon, the guy I had one date with before he flew off to the Galapagos Islands for three months. In spite of the technical restrictions, we are writing to each other, me from Clapham, him from the middle of the Pacific Ocean, and we have arranged to meet up the moment he is back in the country.

Some things are a work in progress. I'm still doing BMF and have already booked on their skiing holiday next year (10 men, 20 women, but we're staying in an après-ski-heavy resort, apparently). I've joined another running club, am going back to playing poker and have joined a very posh dating website, which seems to be full of extremely good-looking entrepreneurs. I am never again going along to single-specific events such as single dinners, speed-dating, singles drinks and all those torturous singles quiz-dating evenings. I shall also cancel most of my internet dating-site memberships and, on the remaining ones, actually get a decent picture up on my profile for once.

The internet dating is actually starting to take off. I have a date next week and two the following week. Now that I've relaxed, culled the pointless singles things from my life and learned to treat it all as a series of mini-adventures rather than a last-gasp, highly pressured attempt to grab a guy before it's too late, it has started to become fun again.

My two hours spent dog walking in Battersea Park were great fun too and something I'm going to try to make a habit of. Archie the dog was perfect – a bouncy, friendly, black and white cocker spaniel – and he was brilliant at zooming off round the park rustling up good-looking men.

It wasn't all plain sailing though. The moment we arrived in the park I took him off his lead and he bounded up to an eligible-looking guy who was walking his dog. As his dog ran up to me to say hello, it seemed entirely appropriate for me to give the guy my most cheerful and winning smile and say to him, with a laugh, 'I think we've swapped dogs!'

Much to my surprise, rather than coming back with an equally winning smile and suitably witty rejoinder before suggesting we go for coffee and then maybe spend the rest of our lives together, he just glowered at me, said precisely nothing and stomped off. I stood there, bewildered. Did he not understand that we were all here to flirt?

Thankfully, there were other men and women to chat to on our circuits round the park as Archie zoomed in and out of the bushes, disappearing occasionally but always finding me again, while I subtly managed to turn my footsteps past every cute guy in a square mile radius.

I have had much more practice walking my friends' small children than large dogs, so when I called out, 'Look, Archie! A train!' out of habit, one man did actually turn around and laugh at me, but in a friendly way. There does seem to be a lot of potential in dog walking, especially if I head out at the weekends rather than just before work.

'Thank you so much for lending me Archie,' I said to his owner, once the pair of us had made it home in one piece. 'He's lovely, isn't he?'

She smiled. 'He is indeed,' she said, 'although he is actually called Alfie.'

Poor sausage! Next time, I promise to get your name right, Alfie.

I have no idea whether any of the things that I've done, or continue to do, will come to fruition at all, but I think it will be a lot of fun finding out. I remain cheerfully optimistic. And it seems that I'm not the only one. I recently got an email from a guy who had only just seen my advert in *Private Eye*.

> Dear Sarah. You don't know me from Adam but I saw your ad in Private Eye and although this is not the type of reply you were looking for – for I am happily married – your ad did inspire me to write one of my comic verses, which I performed at a gig in Inverness last week. Would you like to see it?'

I would, I replied, so long as it didn't make me feel utterly depressed.

It was called 'Body Clock'.

Single female, nineteen years,
Just wiped away my first love's tears,
Would love to meet a handsome stud,
For rolling naked in the mud.

Single female, twenty-two,
Would love to meet a man like you,
If you liked naked fun and frolics,
And can refrain from talking bollocks.

Single female, twenty-five,
Into lindy hop and jive,
Would love to meet a fellow dancer,
Not a two-left-footed chancer.

Single female, twenty-nine,
I know I prob'ly shouldn't whine,
I'm just wanting love and wedlock,
Not continued breeding deadlock.
Are there any decent blokes,
Who don't tell bloody silly jokes,
Who put the seat up, flush the chain,
And when required unblock the drain?

Single female, nice and flirty,
Just the wrongish side of thirty,
Keen, but not too des-per-ate,
Just looking for a lifelong mate.

Single female, thirty-four,
I know you've seen my ads before,
My friends are busy having kids,

So now I'm entertaining bids
From men as old as forty-two,
Even forty-five might do.

Single female, thirty-eight,
Take me now, it's not too late,
I've spent a bloody fortune here,
With personal ads four times a year,
My men don't seem to stick around,
I think they hear that ticking sound,
I'm quite attractive; sexy legs,
Won't someone fertilise my eggs?

Single female, thirty-nine,
Quick, I'm running out of time,
My desperation's hard to mask,
It isn't really much to ask,
Frogs and toads and rainbow trout,
Spread semen liberally about,
And even chimps and pachyderms,
Regularly share their sperms.
I'd take some reproductive fluid,
From a doctor or a druid,
Or from a Duke or lowly waster,
I'm ready with my turkey baster.

Married female, forty-one,
My little baby is such fun.
The turkey baster wasn't needed,
I have been naturally seeded,
I met a lovely man called Drew,
Whose body clock was ticking too.

Here's hoping . . .